WORKBOOK FOR WRITERS

CELIA MILLWARD
LINDA BOWIE

HOLT, RINEHART and WINSTON
NEW YORK CHICAGO SAN FRANCISCO ATLANTA
DALLAS MONTREAL TORONTO

Editor	Kenney Withers
Development Editor	Lauren S. Bahr
Cover and Interior Designer	Diane Daugherty
Production Manager	Vic Calderon

Library of Congress Cataloging in Publication Data

Bowie, Linda.
  Workbook for writers.

  1. English language—Grammar—1950-   2. English
language—Composition and exercises.   3. English
language—Rhetoric.   I. Title.
PE1112.B65   425   79-22781

ISBN 0-03-040721-4

ACKNOWLEDGEMENTS

Excerpt from "On the Beach," by Russell Baker, *The New York Times Magazine*, July 8, 1979. Copyright © 1979 by the New York Times Company. Reprinted by permission.

Excerpt from "On His Centennial: The Spirit of Einstein Abides in Princeton," by Lincoln Barnett. Copyright © 1979 Smithsonian Institution, from SMITHSONIAN magazine, February 1979.

Excerpt from *The Decorative Thirties* by Martin Battersby. Copyright © 1971 by Martin Battersby. Used with permission of the publisher, Walker and Company.

(Continued on page 314)

TABLE OF CONTENTS

PREFACE

The purpose of this workbook is to help students strengthen their abilities to use correct grammatical forms and effective rhetorical devices in their writing. All of us have writing problems that we would like to ignore or that we use as excuses to avoid writing altogether. Avoiding the problem, however, often keeps us from experimenting and learning in an area that is essential to success in modern life—clear communication.

This book attempts to give students practice in fundamental usage so that as they master the rules and concepts they build the confidence necessary to express themselves with more honesty and with less fear of criticism.

Many instructors argue that little is learned from rote memorization of rules and from completion of grammar exercises. They may be correct, to a degree, but a large part of the problem with grammar exercises arises from the fact that the exercises are often isolated from the real writing experience of the students. I have tried to solve this problem by including in this workbook two kinds of exercises: ones that provide traditional "drill" in a rule or concept followed by ones that ask students to apply what they have learned in some form of original writing. Thus, students can see at once how the particular rule or concept can work in their writing and can identify what, if anything, about that particular rule or concept causes problems for them. In addition, "Troubleshooting" sections point out the most common problem areas and the most often abused rules.

Many people shared in the creation of this book. I am deeply indebted to my friend and teacher, Celia Millward, who invited me to collaborate on *Handbook for Writers* and *Workbook for Writers.* Working with her, a privilege and pleasure, has taught me many things—the development of self-discipline, the virtue of patience, the necessity for impatience, the wisdom of humor, and, I am pleased to say, a few spelling rules.

I am also indebted to my husband, Aubrey, for his immense help and support as well as to the other members of my household—my children, Dixie, Don, and Alice; my dear friend (and best proofreader), Gary; and my dog, Grendel, who often kept me company until the wee hours of the morning when I had long been deserted by all of the others.

Others who offered invaluable assistance and encouragement include Lynn Brownlee, Patty Dellinger, Harriett Domnitz, Clelia Hendrix, Dr. Louis Henry, Patti Joplin, and the late Dr. Thomas E. Douglass, who motivated me to pursue my interest in grammar and writing. I would also like to express my appreciation to Santi Buscemi and Ken Rader, both of Middlesex County College, for their helpful comments and suggestions. In addition, I would like to extend special thanks to Lauren Bahr, Vic Calderon, Diane Daugherty, Judith Rothman, Norma Scheck, and Kenney Withers of Holt, Rinehart and Winston for making it all possible.

Many of the creative sparks in this workbook were the suggestions of friends. All of the faults are, I fear, mine.

Linda Julian Bowie

1/SENTENCE PATTERNS

A **sentence** is a group of words that can stand alone. In other words, it is an independent statement. Every sentence contains at least one subject (what or who is talked about) and at least one predicate (what is said about or asked about the subject). The predicate must include a verb phrase, which is a word or words that express an action done by the subject or a state of existence of the subject.

Every English sentence will be one of five types, depending on what elements it is composed of. Some sentences have only a *subject* (S) and a *verb phrase* (VP). Other sentences have a *direct object* (DO), an *indirect object* (IO), a *subject complement* (SC), an *object complement* (OC), or various combinations of several of these elements. (Each of the last four terms is explained in the following discussions.)

1a SUBJECT + VERB PHRASE (S + VP)

>   S   VP
> The crowd roared.
>   S VP
> Frodo lives.
>   S   VP
> That pigeon is flying.

To identify the **subject** of a verb, ask yourself who or what performed the action or is being described by the verb. The **verb** is the easiest part of a sentence to find because it always expresses action or a state of being. The verb is the heart of the sentence.

In the first sentence, the word expressing action (that is, the verb phrase) is *roared*; and if we ask who or what roared, the subject clearly is *crowd*. In the second sentence, *lives* is the verb phrase because it expresses a state of being; and if we ask who or what lives, the answer is *Frodo; Frodo* is the subject of the sentence. *Is flying,* in the third sentence, expresses action and is thus the verb phrase. The thing flying is the pigeon, so *pigeon* is the subject. The verb phrase *is flying,* like many verb phrases, is made up of two words. Some verb phrases have two or more words. This is because verbs have a number of forms, and often two or more of these forms are combined into a single verb phrase. A fuller discussion of verb phrases may be found in section 4 on verbs.

If all our sentences contained only one subject and one verb, our language would be very abrupt, choppy, and generally unsophisticated. We gain variety in our speech and writing through building onto this basic pattern of S + VP. The marvel of language is that each individual develops his or her own unique ways of adding to this basic sentence pattern.

1b SUBJECT + VERB PHRASE
+ SUBJECT COMPLEMENT (S + VP + SC)

One way to expand the basic pattern of S + VP is to add a subject complement. A **complement** is a word or a group of words that completes the meaning of another word or group of words. Notice that the words *complete* and *complement* are similar. The complement may complete meaning by describing or defining. If the complement is a subject complement (SC), the word whose meaning is being defined or described—completed, in short—is the subject.

```
        S    VP  SC
Sunshine is soothing.
        S            VP       SC
Limburger cheese smells terrible.
        S  VP  SC
The car was flashy.
        S  VP        SC
The car was a Volkswagen.
           S     VP      SC
The audience became restless.
           S     VP SC
The intruder was she.
```

In the first sentence, *soothing* describes *sunshine,* the subject. (We know that *sunshine* is the subject because if we ask what is soothing, the answer is *sunshine.*) *Terrible* describes *Limburger cheese* in the second example, *flashy* describes *car* in the third, *Volkswagen* defines *car* in the fourth sentence, *restless* describes *audience* in the fifth sentence, and *she* defines *intruder* in the last example. Notice that, in all of these sentences, the verbs are verbs of being, becoming, or sensing. Such verbs are known as *linking verbs* because they link the subject with a complement. Think of these as equal signs that equate the subject and the complement: *sunshine = soothing*; *car = Volkswagen.*

1c SUBJECT + VERB PHRASE + DIRECT OBJECT (S + VP + DO)

Another way to expand sentences is by adding a direct object (DO) to the basic pattern of S + VP. The **direct object** is the person or thing that receives the action of the verb. The direct object tells who or what receives the action performed by the subject.

```
          S          VP           DO
The fire fighter extinguished the blaze.
     S        VP       DO
A rabbit was chewing lettuce.
     S      VP        DO
The boys hugged their father.
```

In the first sentence, *blaze* tells what the fire fighter extinguished. In the second sentence, *lettuce* tells what a rabbit was chewing. In the last sentence, *father* tells whom the boys hugged.

1d SUBJECT + VERB PHRASE + INDIRECT OBJECT
+ DIRECT OBJECT (S + VP + IO + DO)

If we wish to say to whom or for whom something is done, we often use an **indirect object** (IO) to indicate this relationship.

2

```
       S         VP     IO        DO
The salesperson handed John the perfume.
       S       VP    IO        DO
A clown showed them his costumes.
    S   VP      IO    DO
Eric gave the table a kick.
```

In the first sentence, *John* tells to whom the salesperson handed the perfume. In the second sentence, *them* tells to whom the clown showed his costumes. In the third sentence, *table* tells to what Eric gave a kick.

1e SUBJECT + VERB PHRASE + DIRECT OBJECT + OBJECT COMPLEMENT (S + VP + DO + OC)

Just as the subject complement describes or defines the subject, the **object complement** (OC) completes the meaning of the direct object by describing or defining it.

```
       S    VP  DO    OC
The jury found him innocent.
       S       VP        DO        OC
The crew christened the yacht Scholar-Gypsy.
```

In the first sentence, *innocent* describes the direct object *him,* and in the second example, *Scholar-Gypsy* defines the direct object *yacht.*

Enriching these five basic sentence patterns are *modifiers,* or words interspersed among the basic elements (subjects, verb phrases, objects, and complements). **Modifiers** (M) are words that describe, define, or limit other words.

```
   M     M        M                M         M        M   M
The weary, sunburned fisherman carefully and slowly unloaded his worn,
     M
tangled nets.
```

The, weary, and *sunburned* all describe the subject, *fisherman; carefully* and *slowly* describe the verb, *unloaded;* and *his, worn,* and *tangled* describe the direct object, *nets.*

TROUBLESHOOTING

1. Do not confuse the subject complement and the direct object. Remember that the subject complement must follow a linking verb and that it further explains the subject. A direct object, on the other hand, never follows a linking verb. The direct object adds nothing to our understanding of the nature of the subject. It tells only what receives the action of the verb.

The shrub grew tall (*Tall* tells about the subject, *shrub*; and *grew* is here a linking verb meaning "became.")

The shrub grew buds. (*Buds* is the direct object and tells what was grown by the shrub.)

3

2. Remember that a sentence cannot have an indirect object unless it also has a direct object. However, not all sentences with direct objects have indirect objects.

3. Do not confuse indirect objects with groups of words that appear after the direct object. Indirect objects always precede direct objects.

DO

Toby made Kirsten a <u>table</u>.

DO

Toby made a <u>table</u> for Kirsten.

NAME _____ DATE _____

PART A

DIRECTIONS: For each of the following sentences, write *S* above each subject, *VP* above each verb phrase, *DO* above each direct object, *SC* above each subject complement, and *OC* above each object complement. Some sentences may have more than one subject, object, or complement. Then, in the blank, write the letter from the list below that identifies the structural type of the sentence. If the group of words is not a sentence, write *NS*.

    A. S + VP (Subject + Verb Phrase)
    B. S + VP + SC (Subject + Verb Phrase + Subject Complement)
    C. S + VP + DO (Subject + Verb Phrase + Direct Object)
    D. S + VP + IO + DO (Subject + Verb Phrase + Indirect Object + Direct Object)
    E. S + VP + DO + OC (Subject + Verb Phrase + Direct Object + Object Complement)

EXAMPLE: __*D*__ Clara blew him a kiss.

_____ 1. Blowing, thick sleet lashed the windowpanes.

_____ 2. The crash of the vase onto the hall floor sometime after midnight.

_____ 3. Peter mailed the girl a picture of his moped.

_____ 4. Hot mint tea and toasted bagels with cream cheese taste yummy as a

midmorning snack.

_____ 5. The repairman gave the typewriter a thorough going-over.

_____ 6. Finally, the shiny, blue motorcycle with its driver and female

passenger.

_____ 7. After the almost interminable biology lab, Leroy dashed back to his room for an afternoon of his favorite TV shows.

_____ 8. Having a personality like her father's, Terri also joined the air force.

_____ 9. In an ill-fated decision, Lisa lent her best friend her boyfriend's new camera.

_____ 10. The Doberman pinscher pinned the burglar to the floor.

_____ 11. Understanding oneself and the frictions within each kind of human relationship.

_____ 12. In the final six seconds of play, the quarterback, with amazing dexterity.

_____ 13. After a hot, dry season, big, splashy drops of rain on the soil smell especially earthy and good.

_____ 14. The ten finalists in the beauty pageant gave each other plastic, toothy smiles.

_____ 15. The insurance examiner called the painting a fake.

NAME _____ DATE _____

PART B

DIRECTIONS: Write a sentence for each of the following specified structural types.

EXAMPLE: S + VP + SC

The sky became black.

1. S + VP + DO

_____

_____

2. S + VP + SC

_____

_____

3. S + VP + IO + DO

_____

_____

4. S + VP + DO + OC

_____

_____

5. S + VP

_____

_____

6. S + VP + DO

_____

_____

7. S + VP + SC

_____

_____

8. S + VP + DO

_____

_____

2/PARTS OF SPEECH

All words are classified into eight parts of speech according to their meanings and functions.

PART OF SPEECH	MEANING OR FUNCTION	EXAMPLES
Noun	Names a person, place, or thing and functions as subject, object, or complement	tennis, love, birds
Pronoun	Substitutes for a noun	him, each, you
Verb	Expresses action or a state of being and forms main element of predicate	admire, dance, become
Adjective	Modifies a noun or pronoun	spiteful, yellow, your
Adverb	Modifies verbs, adjectives, other adverbs, and entire groups of words	carefully, too, soon
Preposition	Links a noun or pronoun to other elements in the sentence to form a modifier	up, under, to
Conjunction	Connects words, word groups, and sentences	because, and, nor
Isolate	Is not grammatically connected to other elements in the sentence	no, whew, hello

2a PHRASES AND CLAUSES

Although phrases and clauses are not among the traditional parts of speech, you should be able to recognize these structural components of sentences. If you cannot distinguish between them, you will have difficulty in understanding how sentences are put together, an understanding essential to the analysis and improvement of your own writing.

A **phrase** is a group of words arranged grammatically but not containing both a subject and a predicate. There are many different kinds of phrases, as the following examples illustrate.

this tattered old Levi shirt	would have been announced
under the pier	Caesar's having conquered Gaul
finding the gold	

A **clause** is a group of words arranged grammatically and containing both a subject and a predicate. Some clauses can stand alone as complete sentences. These are called **independent clauses**. Other clauses, called **dependent clauses**, must be attached to an independent clause in order to form a complete sentence.

INDEPENDENT CLAUSES	DEPENDENT CLAUSES
The hawk circled lazily.	while the hawk circled lazily
The car zoomed off.	after the car zoomed off
A dog ran through the park.	that a dog ran through the park

As these examples show, a dependent clause is very often signaled by a conjunction that makes the clause dependent. If you remove the conjunction *while* from the first dependent clause, you will have an independent clause (*the hawk circled lazily*). Similarly, the conjunction *after* makes the second example a dependent clause, and the conjunction *that* makes the third example a dependent clause.

3/PARTS OF SPEECH: NOUNS

Nouns are the names of persons, places, things, or ideas.

3a CHARACTERISTICS

The form of a noun is changed (or inflected) in English to show certain grammatical features.

    1. Number—**singular**, or restricted to one (*book, calf*), and **plural**, or referring to more than one (*books, calves*).

    2. Case—**common** (if the noun serves as a subject, object, or complement: *doctor, the Smiths*) and **possessive** (if the noun functions as a modifier: *doctor's, the Smiths'*).

    Nouns are often made from other parts of speech by the addition of endings called **suffixes.** The following are a few of the suffixes that clearly label a word a noun.

-ness (kind, *kindness*)	- ity (noble, *nobility*)
-dom (king, *kingdom*)	- ment (move, *movement*)
-tion (abstract, *abstraction*)	- ance (convey, *conveyance*)
-hood (child, *childhood*)	- ism (natural, *naturalism*)

    Nouns may function in nine different ways in sentences. To illustrate these nine functions, the word *cat* is used differently in each of the following sentences.

    1. Subject. The *cat* was very old. (If you ask what was very old, the answer—and subject of the verb *was*—is *cat*.)

    2. Subject Complement. The child's birthday present was a *cat*. (If you ask what the *present,* the subject, was, it equals *cat*, the subject complement, attached to the subject by the linking verb *was*.)

    3. Direct Object. Alice's husband brought home a stray *cat*. (If you ask what it was that the *husband*, the subject, brought home, the answer is *cat*, the direct object, which receives the action of the verb *brought*.)

    4. Object Complement. The toddler called every animal a *cat*. (If you ask what it was that the *toddler*, the subject, called every *animal*, the direct object, the answer is *cat*, the object complement, which completes the meaning of the direct object *animal*.)

5. Indirect Object. He gave the *cat* a ball of yarn. (If you ask to whom *he*, the subject, gave the *ball*, the direct object, the answer is *cat*, the indirect object. Notice that the indirect object is not preceded by the words *to* or *for*.)

6. Object of a Preposition. During thunderstorms our dog always huddles beside the *cat*. (If you ask what noun follows the preposition *beside*, we see that it is *cat*. The noun following a preposition is called the object of the preposition. The preposition connects that noun in a meaningful way with the rest of the sentence. In this sentence, the preposition relates *cat* to the subject, *dog*, showing a spatial relationship between the two.)

7. Appositive. The pet, a *cat*, terrorized everyone but its owner. (If you ask what noun means the same thing as *pet*, the subject, the answer is *cat*, which is said to be in apposition to *pet* because it renames the first noun in different terms. Any noun in a sentence—not just the subject—may be followed by an appositive).

8. Direct Address. "*Cat*, if you jump onto the dining table again, I'll swat you!" Mrs. Schneider threatened. (If you ask what person or object is being addressed by the speaker, the answer is *cat*.)

9. Nominative Absolute. The *cat* having disappeared, the family launched a search of the neighborhood. (The noun *cat* and the following verb form modify the rest of the sentence. Note that nominative absolutes are not independent clauses and cannot stand alone as separate sentences: *The cat having disappeared* is not a complete sentence.)

3b CLASSES

Nouns are of several classes.

1. Simple and Compound Nouns. A simple noun is one word: *bird, energy, light*. A compound noun contains two or more parts of speech that work together as a single noun: *pancake, salesperson, namesake, boardwalk*.

2. Countable and Mass Nouns. A countable noun has both a singular and a plural form. The singular form may be modified by both *a* and *the*: *a carpet, the carpet, the carpets*. A mass (or uncountable) noun has no plural form and cannot be modified by the words *a* or *one*: *garbage, air, magic*.

3. Proper and Common Nouns. A proper noun, which may consist of more than one word, names a particular person, place, or thing (bridges, titles, people's names, holidays, ships, and so on). All proper nouns or groups of proper nouns are capitalized (except for those prepositions, articles, and conjunctions that are not the first word in the group): *the Chrysler Building, the Fourth of July, Dustin Hoffman, A Chorus Line, Close Encounters of the Third Kind*. A common noun is any noun that is not a proper noun: *bridge, day, woman, film*.

4. Concrete and Abstract Nouns. A concrete noun, which may be either countable or mass, names something that we can see, hear, touch, smell, or taste: *sunshine, velvet, fish, stadium*. An abstract noun, which is normally a mass noun, names an idea or concept—an intangible: *admiration, deceit, imagination, nobility, snobbishness*.

5. Collective Nouns. A collective noun names a group of countable people or things: *faculty, herd, team, class*.

TROUBLESHOOTING

1. Do not confuse a subject complement and an appositive. Both of these constructions rename and further define another word, but a subject complement renames *only* the subject and is separated from the subject by a linking verb. An appositive may follow *any* noun or pronoun in the sentence (or any group of words functioning as a noun or pronoun). The appositive with its modifiers comes immediately after the word it describes.

The snake, a copperhead, was dead. (appositive)

The snake was a copperhead. (subject complement)

NAME _____ DATE _____

PART A

DIRECTIONS: Underline all nouns in the following sentences. Above each noun you have underlined, write the letter from the list below that describes that noun's function in the sentence.

A. Subject   F. Object of a Preposition
B. Subject Complement   G. Appositive
C. Direct Object   H. Direct Address
D. Object Complement   I. Nominative Absolute
E. Indirect Object

         A   *C*   *F*
EXAMPLE: Carlos proposed marriage to the astonished girl.

1. By early evening the tent had become an oven.

2. Luigi bought his girlfriend, Rita, the present of her dreams, a bracelet made of

gold and diamonds.

3. Renée considered her father-in-law a pompous bore.

4. Scott recognized the girl, a pretty redhead with green eyes.

5. The dance having ended, the three couples went across the street for breakfast

at a Greek restaurant.

6. But, Dad, these new skis are the best brand on the market!

7. A storm clearly threatening, the men quickly sailed the sloop into the harbor.

8. Giggly and squealing, the toddler hopped lopsidedly, fell down, climbed up,

and hopped some more.

9. On her sixteenth birthday, Jan wore the pearls, a gift from her grandmother, for the first time.

10. Daniel quickly became the best quarterback in the history of the team.

11. Sunlight danced on the dewy leaves of the giant elm outside her window.

12. On Sunday the Wallaces always fought over the comics and the crossword puzzle in the newspaper.

13. Herb had lent Angela his best albums for her party.

14. Herb had lent his best albums to Angela for her party.

PART B

DIRECTIONS: Write one sentence for each of the following patterns using nouns in the function specified for each. Do not use any nouns other than those asked for. Your five sentences may make up a unified paragraph, or they may be independent of each other.

EXAMPLE: Nominative Absolute—Subject Complement

The movie having ended, Madelyn fell asleep.

1. Subject—Indirect Object—Direct Object

_____

2. Object of a Preposition—Subject—Subject Complement

_____

3. Direct Address—Subject

_____

4. Nominative Absolute—Subject

_____

4/PARTS OF SPEECH: VERBS

The primary function of a **verb** is to form the main element of the predicate—to explain what is going on.

4a CHARACTERISTICS

Verbs have three principal parts on which all other forms are based: the **infinitive**, the **past tense**, and the **past participle**. The principal parts of the verbs *to see* and *to watch,* for example, are:

INFINITIVE	(to) see	(to) watch
PAST TENSE	saw	watched
PAST PARTICIPLE	see	watched

The infinitive of the verb is always made up of the base verb, either with or without the word *to.*

Various endings and auxiliary or "helping" verbs combine with these three principal parts to show the **tense** (time or duration of the action), the **mood** (the attitude of the speaker), and the **voice** (the relationship of the action of the verb to the subject of the verb).

The tense of a verb may be **present, past, future, perfect, progressive,** or various combinations of these. (See the following summary of the verb *to watch.*)

PRESENT	Diana watches the street-cleaner.
PAST	Diana watched the street-cleaner.
FUTURE	Diana will watch the street-cleaner.
(PRESENT) PERFECT	Diana has watched the street-cleaner.
(PRESENT) PROGRESSIVE	Diana is watching the street-cleaner.

The **indicative mood** makes a statement or asks a question. The **imperative mood** expresses a command. The **subjunctive mood** expresses something unreal, doubtful, or contrary to fact.

INDICATIVE	He closed the door. Does he close the door?
IMPERATIVE	Close the door.
SUBJUNCTIVE	I asked that he close the door. If he closed the door, I would be warmer.

A verb is said to be in the **active voice** when the subject is the doer of the action. A verb is in the **passive voice** when the subject is the receiver of the action of the verb.

ACTIVE VOICE	Diana watched the street-cleaner.
PASSIVE VOICE	The street-cleaner was watched by Diana.

To help you understand the tenses, moods, and voices of verbs, a complete **conjugation** (list of forms) of the verb *to take* is given on pages 17-18.

4b CLASSES

All verbs are either main verbs or auxiliary verbs. **A main verb** carries most of the meaning of the verb phrase in which it appears. Two major classifications of main verbs are (1) regular and irregular verbs, and (2) transitive, intransitive, and linking verbs.

Regular verbs form both their past tense and their past participle by adding *-ed*. The 200 or so **irregular verbs** form their past tenses and past participles in a variety of ways, but, because they are so frequently used, the principal parts of most irregular verbs are familiar.

REGULAR VERB	(to) kiss, kissed, kissed
IRREGULAR VERB	(to) go, went, gone

Transitive verbs take a direct object, and **intransitive verbs** do not take a direct object.

TRANSITIVE VERB	The boy rang the bell.
INTRANSITIVE VERB	The bell rang.

Transitive verbs with direct objects that refer to the subject of the sentence are called **reflexive verbs**: *He scratched himself.* Verbs that are followed by a subject complement are **linking verbs** (they link the subject with a word that is equivalent to it or that modifies it). Linking verbs include *to be*, *become*, *seem*, *appear*, and verbs of sensing (*look*, *feel*, *taste*, *smell*, *sound*).

LINKING VERBS

I am magnificent.   My velvet dress feels soft.

Xavier was a plumber.   What smells so funny?

This room seems stuffy.

Many verbs can be transitive in one sentence, linking in another, reflexive in another, and intransitive in yet another. Generally, these labels apply, not to the verb itself, but to the way the verb functions in a given sentence.

TRANSITIVE	The dog smelled the kitten.
INTRANSITIVE	The dog smelled cautiously.
REFLEXIVE	The dog smelled himself.
LINKING	The dog smelled clean.

Auxiliary verbs (also called **helping verbs**) are used in forming verb phrases, but do not form a complete verb phrase by themselves. The auxiliary verbs are (1) *be*, (2) *have*, (3) *do*, and the **modal auxiliaries**—*will*, *would*, *shall*, *should*, *can*, *could*, *may*, *might*, *dare*, *need*, *ought*, and *must*.

AUXILIARY VERBS

Barney is singing.   Barney will decide.

Barney has fallen.   Barney must go.

Does Barney know?   Barney must have gone.

COMPLETE CONJUGATION OF THE VERB *TO TAKE*

Note: Some of the following combinations occur only rarely, but all are grammatical and possible.

INDICATIVE MOOD

ACTIVE VOICE

		PRESENT	PAST	FUTURE
Simple	I	take	took	will take
	you/we/they	take	took	will take
	he/she/it	takes	took	will take
Progressive	I	am taking	was taking	will be taking
	you/we/they	are taking	were taking	will be taking
	he/she/it	is taking	was taking	will be taking
Perfect	I	have taken	had taken	will have taken
	you/we/they	have taken	had taken	will have taken
	he/she/it	has taken	had taken	will have taken
Progressive Perfect	I	have been taking	had been taking	will have been taking
	you/we/they	have been taking	had been taking	will have been taking
	he/she/it	has been taking	had been taking	will have been taking

PASSIVE VOICE

		PRESENT	PAST	FUTURE
Simple	I	am taken	was taken	will be taken
	you/we/they	are taken	were taken	will be taken
	he/she/it	is taken	was taken	will be taken
Progressive	I	am being taken	was being taken	will be being taken
	you/we/they	are being taken	were being taken	will be being taken
	he/she/it	is being taken	was being taken	will be being taken
Perfect	I	have been taken	had been taken	will have been taken
	you/we/they	have been taken	had been taken	will have been taken
	he/she/it	has been taken	had been taken	will have been taken

	I	you/we/they	he/she/it
Progressive			
Perfect	have been being taken	had been being taken	will have been being taken
	have been being taken	had been being taken	will have been being taken
	has been being taken	had been being taken	will have been being taken

SUBJUNCTIVE MOOD

		PRESENT	PAST
ACTIVE VOICE			
Simple	All persons	(that he) take	(if he) took
Progressive	All persons	(that he) be taking	(if he) were taking
Perfect	All persons	(that he) have taken	(if he) had taken
Progressive Perfect	All persons	(that he) have been taking	(if he) had been taking
PASSIVE VOICE			
Simple	All persons	(that he) be taken	(if he) were taken
Progressive	All persons	(that he) be being taken	(if he) were taken
Perfect	All persons	(that he) have been taken	(if he) had been taken
Progressive Perfect	All persons	(that he) have been being taken	(if he) had been being taken

IMPERATIVE MOOD

Active Present	take
Passive Present	be taken

Infinitive	(to) take
Gerund	taking

NAME _____ DATE _____

PART A

DIRECTIONS: Match the italicized verbs on the left with the correct tense from the list on the right. Write the letter of the correct tense in the space before the verb.

EXAMPLE: __*F*__ they *are talking*

_____ 1. it *has rained*	A.	Future perfect
_____ 2. they *will be going*	B.	Past
_____ 3. he *fidgets*	C.	Present
_____ 4. it *crashed*	D.	Future
_____ 5. they *are clamoring*	E.	Past perfect
_____ 6. it *will have exploded*	F.	Present perfect
_____ 7. she *will dream*	G.	Present progressive
_____ 8. he *was yelling*	H.	Past progressive
_____ 9. she *had arrived*	I.	Present perfect progressive
_____ 10. he *has been jogging*	J.	Future progressive

PART B

DIRECTIONS: Indicate the mood of the following italicized verbs as *A*—indicative, *B*—subjunctive, or *C*—imperative by writing the appropriate letter in the space before the verb.

EXAMPLE: __*B*__ If it *be* he

_____ 1. *Stay* away.	_____ 6. that he *be* still
_____ 2. *Avoid* the rush.	_____ 7. it *is evolving*
_____ 3. that she *run*	_____ 8. *Did* he *speak?*
_____ 4. *Has* it *fallen?*	_____ 9. if he *were*
_____ 5. *Copy* it.	_____ 10. *Have* some more.

PART C

DIRECTIONS: Indicate the voice of the following italicized verbs as *A*—active or *B*—passive by writing the appropriate letter in the space before the verb.

EXAMPLE: ___*B*___ they *will be allowed*

_____ 1. he *has been caught*   _____ 6. she *was telling*

_____ 2. he *has caught*   _____ 7. she *will be telling*

_____ 3. it *has been found*   _____ 8. she *will be told*

_____ 4. it *is observed*   _____ 9. they *were playing*

_____ 5. she *was told*   _____ 10. they *were spanked*

PART D

DIRECTIONS: Complete the following sentences by writing the specified tense, mood, and voice of the italicized infinitive on the line provided.

EXAMPLE: The storm probably _____*will hit*_____ around
(*to hit*, future tense, active voice)
noon.

1. The sun _____ all day.
(*to shine*, present perfect tense progressive)

2. The crew _____ immediately that the mine
(*to tell*, past tense, passive voice)

_____ .
(*to close*, past perfect, passive voice)

3. Mrs. Panwitz _____ to buy the cheese on her way
(*to plan*, past tense progressive)
home.

4. Roy _____ on the last flight.
(*to come*, future tense progressive)

20

NAME _____ DATE _____

5. You _____ the lab assistant that she
        (*to tell,* future tense)

   _____ .
   (*to fire,* present perfect tense, passive voice)

6. They _____ for half the day before they
        (*to swim,* past perfect tense)

   _____ on the warm sand to rest.
   (*to lie,* past tense)

7. The moment _____ very awkward for both Kate and Tim.
        (*to be,* past perfect tense)

8. Phil _____ that we _____ the camping
        (*to know*, past tense)   (*to plan*, past tense progressive)
   trip.

9. When Nat _____, Chris and Shirley
        (*to arrive,* past tense)

   _____ a nasty argument.
   (*to have*, past perfect tense progressive)

10. Sita _____ an angel for a change.
        (*to be*, present perfect tense progressive)

11. The violin _____ to José by his grandfather.
        (*to give,* past tense, passive voice)

12. *Superman* _____ a much better movie than David and Sara
        (*to be,* past tense)

   _____ .
   (*to expect,* past perfect tense)

13. If it _____ not so far to Atlanta, Dick would do all his
        (*to be,* subjunctive mood)
   shopping there.

21

14. The child _____ it difficult to endure the cruel comments of
          (*to find*, present tense)
   his classmates.

15. Mrs. Schimel _____ the package on the kitchen table be-
          (*to lay*, past perfect tense)

   fore she _____ down for her nap.
          (*to lie*, past tense)

16. After they _____ the punch, all of them _____
          (*to drink*, past tense)   (*to begin*, past tense)
   to feel sick.

17. Mei-ling _____ to play such jokes as
          (*to know*, present perfect tense, passive voice)
   these.

18. Henri _____ a VW for the last two months.
          (*to drive*, present perfect tense progressive)

19. "When we get there, the cat _____ , and
                         (*to feed*, future perfect tense, passive voice)

   the dishes _____," Maggie said to Curtis,
          (*to do*, future perfect tense, passive voice)

   who _____ .
          (*to drive*, past tense progressive)

20. Because Kent _____ that picture so quickly, we
          (*to hang*, present perfect tense)

   _____ him to do the others.
   (*to beg*, present tense progressive)

NAME _____ DATE _____

PART A

DIRECTIONS: Identify the function of each form of the verbs *be*, *have*, and *do* in the following sentences by writing either an *A* (auxiliary verb) or *M* (main verb) in the blank following the verb.

>   EXAMPLE: The professor has ___*A*___ never told us when the exam will be
>   ___*M*___.

1. Didn't _____ Margie say that she has _____ never had _____ a boy-friend who was _____ her intellectual equal?

2. Rainy mornings have _____ always been _____ Peter's favorite time for playing the piano.

3. The girl was _____ being _____ especially careful to divert suspicion.

4. Does _____ the man always do _____ that when he has _____ been _____ out late?

5. Diego has _____ never been _____ one to admit that he is _____ wrong.

6. The plane will have _____ been _____ on the ground half an hour before the authorities are _____ able to capture the terrorist.

7. The child did _____ it, though he was _____ being _____ watched every second.

8. His mother has _____ no idea how he has _____ done _____ all of the paintings in only two months.

9. I was _____ unable to see what he was _____ doing _____ when I arrived.

10. We were _____ not the only ones who had _____ not been _____ invited.

11. Chip's brown eyes were _____ slowly filling with tears as he was _____ told that he was _____ no longer a member of the team.

12. "Don't _____ be _____ so selfish!" shouted Gina, who had _____ been _____ growing angrier by the second.

13. They did _____ do _____ everything they had _____ been _____ planning for so long.

14. The old man was _____ having _____ a difficult time because the fish was _____ thrashing about wildly in a desperate death-struggle.

15. As the fog was _____ just lifting and the first rays of the sun were _____ heralding the dawn, the farmhands were _____ already in the fields.

PART B

DIRECTIONS: Write one sentence to fit each of the following specifications.

EXAMPLE: Use a form of the verb *to have* as an auxiliary verb.

I have spent a great deal of time on this project.

1. Use a form of the verb *to do* as an auxiliary verb.

_____

2. Use a form of the verb *to do* as a main verb.

_____

3. Use a form of the verb *to be* as a main verb.

_____

4. Use a form of the verb *to be* as an auxiliary verb.

_____

5. Use a form of the verb *to have* as an auxiliary verb.

_____

6. Use a form of the verb *to have* as a main verb.

_____

5/PARTS OF SPEECH: ADJECTIVES

Adjectives modify, that is, describe, define, or qualify, nouns or pronouns.

5a CHARACTERISTICS

Some adjectives are inflected (take special endings) to show comparison. The positive degree of an adjective has no ending (a *small* cave), the comparative usually ends in *-er* (a *smaller* cave), and the superlative degree usually ends in *-est* (the *smallest* cave). Most one-syllable adjectives and many two-syllable adjectives that end in *-y*, *-ly*, *-le*, *-er*, and *-ow* follow this pattern in their comparative forms. Adjectives with more than two syllables and some two-syllable adjectives are compared by means of *more* and *most*.

> the <u>more</u> <u>stubborn</u> of the two
> the <u>most</u> <u>delicious</u> lobster

A few two-syllable adjectives may be compared by either the *-er/-est* endings or by *more* and *most*: *handsomest* or *most handsome*. And some adjectives have irregular comparisons that must be learned separately.

POSITIVE	COMPARATIVE	SUPERLATIVE
good	better	best
bad	worse	worst
a little	less	least
many/much	more	most
far	farther/further	farthest/furthest
old	older/elder	oldest/eldest

5b CLASSES

Adjectives can be divided into a number of different classes, depending on their forms and their functions in a sentence.

    1. **Descriptive adjectives** describe; that is, they specify a quality or state of the nouns they modify. Only descriptive adjectives may be compared. Examples of descriptive adjectives are *bashful, distinguishable, green, lurid.*

> His <u>bashful</u> cousin found that faces were barely <u>distinguishable</u> in the <u>lurid</u> light of the <u>green</u> lamps.

    2. **Proper adjectives** are made by adding a suffix to proper nouns: *French, Amish, Athenian, Elizabethan.*

> The <u>French</u> tourist insisted that he saw both <u>Athenian</u> and <u>Elizabethan</u> influences in <u>Amish</u> customs.

    3. **Possessive adjectives** are made from personal pronouns: *my, your, his, her, its, one's, our, their.*

> <u>My</u> cat is braver than <u>her</u> dog, but <u>your</u> guinea pig terrifies all <u>our</u> pets whenever it escapes from <u>its</u> cage.

4. **Demonstrative adjectives** indicate that the following nouns are "nearer" (*this, these*) or "farther" (*that, those*) from the speaker or writer.

This saucer is dirty and those cups are stained; these dishes should be washed in that hot soapy water in the sink.

5. **Numerical adjectives** indicate the number of a following noun or order in a series of a following noun: *one, first; six, sixth; twenty-nine, twenty-ninth.*

One thing to remember about Jacques is that he will not be six years old on his sixth birthday because he was born on the twenty-ninth day of February.

6. **Indefinite adjectives** refer to an unspecified person or thing: *another, each, either, few, little, much, neither, no, all, both, many, several, any, enough, other, some, such,* and so on.

All my glasses have several defects; no pair fits my nose, and some people would take little pleasure in wearing any glasses with adhesive tape on both bows.

7. **Interrogative adjectives** modify nouns in questions: *which, what, whose.*

Which ceiling do you want painted, what color should it be—and whose idea was it to redecorate?

8. **Relative adjectives** introduce dependent clauses: *which (ever), what (ever), whose (ever).*

The man whose ladder you borrowed will also lend you whatever tools you need.

9. **Articles** include the *indefinite article a (an)* and the *definite article the.*

The little boy begged for a story about an ostrich and a camel that took a trip to the moon.

Most of the classes of adjectives can also function as pronouns. Whether the word in question is an adjective or a pronoun is determined entirely by its function in the given sentence.

Which do you think will be the most entertaining? (*Which* is a pronoun here because it functions as the direct object, a function served only by nouns and pronouns or phrases or clauses acting as nouns.)

Which movie do you think will be the most entertaining? (Here *which* is functioning as an adjective. It is an interrogative adjective that modifies *movie*.)

Each costs us twenty-three cents. (*Each*, as the subject of the verb *costs*, must be a pronoun.)

Each invitation cost us twenty-three cents. (Here *each* modifies the noun *invitation*. It is an indefinite adjective.)

TROUBLESHOOTING

1. Do not confuse the possessive pronoun *its* with the contraction *it's*, which always means "it is."

2. Do not form the comparative or superlative by using both an ending (*-er* or *-est*) and (*more* or *most*).

INCORRECT	Ted was the <u>more</u> awkward<u>er</u> of the two players.
CORRECT	Ted was the <u>more</u> awkward of the two players.
CORRECT	Ted was the awkward<u>er</u> of the two players.
INCORRECT	Kathryn was one of the <u>most</u> friendli<u>est</u> people Todd had ever met.
CORRECT	Kathryn was one of the <u>most</u> friendly people Todd had ever met.
CORRECT	Kathryn was one of the friendli<u>est</u> people Todd had ever met.

3. Do not confuse the indefinite adjectives *fewer* and *less*. Use *fewer* to modify plural nouns and *less* to modify mass nouns (nouns that cannot be made plural and cannot be preceded by *a* or *one*).

4. Do not confuse the comparatives *farther* and *further*. *Farther* is preferred when a literal physical distance is being discussed, and *further* is preferred when a degree or figurative distance is meant.

The man refused to go a mile <u>farther</u>.

The judge refused to hear <u>further</u> testimony.

5. Do not confuse the interrogative adjectives and the relative adjectives. The same words—*what, which,* and *whose*—can serve either function. The interrogative adjective asks a question (*Which* boy found the wallet?). The *relative* adjective relates a dependent clause, that is, a clause that depends on the main clause, to the main or independent clause. (This is the lady *whose* wallet the boy found.)

NAME _____ DATE _____

PART A

DIRECTIONS: Underline all adjectives in the following sentences. Then, on the line beneath each sentence, write each adjective and the letter from the list below that identifies what kind of adjective it is.

A. Descriptive   F. Indefinite
B. Proper   G. Interrogative
C. Possessive   H. Relative
D. Demonstrative   I. Article
E. Numerical

EXAMPLE: The large platter was painted in a colorful Pennsylvania Dutch design.

The — I, large — A, a — I, colorful — A, Pennsylvania Dutch — B

1. In the lush pasture, each blade of grass seemed an individual thread in a gigantic green carpet.

   _____

   _____

2. Four of the guides went ahead with the supplies, but two waited until all twenty-three campers had arrived and checked out their equipment.

   _____

   _____

3. Which do you think would be a better buy?

   _____

   _____

4. Neither car would start on that stormy morning.

   _____

   _____

5. "Those goblins are real in his mind," the pediatrician, in a serious tone, said to Mrs. Mandel.

_____

_____

6. The Norman Invasion is his favorite of the many military campaigns that he has studied.

_____

7. Few onlookers seemed concerned about the two lost and frightened children.

_____

8. Few realize that all kinds of bizarre threats pour into the main office with regularity.

_____

_____

9. Neither boy seemed to remember which man had gotten on the first bus and which on the second.

_____

_____

10. "Japanese food is my favorite," the shy boy replied, "because it tastes healthful."

_____

11. "Little furry dogs always seem like overgrown cats," Marilyn said.

_____

12. Several herbs can be grown easily indoors if the lighting is average and the humidity is fairly high.

_____

_____

NAME _____ DATE _____

13. Whose jacket did you find when you were cleaning up after the New Year's Eve party?

_____

_____

14. Nicky, a husky, was humiliated when her owners had all of her hair shaved off so that she could bear the sweltering days of August.

_____

_____

15. Both suggestions were unusually good, but Chris, always indecisive, just couldn't make up his mind.

_____

_____

16. Although their birthdays fall on the same day, our daughters insist on having separate parties.

_____

_____

17. Ellen wouldn't tell me which boy she wanted most to date.

_____

18. Four hours of class without a break is too much for Jack to bear.

_____

19. Whose brown gloves are those lying on the table?

_____

20. The heavy cast-iron skillet, which Gary had heated until it was red-hot, cracked when he rinsed it in cold water.

_____

_____

DIRECTIONS: Write a sentence using each of the following specified forms of the adjective. Consult your dictionary, if necessary, for correct forms. Be certain that you have used the words as adjectives.

> EXAMPLE: The superlative of *droopy*
>
> *That is the droopiest salad you have ever served.*

1. The comparative of *good*

   _____

2. The superlative of *bad*

   _____

3. The comparative of *evil*

   _____

4. The superlative of *lucid*

   _____

5. The comparative of *subtle*

   _____

6. The superlative of *cheerful*

   _____

7. The positive of *tremendous*

   _____

8. The superlative of *cruel*

   _____

6/PARTS OF SPEECH: ADVERBS

Adverbs modify verbs, adjectives, other adverbs, and entire clauses or sentences.

6a CHARACTERISTICS

Adverbs perform their functions in a sentence by expressing several different things.

MANNER	The deer leapt gracefully.	(*Gracefully* modifies the verb *leapt*, telling how the deer jumped.)
DEGREE	The sun was very hot.	(*Very* modifies the adjective *hot*, telling the degree of hotness.)
FREQUENCY	Sometimes the dog goes with her.	(*Sometimes* modifies the verb *goes*, telling how often the dog goes.)
TIME	He expects the letter today.	(*Today* modifies the verb *expects*, telling when the letter is expected.)
PLACE	The children followed her everywhere.	(*Everywhere* modifies the verb *followed*, telling where the children followed her.)
NEGATION	The boss did not know.	(*Not* modifies the verb *did know*, negating it.)
AFFIRMATION	The magnolia really has grown.	(*Really* modifies the verb *has grown*, affirming it.)
QUALIFICATION	He probably forgot to check it.	(*Probably* modifies the verb *forgot*, expressing likelihood.)

Adverbs made from adjectives form comparatives in the same way as adjectives (see 5). Some adverbs have irregular comparisons.

POSITIVE	COMPARATIVE	SUPERLATIVE
well	better	best
badly	worse	worst
far	farther/further	farthest/furthest

6b CLASSES

There are several classes of adverbs.

1. **Adjectival adverbs** are made from adjectives, usually by the addition of the suffix *-ly* (*rashly, quietly, effortlessly, calmly*). Some adverbs, called **plain adverbs**, have the same form as adjectives (*fast, long, monthly*).

> Louie rashly stuck his hand through the window, and Mrs. St. Lawrence quietly and effortlessly bandaged his cuts.
> Mr. McQueen still plays tennis monthly, but he doesn't play as fast or as long as he did twenty years ago.

2. **Prepositional adverbs** are identical in form to prepositions. Most express spatial relationships.

> It's going to fall off!
> Inside, the humidity is high.

Contrast the use of the same words as prepositions.

He fell off his horse.
She waited inside the car.

3. **Interrogative adverbs** (*why, when, where,* and *how*) ask questions.

Where have you been?
How can they afford a new car?

4. **Relative adverbs** (*why, when, where,* and *how*) introduce dependent clauses.

Do you understand how he does it?
Lori doesn't know why he called.

5. **Adverbial conjunctions** (also called **conjunctive adverbs**) are used to join independent clauses. They may appear at the beginning of a clause or within a clause. Conjunctive adverbs express such meanings as illustration (*for instance, namely*), addition (*moreover, also*), contrast (*however, nevertheless*), qualification (*perhaps, certainly*), result (*therefore, consequently*), attitude (*fortunately, unhappily*), summary (*finally, in other words*), and time (*then, thereafter*).

Virginia has strange tastes in food. For instance, she recently invented shrimp ice-cream. Moreover, she eats salami and jelly sandwiches for breakfast. Her family, however, does not share all her enthusiasm for exotic combinations; certainly, they are not as open-minded as she about chocolate-covered ants. Consequently, Virginia is seldom asked to prepare a meal. Her friends, fortunately, find Virginia's culinary ideas entertaining, if not appetizing. In other words, they encourage her to invent new combinations, but then they politely offer excuses for not eating them.

6. **Miscellaneous adverbs** are not derived from other parts of speech and are recognizable as adverbs only by their function in the sentence (*very, rather, quite, ever, so, somehow, always, not, never,* and so forth).

Hal is always very eager to begin new projects, but somehow he is never able to complete them.

TROUBLESHOOTING

1. Do not confuse adverbs with adjectives that have the same form. Remember that adjectives modify only nouns and pronouns and that adverbs modify adjectives, other adverbs, verbs, and entire sentences.

She was arriving on the early train. (*Early* tells something about the noun *train*, and because it modifies a noun, it is an adjective.)
She was arriving early by train. (*Early* tells something about the verb *was arriving*, and because it modifies a verb, it is an adverb.)

2. Be especially careful to choose correctly between adjective and adverb forms, particularly when the verb is a linking verb.

John felt badly. (*Badly* is the adverb form and because it is an adverb, the reader is concerned about John's poor sensory ability.)
John felt bad. (Because *bad* is the adjective form, we know that it modifies *John* and communicates the idea that John was sick or in poor spirits.)
INCORRECT   Things are going good for me. (*Good* is always the adjective form and cannot explain how things are going.)
CORRECT   Things are going well for me. (*Well* is the adverbial equivalent of the adjective *good*.)

NAME _____ DATE _____

DIRECTIONS: Underline all adverbs in the following sentences. Then choose one adverb from those underlined and use it in an original sentence to be written on the line provided.

EXAMPLE: The cat <u>rather</u> <u>haughtily</u> peered <u>down</u> from the top of the refrigerator.

The man haughtily demanded to see the messenger.

1. Darlene seldom had seen Jessica react so furiously to criticism as she did then.

_____

2. When has her mother-in-law ever treated her so well as she did yesterday?

_____

3. The police temporarily blocked the road and were routinely questioning all passersby.

_____

4. Mark's entry was not good enough to win first prize; however, it did earn him a job interview later with one of the judges.

_____

5. Sally, the chimpanzee, responded intelligently to all of the questions and, in fact, seemed intensely stimulated by all of the attention lavishly paid her during the experiments.

_____

6. "Gene always brought his sister along when he came to football practice, and eventually she became a pretty good quarterback," the coach said, grinning broadly.

_____

7. How did the crew discover that a man had fallen overboard?

_____

8. Nancy, appropriately dressed for every occasion, always looked somewhat like a mannequin.

_____

9. Tom flinched only slightly when the dentist accidentally hit a nerve.

_____

10. First the mechanic slowly shook his head and then, coughing nervously, he handed Mr. Joplin the outrageously high bill for the repair job.

_____

11. Andrew really did not know how the warped record had gotten mixed in with the others.

_____

12. Mr. O'Brien had scarcely eaten a bite of his toast before the piercing buzz of the doorbell summoned him quickly to his feet.

_____

13. Why would Mr. Pienta rather drive to work than take the commuter train?

_____

14. The girl tiptoed very cautiously into the dark room, hesitating only momentarily at the door.

_____

15. Usually the bank had already closed when Lauren got there, but on Friday she miraculously arrived in time.

_____

16. "The whole disaster was entirely your fault," Bert's father said firmly, gripping the arms of his chair so hard that his knuckles whitened.

_____

17. Mr. Huff always welcomed his guests warmly, jovially introduced them to each other, and then promptly sneaked off to bed, leaving the partygoers to fend for themselves.

_____

NAME _____ DATE _____

PART A

DIRECTIONS: Write *adj.* in each blank following an italicized adjective and *adv.* in each blank following an italicized adverb.

EXAMPLE: The sun was *already*   _adv._   high   _adj._   when we set
out   _adv._ .

1. Watching crowds milling *around* _____ in a public place is a fascinating pastime, and *no* _____ place provides a *better* _____ setting for an *intense* _____ look at our fellow beings than a passenger lounge at the airport does.

2. A *strange* _____ robotlike man in a rumpled brown suit scurries *past* _____ so that he can be *first* _____ at the check-in counter to get his tickets and get rid of his baggage.

3. He tries *hard* _____ to appear calm, but he *nervously* _____ brushes imaginary dandruff from his shoulders as he asks, in a *timid* _____ voice, if the plane is *late* _____.

4. Going *first* _____ left and then *right* _____ in the waiting room, he settles into a *plastic* _____ chair, *not* _____ to read or to watch the other people checking in, but to stare at the *least* _____ interesting things—the specks in the tile floor and the *splotchy* _____ ceiling.

5. The waiting room fills *fast* _____, and the *early* _____ silence of the *open* _____ area grows to a *hypnotic* _____ drone.

6. Some passengers speak of *past* _____ travels; others seem calloused by *daily* _____ flights; and *still* _____ others cower in dread, wishing that they were *outside* _____ in the warm sunshine like the maintenance people servicing *several* _____ planes on the ground *far* _____ below the terminal.

7. *Three* _____ boisterous children head *straight* _____ for the window, *quickly* _____ smudging it with handprints as they watch a *very* _____ shiny jet take off and fly *east* _____ into a patch of clouds.

8. A *tearful* _____ woman who obviously visits her grandchildren *only* _____ once or twice a year at last turns her back to her family and walks *resolutely* _____ to the counter, her head held high.

9. Two businessmen who are *uncomfortably* _____ hot _____ from their three-piece suits and *overly* _____ tight _____ collars sit conversing *casually* _____, fanning themselves with today's *Wall Street Journal*, hoping that the plane will *soon* _____ be *ready* _____ for boarding.

10. And, as *always* _____ happens, just as the *final* _____ call is being made, a straggler appears, striding *boldly* _____ to the ticket agent, *coolly* _____ demanding his choice of seats in an *egotistical* _____ tone that denies that he could be anything but *right* _____ or that he has *ever* _____ arrived anywhere *too* _____ *late* _____ to be given *first* _____ priority.

11. The passengers crowd into the jetway, *politely* _____ jostling each other as they imagine themselves arriving at their *faraway* _____ destinations.

12. Another flight has been *successfully* _____ filled, and as the plane rolls *back* _____ from the terminal, *inside* _____, another *frantic* _____ little man finds it imperative to hurry to the head of the line for the *next* _____ flight.

PART B

DIRECTIONS: Write one sentence to meet each specification.

    EXAMPLE: Use *small* as an adjective.

    She has a small head and can't find hats to fit her.

1. Use *high* as an adverb.

    _____

2. Use *high* as an adjective.

    _____

3. Use *far* as an adverb.

    _____

4. Use *far* as an adjective.

    _____

5. Use *hard* as an adverb.

    _____

6. Use *hard* as an adjective.

    _____

7. Use *good* as an adjective.

    _____

8. Use *well* as an adverb.

    _____

7/PARTS OF SPEECH: PRONOUNS

A **pronoun** is a word that is used as a substitute for a noun.

7a CHARACTERISTICS

Although there are a number of different kinds of pronouns, they all are used instead of nouns (or instead of phrases or clauses serving as nouns).

> Noun   Pron
> The actor performed well. He was applauded warmly. (*He* substitutes for *The actor*.)
>
> Noun   Pron
> Felice, who wants to be a teacher, now works in a day-care center. (*Who* substitutes for *Felice*.)
>
> Pron   Phrase
> It is very hard to find a good carpenter. (*It* substitutes for *to find a good carpenter*.)

In addition, a pronoun is used when the appropriate noun is unknown or unspecified, or when there is no appropriate noun to act as subject.

> Someone must go to the store. (It is not known exactly who will go.)
>
> It has been raining all day. (There is no appropriate noun subject for *has been raining*.)

The **antecedent** of a pronoun is the noun (or phrase or clause) that is replaced by the pronoun. Pronouns always have the same number (singular or plural) as their antecedents.

Pronouns serve the same functions in sentences that nouns do.

SUBJECT	They are not coming.
SUBJECT COMPLEMENT	The culprit was she.
DIRECT OBJECT	John kicked it across the floor.
INDIRECT OBJECT	Anna gave her the letters.
OBJECT COMPLEMENT	I am not an expert, but I consider him one.
OBJECT OF A PREPOSITION	The platter was on the shelf above him.
APPOSITIVE	Glenda bought a new refrigerator, one with an ice-maker.
DIRECT ADDRESS	Hey, you with the stars in your eyes!
NOMINATIVE ABSOLUTE	Everything having been decided by the lawyers beforehand, the hearing was a mere formality.

7b CLASSES

Pronouns can be divided into a number of different classes, depending on their form and their function in a sentence.

1. **Personal pronouns** indicate the category known as **person.** They distinguish the individual who is speaking (*first person*), the one spoken to (*second person*), and the person or thing being talked about (*third person*). For each person, singular or plural, there are three **cases**: the **subject case,** used for subjects and subject complements; the **object case,** used for objects of all kinds; and the **possessive case,** which substitutes for a possessive adjective and its noun. The third-person singular personal pronoun is also inflected for **gender,** which indicates whether a person or thing being talked about is a male (*masculine gender*), a female (*feminine gender*), or neither (*neuter gender*). The following table summarizes all the forms of the personal pronoun.

PERSON	CASE	NUMBER	
		SINGULAR	PLURAL
First	Subject	I	we
	Object	me	us
	Possessive	mine	ours
Second	Subject	you	you
	Object	you	you
	Possessive	yours	yours

		GENDER		
		MASCULINE	FEMININE	NEUTER
Third	Subject	he	she	it they
	Object	him	her	it them
	Possessive	his	hers	its theirs

2. **Reflexive pronouns** indicate that the object of the verb or preposition is the same as the subject of the clause. Reflexive pronouns are formed by adding *-self* (singular) or *-selves* (plural) to the personal pronouns (*myself, yourself, himself, herself, itself, oneself, ourselves, yourselves, themselves*).

Geraldine treated <u>herself</u> to a manicure.
We looked at <u>ourselves</u> in the mirror.

3. **Intensive pronouns** emphasize a noun or pronoun, usually following it or coming at the end of a clause. Intensive pronouns have the same form as reflexive pronouns.

The doctor <u>herself</u> had told him.
The doctor had told him <u>herself</u>.

4. **Demonstrative pronouns** indicate that particular things are "nearer to" (*this, these*) or "farther from" (*that, those*) the speaker.

<u>This</u> is too small, but <u>that</u> fits perfectly.

5. **Interrogative pronouns** introduce questions. The interrogative pronouns are *what, which, who, whose, whom,* and their forms in *-ever* (*whatever, whichever, whoever, whosever, whomever*).

What does Milton want?
Whoever told you that?

6. **Relative pronouns** introduce dependent clauses and serve as subjects or objects in those clauses. Relative pronouns are identical in form to interrogative pronouns (*what, which, who, whose, whom*, and their forms in *-ever*). In addition, *that* is also used as a relative pronoun. *What* and *which* refer to things, *who* and *whom* to persons, and *that* and *whose* to either persons or things.

Do you know what Milton wanted?
She tells whoever will listen all her problems.

7. **Indefinite pronouns** refer to members of a category or a part of a category without specifiying which particular members or parts. Indefinite pronouns include *another, each, either, neither, one, both, few, many, several, all, enough, more, most, other, some, such, less, little, much, any*, and *none*. (Many of these words are also used as indefinite adjectives.) Compound indefinite pronouns, which are all singular, include *anybody, anything, anyone, somebody, something, someone, everybody, everything, everyone, nobody, nothing, no one.*

Both have enough; neither needs more.
Everybody has promised to be at the meeting. (Notice that *everybody* takes a singular word grammatically, although the sense of it is plural.)

8. **Reciprocal pronouns** indicate interaction between two or more persons or things. *One another* indicates interaction between two parties, and *each other* indicates interaction of more than two parties.

The two children splashed one another.
The four secretaries are rude to each other.

9. **Expletive pronouns** serve as subjects of sentences and clauses when no other subject is appropriate or when the true subject is a long clause. The expletive pronouns are *it* and *there*.

It is already too late to go to the beach.
There was no one else to do the job.

TROUBLESHOOTING

1. Do not confuse relative pronouns with relative adjectives. In both cases, the relative word introduces a dependent clause, but the relative adjective modifies a noun or a pronoun and the relative pronoun replaces a noun.

Mr. Beveliaque did not say which he was bringing. (*Which* replaces a noun and introduces a relative clause, so it is a relative pronoun.)

Mr. Beveliaque did not say <u>which painting</u> he was bringing. (*Which* modifies the noun *painting*, so it is a relative adjective.)

2. Do not confuse demonstrative pronouns with demonstrative adjectives.

<u>This</u> vacation was a real treat! (*This* modifies *vacation*, so it is an adjective.)
<u>This</u> was a real treat! (*This* is a pronoun.)

3. Do not confuse interrogative pronouns with interrogative adjectives.

<u>Whose towel</u> is that lying on the sand? (*Whose* is an adjective.)
<u>Whose</u> is that lying on the sand? (*Whose* is a pronoun.)

4. Remember that the possessive forms of the personal pronoun are *never* written with an apostrophe: *its, his, hers, ours, yours, theirs.* (*It's* always means "it is.")

5. Do not confuse the relative pronoun *that* with the subordinating conjunction *that*. *That* as a relative pronoun always has a grammatical function *within* the clause; *that* as a conjunction simply links the subordinate clause to an independent clause.

We saw the trail <u>that</u> was at the top of the mountain. (*That* is the subject of the verb *was*.)
We saw <u>that</u> the trail would end at the top of the mountain. (*That* is a conjunction here; it could be omitted.)

NAME _____ DATE _____

PART A

DIRECTIONS: Underline all pronouns in the following sentences. Then, above each pronoun, write the letter from the list below that indicates the function of the pronoun in the sentence.

A. Subject   E. Object complement
B. Subject complement   F. Object of a preposition
C. Direct object   G. Appositive
D. Indirect object   H. Direct address
                              I. Nominative absolute

EXAMPLE: Jenkins punched <u>him</u> in the nose, and then <u>he</u> [*E*, *A*]
rushed from the room.

1. No one seemed the least bit amused by the trick, one which Uncle Walter had

practiced before with great success.

2. That was it for Wallace; he swore never to return.

3. We wanted to give her something really wacky.

4. The senator's defeat was a surprise to no one, least of all to him.

5. Sally and Edith gave one another very cool stares when they met at the party

wearing identical dresses.

6. Several of them had planned to attend the convention, but the flu sent them to

the infirmary instead.

7. "It's the one I want," Mrs. Miller insisted, "and don't think for a minute that you can trick me with a cheap imitation."

8. The cabinet above him burst open, and Ken watched as four antique serving dishes crashed into pieces around his feet.

9. Sylvia found David something amusing to read while he was convalescing.

10. No one having answered the door, both of them returned to the dark street.

11. Albert wanted a wife, someone to care for him always.

12. They do not consider a visit from their cousins anything special.

13. We have never seen them as angry with one another as they are this time.

14. "That is exactly the book Harry lost, and this is just like my broken vase," Mrs. Brundige said as she surveyed the bargains at the flea market.

15. "You there, halt!" the policeman shouted as he raised his gun and aimed it.

PART B

DIRECTIONS: Underline all the pronouns in the following sentences. Above each, write the letter from the list below that identifies the kind of pronoun it is.

A. Personal	F. Relative
B. Reflexive	G. Indefinite
C. Intensive	H. Reciprocal
D. Demonstrative	I. Expletive
E. Interrogative	

NAME _____ DATE _____

EXAMPLE: <u>There</u> is no sense in <u>anything</u> <u>that</u> <u>she</u> says.
            I   *G*   *F* *A*

1. Athena is the one who suggested that we visit one another more often.

2. The professor herself assured me that I could take the exam early.

3. The child's imagination ran away with him, and no one knew exactly what to

   do about his bewildering creativity.

4. "This is not what I ordered," Mrs. Brownlee assured that clerk.

5. The kittens chased each other through the house, their claws snagging furniture,

   draperies—everything they touched.

6. "The men only cheat themselves if they don't want to see the wisdom of this

   plan," the foreman told his boss.

7. "Everything that mechanic touches," Henry said, "begins to hum as if it were a

   brand-new machine."

8. What on earth is Scott planning to make out of that mound of pop tops?

9. Helen never knew who it was that told them about her past.

10. We promised to mail both of those to Lucy.

11. Didn't Matt say that someone would be waiting for us at the airport?

12. There was no relief from the blizzard; the storm drove its furious cold into

every chink and crevice of their cabin.

13. Someone standing on the side of the freeway was signaling for help, but

nobody was paying him any attention.

14. "Whose is this?" Gary's mother asked as she picked up Jane's scarf.

15. Several had been broken, but the others were like new.

PART C

DIRECTIONS: Write several (five or six) sentences about strangers you have watched interact in a public place. In your sentences use each class of pronoun at least once (see Part B of this set of exercises for a list of the classes of pronouns). Underline each pronoun in your sentences, and in the margin write what kind it is.

_____

_____

_____

_____

_____

_____

8/PARTS OF SPEECH: PREPOSITIONS

Prepositions are words used before nouns or pronouns (or phrases or clauses serving as nouns) to form phrases that modify other parts of the sentence. The following noun or pronoun is called the **object of the preposition**, and the combination of the preposition and its object is called a **prepositional phrase**.

PREPOSITIONAL PHRASES

Prep   Object
<u>about</u> your <u>story</u>

Prep   Object
<u>because of</u> <u>him</u>

Prep Object
<u>until</u> <u>tomorrow</u>

Prep   Object
<u>without</u> a <u>leg</u> to stand on

The following are some of the many English prepositions. Notice that some prepositions consist of more than one word.

about	at	but	near	through
above	because	by	next to	to
according to	before	down	of	toward
across	behind	during	off	under
after	below	except	on	underneath
against	beneath	for	out	until (till)
among	beside	from	over	up
around	between	in (into)	past	with
as	beyond	like	since	without

TROUBLESHOOTING

1. Do not confuse prepositions with adverbs or conjunctions that have the same form.

<u>Until</u> today, Laura did not think it possible. (*Until* is a preposition.)

<u>Until</u> Laura saw it, she did not think it possible. (*Until* is a subordinating conjunction because it introduces a dependent clause.)

No one was there <u>but</u> Larry. (*But* is a preposition.)

No one was there, <u>but</u> Larry was not lonely. (*But* is a coordinating conjunction, linking two independent clauses.)

<u>Inside</u> the hotel, crowds were trying to see the actress. (*Inside* is a preposition.)

<u>Inside</u>, crowds were trying to see the actress. (*Inside* is an adverb modifying the following clause.)

2. Do not confuse the preposition *to* and the word *to* that precedes an infinitive.

We wanted <u>to</u> see the magician. (*To see* is a verbal form, the infinitive.)

We walked <u>to</u> the beach. (*To* is a preposition followed by its object, *beach*.)

NAME _____ DATE _____

PART A

DIRECTIONS: Underline all prepositional phrases in the following sentences. Then choose *one* preposition from those underlined and use it in an original sentence to be written on the line provided.

EXAMPLE: Just out of the blue, Zach asked for a date.

I'm still waiting for that letter he promised to write.

1. Throughout the season, the team continued to improve its passing game.

   _____

2. Before the mail had come, Fred had been sure that he would never again hear from Cora.

   _____

3. Since Thursday, Flo and Anna have been on a strict diet.

   _____

4. The brightly colored hot-air balloon floated gracefully above the crowd like a giant buoy bobbing up and down in the water.

   _____

5. All of the boys except Tony must have walked past that store a dozen times before they summoned up enough courage to go in.

   _____

6. The hikers stopped several times along the trail to rest and to take pictures of the beautiful wildflowers around them.

   _____

7. Jane tried tapping the wall underneath the stairs, for that was without a doubt where she expected to find the safe.

   _____

8. After the sun had set, the crickets began their serenade and fireflies appeared down by the creek.

   _____

9. Wilbur's mother had forbidden him to walk across the neighbors' lawn because of all the complaints the neighbors had made about the rowdy children who lived in the area.

_____

10. As a prank, Joe's roommate refused to let him in, pretending that he had never seen Joe before in his entire life.

_____

11. Nora would have done anything for the job with the ad agency, but circumstances were beyond her control.

_____

12. Because he was held up for two hours in a traffic jam, Kevin did not come over at seven, as he had promised when they had talked during lunch.

_____

13. For some crazy reason, the campers all liked to be outside during rainstorms.

_____

14. Daniel saw straight through his parents' plan to send him away to boarding school in Connecticut.

_____

PART B

DIRECTIONS: Look for prepositional phrases in the titles of songs, books, movies, and television programs. On each line below write the title of one work and then put parentheses around the prepositional phrase or phrases in it. (Book and movie titles are underlined, song titles are enclosed in quotation marks, and television programs are either underlined or enclosed in quotation marks.)

_____

_____

_____

_____

_____

_____

9/PARTS OF SPEECH: CONJUNCTIONS

Just as railway or roadway *junctions* are places where tracks or roads come together, **conjunctions** are the places in sentences where words or phrases or clauses are hooked together. Conjunctions are *joining* words. There are three major kinds of conjunctions: coordinating conjunctions, adverbial conjunctions, and subordinating conjunctions.

9a COORDINATING CONJUNCTIONS

Coordinating conjunctions join elements that serve the same function in a sentence. For example, they may join two (or more) subjects, or two objects, or two independent clauses. The four principal coordinating conjunctions are *and, but, or,* and *nor. Yet*, often used as an adverb, may also function as a coordinating conjunction meaning "but." Even though they connect elements that are not completely parallel, *for* and *so* are often considered coordinating conjunctions because they are punctuated like coordinating conjunctions.

So, *for*, and *nor* (used without *neither*) join *only* clauses, but the other four conjunctions connect elements of all levels—words, phrases, and independent clauses.

> The desk was littered with crumbs and ashes. (*And* connects two nouns, *crumbs* and *ashes*, which are objects of the preposition *with*.)
>
> He would like to play golf or to explore the beach. (*Or* connects two infinitive phrases, which serve as direct objects—*to play golf* and *to explore the beach*.)
>
> Marion likes outdoor sports, but she really prefers chess to any other hobby. (*But* connects independent clauses.)
>
> The dog would not eat, nor did she seem at all playful. (*Nor* connects independent clauses.)
>
> Amanda ate pastry constantly, yet she never gained weight. (*Yet* joins independent clauses.)
>
> The manager appeared at once, for we had refused to pay our bill. (*For* joins independent clauses. The second clause expresses the cause for the action of the first.)
>
> Richard's mother begged him to get his shoulder-length hair trimmed, so he resorted to a G.I. cut. (*So* joins independent clauses. The second clause expresses the result of the action of the first.)

Correlative conjunctions are special kinds of coordinating conjunctions. They occur *only* in pairs. Frequently used correlative conjunctions are the following:

both . . . and	as . . . as
either . . . or	(just) as . . . so
neither . . . nor	such . . . as
not only . . . but (also)	no (*or* not) . . . or
whether . . . or	not so much (that) . . . as
the . . . the	

Frederick could <u>neither</u> play an instrument <u>nor</u> dance.

<u>The</u> more you race the engine, <u>the</u> deeper the wheels will sink.

<u>Such</u> houseplants <u>as</u> philodendron are easy to grow.

Greta was <u>not only</u> very loud <u>but</u> she was <u>also</u> boring.

9b ADVERBIAL CONJUNCTIONS

Adverbial conjunctions (also called **conjunctive adverbs**; see 6) are like coordinating conjunctions in that they join independent clauses, but, while coordinating conjunctions always appear at the *beginning* of a clause, adverbial conjunctions sometimes appear within a clause. Adverbial conjunctions express such diverse meanings as illustration (*for instance, namely*), addition (*moreover, also*), contrast (*however, nevertheless*), qualification (*in fact, undoubtedly*), result (*therefore, consequently*), attitude (*fortunately, unhappily*), summary (*finally, in other words*), and time (*then, thereafter*).

> The test is tomorrow; <u>therefore</u>, Henry is cramming tonight. (Henry is cramming tonight as a result of the fact that the test is tomorrow.)
> The test is tomorrow. <u>Therefore</u>, Henry is cramming tonight.
> The test is tomorrow; Henry is, <u>therefore</u>, cramming tonight.

> Michael is handsome; <u>however</u>, his brother is both handsome and witty. (*However* expresses a contrast between Michael and his brother.)
> Michael is handsome. <u>However</u>, his brother is both handsome and witty.
> Michael is handsome; his brother, <u>however</u>, is both handsome and witty.

Notice that when an adverbial conjunction is at the *beginning* of a clause, it is either (1) preceded by a semicolon and followed by a comma, or (2) begins an entirely new sentence and is followed by a comma. When the conjunctive adverb is *within* the clause, it is set off by commas.

9c SUBORDINATING CONJUNCTIONS

Subordinating conjunctions connect clauses that are not grammatically parallel. That is, the subordinating conjunction makes the idea in the following clause dependent on the independent clause, to which it *must* be connected. Adding a subordinating conjunction to an independent clause makes that independent clause "lower in rank" than an independent clause.

> They went to the costume party. (This is an independent clause.)
> <u>When</u> they went to the costume party. (This is not a sentence or an independent clause because the subordinating conjunction *when* makes it dependent on an independent clause. Read aloud, the *when* clause is obviously an incomplete idea, though the idea as expressed before the *when* was added is a complete thought.)

Among the most frequently used subordinating conjunctions are *after, (al)though, as, as if, because, before, if, since, that, unless, when*, and *while*.

After he had finished his biology homework, Stan went outside to play Frisbee. He locked his dog inside when he left because Woofer always got too excited over Frisbee games. While he was gone, Woofer chewed up his lab notebook.

Some subordinating conjunctions occur in pairs: *if. . .then, no sooner. . .than, scarcely. . .when, so. . .that*, and *such. . .that*.

If you leave your bicycle unlocked, then it will surely be stolen.
No sooner had it begun to thunder than the rain began to pour.

Some subordinating conjunctions occur in *elliptical* clauses, or clauses in which the verb or both the subject and verb have been omitted, though they are obvious to the reader.

If possible, I will call you tonight. ("If *it is* possible" is understood.)
Sasha is as tall as Dora. ("As Dora *is*" is understood.)

TROUBLESHOOTING

1. Do not confuse conjunctions with adverbs or prepositions that have the same form as the conjunctions.

After the trial had ended, the crowds quickly dispersed. (*After* functions here as a subordinating conjunction.)
After the trial, the crowds quickly dispersed. (*After* functions here as a preposition.)
Everyone came, but no one seemed to have any fun. (*But* is a coordinating conjunction in this sentence.)
Everyone came but Joe. (*But* functions here as a preposition.)

2. Remember that when adverbial conjunctions join two main clauses in one sentence, the clauses *must* be separated by a semicolon. If you use a comma here, the result is a comma splice. If you use no punctuation, the result is a fused sentence. Both comma splices and fused sentences are serious punctuation errors.

COMMA SPLICE	Eileen has just been promoted, consequently, she is celebrating.
FUSED SENTENCE	Eileen has just been promoted consequently she is celebrating.
CORRECT	Eileen has just been promoted; consequently, she is celebrating.

NAME _____ DATE _____

PART A

DIRECTIONS: Underline all the conjunctions in the following paragraphs. Then, on the lines following each passage, list each conjunction and tell what kind it is (coordinating or subordinating). Don't forget to underline and list both elements of correlative conjunctions and subordinating conjunctions that occur in pairs.

> EXAMPLE: Lunch was the principal meal of the day, and its main course often featured spaghetti or macaroni, for Einstein had a special liking for Italian food, perhaps as a consequence of a happy year he had spent with his parents in Milan as a boy. After lunch he would ascend to his study, sometimes to nap, but often as not to continue his calculations. In the evening after a light supper, if there were no guests he would return to his study and work far into the night on his lonely quest.
>
> —Lincoln Barnett, *"On His Centennial: The Spirit of Einstein Abides in Princeton," Smithsonian*

and — coordinating, or — coordinating,

for — coordinating, but — coordinating,

if — subordinating, and — coordinating

1. The thirties were born prematurely and disastrously on Thursday 24 October 1929 when the New York Stock Exchange closed its doors. The events of that day were to affect the lives of millions, directly or indirectly, for years to come. The previous decade for all its reputation of hectic gaiety had had its realities of disillusion and hardship and to many the depression of the early thirties spelt out the end of any hopes they may have had. But for others—and they were in the majority—the bright bubble of a false prosperity vanished overnight, leaving them in a seemingly endless twilight of poverty and hopelessness. The arts survived as they always do, for there were still a number of rich patrons who were either unaffected by the recurring financial crises or even richer as a result of those same crises.

—Martin Battersby, *THE DECORATIVE THIRTIES*

_____

_____

_____

2. As an 18th-century father, Peale was as concerned for his children's education as he was for the shape of his museum or the quality of a portrait—perhaps more so. Educated in the writings of French and English Enlightenment philosophers and scientists, he shared Rousseau's conviction that children should be led "to the paths of Virtue with a Chain of Flowers," that education provided the answer to most of society's ills. Just as he planned his museum so that its organization as well as its exhibits would instruct the public in nature's order and harmony, so he created a family structure that would allow his children to develop freely within a discipline imposed by an understanding of nature's laws.

—Lillian B. Miller, *"The Peale Family:*
A Lively Mixture of Art and Science," Smithsonian

PART B

DIRECTIONS: Write five or six sentences about an unpleasant dilemma you have experienced. In the sentences be sure that you use and underline at least (1) three different coordinating conjunctions, (2) four subordinating conjunctions, (3) two adverbial conjunctions—one between independent clauses and the other within an independent clause. Indicate what each conjunction is by writing above it *C* for coordinating, *S* for subordinating, and *A* for adverbial.

NAME _____ DATE _____

DIRECTIONS: In the blank following each italicized word, identify that word as one of the following. Be sure to look at the context before deciding how the word functions in the sentence.

Conj. (Conjunction)
Prep. (Preposition)

EXAMPLE: Jeff had nothing valuable with him *but* ___*Prep.*___ his watch.

1. *Once* _____ you have bought a car, either new or used, familiarizing yourself with procedures *for* _____ routine engine maintenance and for keeping the car clean will prolong its life long *after* _____ the demise of less well-kept autos.

2. *Before* _____ raising the hood and tinkering around with wires and caps, read your owner's manual thoroughly *until* _____ you know where the battery is, how to find the oil gauge (or dipstick) *for* _____ checking oil, and where the reservoirs are that hold brake fluid, radiator fluid, and windshield-wiper fluid.

3. *Because* _____ an engine cannot run without oil, you should check the oil level at least once every two weeks.

4. *After* _____ locating the dipstick, simply pull it out, wipe it off with a rag, push it back into the same opening *until* _____ it will not go in any farther, and then pull it out, checking the oil level on the gauge imprinted on the rod.

5. If your motor oil is low by as much as a quart, you should add some oil *before* _____ you drive the car, pouring oil into the engine's reservoir *as* _____ you take care to avoid a spill, which might cause the engine to smoke.

6. *After* _____ you have checked the oil, next check the fluid level in the radiator, brakes, and transmission, *since* _____ lack of fluid in any of these engine parts could lead to serious mechanical problems and dangerous conditions *for* _____ the driver.

7. Brake fluid and radiator fluid (and wiper fluid) can be quickly checked, *for* _____ their levels are easily seen in their translucent reservoirs, *but* _____ checking the transmission fluid requires keeping the motor running *until* _____ the level of the fluid can be read on a dipstick.

8. All of the important routine checks *but* _____ two are made under the hood, *but* _____ these two important checks—noting the condition of the tires and the body—are no less important than the others *for* _____ safety and economy.

9. *As* _____ a result of looking at the tires, especially if it has been more than a couple of weeks *since* _____ the last check, you can tell if the tires are wearing evenly and if a worn mark has yet been exposed.

10. *Because* _____ having the wrong amount of air in your tires can make them wear out faster than they otherwise might, use the air pump at a service station to keep the tires filled, *yet* _____ not over- or underfilled.

11. Maintaining the body of the car is also important *for* _____ a long life and good resale value, *so* _____ don't forget to look for chipped places in the surface, which you should paint *before* _____ rusting occurs.

12. Preventive maintenance will not solve all of your car's problems, *but* _____ setting up a regular schedule *for* _____ checking your car inside and out will keep you from waiting so long that it needs major repairs, and it will keep your car in tip-top shape *until* _____ trade-in time.

10/ISOLATES

Isolates are words and phrases that are used either as separate utterances by themselves or that are independent of (isolated from) the grammar of the sentences in which they appear. Some isolates are onomatopoetic (imitative of sounds not used in normal speech): *Ugh!, Whew!, Yikes!, Hmmm.*

Some isolates are set off by commas; others are completely separated from the sentence and are followed by a period or exclamation point.

<u>No</u>, I think you are mistaken.

He was here, <u>yes</u>, but he's gone now.

<u>Yuk</u>! How can anyone eat snails?

<u>Ah-h-h</u>! That's just what the doctor ordered.

Isolates are used in various kinds of situations.

1. **Agreement and disagreement.** Yes, No, Nix, Yeah, Yep, Roger, Nope, Okay, Right, No way!, Uh-uh, Maybe.

2. **Meeting and parting.** Hello, See you, Good morning, Bye, See you later, Have a good day, Take care, So long, How are you?, How do you do?, Fine, and you?, Nice to see you.

3. **Asking and receiving.** Please, Thank you, Thanks, You're welcome, Think nothing of it.

4. **Apology.** Pardon me, Sorry, Excuse me, Forgive me, Uh-oh, Whoops!, That's all right.

5. **Name-calling.** You numbskull!, Idiot!, Quack!, Dumb-dumb!, Jerk!, Dad, George, Good boy!

6. **Alarm or attention-getting.** Excuse me!, Watch it!, Watch out!, Duck!, Run!, Help!, Psst!, Listen here!, Sssh, Hey!

7. **Hesitation.** Uh, You know, I mean, Of course, Well, Why.

8. **Physical discomfort or comfort.** Ouch!, Yuk!, Ah-h-h!, Whew!, Mmmm!, Yum!, Eek!, Brrr!

9. **Special occasions.** Happy anniversary!, Happy Hanukkah!, Best wishes!, Cheers!, Happy birthday!, Merry Christmas!, Good luck!

10. **Emotional reactions.** These range from mild interjections like *Gosh* or *Gee whiz* to swear words (which usually involve religious terms) and taboo words (which usually refer to bodily functions).

11/PHRASES

A **phrase** is a group of words arranged grammatically but not containing both a subject and a verb. A phrase may serve as a subject, the main part of a predicate, a complement, an object, or a modifier. There are four major kinds of phrases.

11a NOUN PHRASES

A **noun phrase** consists of a noun and all its modifiers. The noun phrase functions just as a single noun does.

SUBJECT	The snaggletoothed kid is her brother.
DIRECT OBJECT	Chuck brought a small pickup truck.
INDIRECT OBJECT	The vet gave the fat, black cat a bath and a shot.
SUBJECT COMPLEMENT	The speaker was a balding, middle-aged man with a squeaky voice.
OBJECT COMPLEMENT	She considered the film a poor representation of the novel.
OBJECT OF A PREPOSITION	She stopped at a rundown fish market.
DIRECT ADDRESS	You with the roller-skates! Get out of my way.
NOMINATIVE ABSOLUTE	The long hot summer drawing to a close, sun-lovers abandoned the beaches.

Notice that a noun phrase may include other kinds of phrases. For example, in the fourth sentence, *with a squeaky voice* is a prepositional phrase included within the larger noun phrase *a balding, middle-aged man with a squeaky voice*. In the fifth sentence, the prepositional phrase *of the novel* is part of the larger noun phrase *a poor representation of the novel*.

11b VERB PHRASES

A **verb phrase** is made up of a main verb and all its auxiliaries. The verb phrase is the chief element in the predicate of a sentence.

He went to the store.
All the strawberries have been eaten.
She has refused to go with us.

11c VERBAL PHRASES

There are three kinds of **verbal phrases**: infinitive phrases, participle phrases, and gerund phrases.

An **infinitive phrase** is made up of the infinitive form of a verb, including the word *to*, and any objects or modifiers of the infinitive. Infinitives function as modifiers, subjects, objects, or complements.

MODIFIER	Jackson's book was too realistic to be forgotten. (*To be forgotten* modifies the adjective *realistic*.)
MODIFIER	Uncle Martin has money to throw away. (*To throw away* modifies the rest of the sentence.)
SUBJECT	To be careless is very uncharacteristic of Florence. (The infinitive phrase, consisting of the infinitive *to be* and its complement *careless*, is the subject.)
OBJECT	I like to watch parades. (*To watch parades* is the direct object of the verb *like*.)
COMPLEMENT	The main point of poker is to win the pot. (*To win the pot* is the subject complement.)

A **participle phrase** is made up of a present participle or past participle and its objects, complements, and modifiers. Participle phrases serve as modifiers.

Whistling loudly, the mail carrier rang the bell. (*Whistling* is a present participle, and *loudly* is an adverb that modifies *whistling*. The participle phrase modifies the rest of the sentence.)

Determined to get some sleep, Jonas drank some warm milk. (*Determined to get some sleep* modifies the subject of the sentence, *Jonas*. It is made up of the past participle *determined*, the infinitive *to get*, and *some sleep*, the direct object of the infinitive.)

Having received her refund, Mrs. Veach stalked angrily out of the store. (*Having received* is a perfect participle, that is, a present participle plus a past participle. The phrase consists of the perfect participle *having received* and its direct object, *her refund*. The entire phrase modifies the subject, *Mrs. Veach*.)

An **absolute phrase** is a special kind of participle phrase, consisting of a noun or pronoun, and a participle. An absolute phrase modifies an entire clause or sentence.

The decision once made, the two men began to set up camp. (*The decision once made* is an absolute phrase consisting of a noun phrase, *the decision*; an adverb, *once*; and a past participle, *made*.)

A **gerund phrase** is made up of a gerund, its modifiers, and its objects, if there are any. A gerund is a noun made from a verb by adding *-ing*. Gerund phrases are subjects, objects, or complements.

SUBJECT	Cleaning the oven is Gerald's least favorite chore. (*Cleaning* is the gerund, and *the oven* is its object.)
OBJECT	We were all in favor of walking out of the meeting. (*Walking* is the gerund, and the adverb *out* and the prepositional phrase *of the meeting* are its modifiers.)
COMPLEMENT	Their favorite pastime is surfing.

11d PREPOSITIONAL PHRASES

A **prepositional phrase** includes a preposition, its object or objects, and any modifiers of the object. Prepositional phrases are usually modifiers.

> A package <u>with no return address</u> was delivered to Mrs. Pahlitzsch. (*With no return address* modifies the noun *package*.)
>
> The sunburned fisherman climbed wearily <u>onto the pier</u>. (*Onto the pier* modifies the verb *climbed*.)

TROUBLESHOOTING

1. Do not confuse participle phrases and gerund phrases. Both the present participle and the gerund end in *-ing*, so that both forms look exactly alike: *going, seeing, discovering.* The difference is in the way they function. Gerunds *always* serve as nouns. Participles are either parts of verb phrases or are modifiers.

> The cat is <u>jumping</u> off the refrigerator. (Here, *jumping* is a participle and part of the verb phrase *is jumping*; it tells what the cat is doing.)
>
> The cat <u>jumping</u> off the refrigerator is Ajax. (Here, *jumping* tells which cat— the one doing the jumping—so it is a modifier and, thus, a participle.)
>
> <u>Jumping</u> off the refrigerator is easy for our cat. (Here, *jumping* is serving as a noun because it is the subject of the sentence. Thus it must be a gerund.)

2. Do not confuse a past participle phrase with the past tense or past participle of a finite verb.

> The child, <u>loved</u> by everyone, was a genius. (Here, *loved* is a part participle describing the child, telling which child—the one loved.)
>
> The child was <u>loved</u> by everyone. (Here, *loved* is part of the main verb, *was loved*, the past tense, passive voice.)

3. Do not confuse an infinitive phrase with a prepositional phrase. Both infinitive phrases and some prepositional phrases begin with *to*, but prepositional phrases are always followed by an object. The *to* of the infinitive is always followed by the infinitive form of the verb.

> Ralph hurried <u>to the store</u>. (*To the store* is a prepositional phrase modifying the verb *hurried*.)
>
> Ralph wanted <u>to hurry</u> to the store. (*To hurry* is an infinitive functioning as the direct object of the verb *wanted*.)

NAME _____ DATE _____

PART A

DIRECTIONS: In the blank after each italicized phrase, write the letter from the first column below that defines the kind of phrase and the number from the second column that explains how that phrase functions. If the italicized phrase contains other phrases, label only the larger element.

A. Verb	1. Main verb
B. Noun	2. Subject
C. Prepositional	3. Direct object
D. Infinitive	4. Indirect object
E. Participle	5. Subject complement
F. Gerund	6. Object complement
G. Absolute	7. Object of a preposition
	8. Modifier

EXAMPLE: *After the game* __*C-8*__ the two couples *had driven* __*A-1*__ out to the beach *to have* __*D-8*__ a quiet seafood dinner.

1. *A thunderstorm threatening* _____, Eric and Rick began *packing* _____ all their fishing gear *into the camper* _____.

2. *Finding this secluded cove* _____ had not been easy, but the two men had searched hard *to find* _____ a place that *would offer* _____ them *a much-needed vacation* _____ from their hectic days *as staff doctors* _____ in a children's hospital.

3. *From the outset* _____, however, the fishing expedition had been doomed *to fail* _____, and *the storm* _____, rumbling and flashing and lashing trees *across the lake* _____, seemed only the latest disaster *to jinx* _____ the excursion.

4. After *parking their camper* _____, they decided *to go fishing* _____ at once, but attempts at *launching their small motor boat* _____ proved frustrating: *the marshy, spongy shoreline* _____ bogged down the boat trailer over and over again.

5. *The boat finally launched* _____, the fishermen found *starting the motor* _____ impossible, and they had to content themselves *with rowing* _____ out into the lake.

6. The lake was *a mirror* _____, *reflecting the outline* _____ *of the boat* _____ as well as the willow branches *drooped over the shore* _____.

7. Eric gave *his fellow fisherman* _____ a smile of contentment as he made *his first cast* _____ into the clear water.

8. *Feeling the line suddenly go taut* _____, Eric, *convinced that he had a bite* _____, jumped *to his feet* _____ *with excitement* _____, *tipping the boat over into the lake* _____.

9. The two men, cold and weary from *struggling to right the boat* _____, realized that the spill had sent *their rods, tackle boxes, bait, cooler, and other equipment* _____ to the bottom of the lake.

10. Sulkily they rowed back to shore, *the oars having been found afloat near the boat* _____, and once back on soggy land, Rick called Eric *"a blinking idiot" and "a blundering, clumsy fool"* _____ over and over until *utter frustration* _____ quieted him.

11. Once their clothes dried, they gradually began *to see the humor of the spill* _____, and they vowed to cook dinner and have a cozy evening *around a roaring fire* _____ —in spite of their misfortune.

12. *To cook dinner* _____, however, seemed *a physical impossibility* _____: Eric *somehow had forgotten* _____ the gas for the stove _____; all the matches they had brought were in their jacket pockets when the boat turned over; and *the box of provisions* _____ turned out to be Rick's son's science project, *mistakenly picked up in Rick's kitchen* _____ in the rush *to leave* _____.

13. *Going home* _____ seemed *the only thing* _____ *to do* _____ (though neither man wanted to be the one to suggest it), and the storm *rumbling and flashing close by* _____ spirited them into *packing their remaining possessions and pulling out* _____.

PART B

DIRECTIONS: Write one sentence using each of the elements specified below and underline the element being used.

EXAMPLE: A prepositional phrase used as an adjectival

It certainly was a house of cards that he had built.

1. A gerund phrase used as a subject

_____

2. A prepositional phrase used as a modifier

_____

3. An infinitive phrase used as a direct object

_____

4. A nominative absolute

_____

12/CLAUSES

A **clause** is a sequence of words that contains a subject and a predicate. There are two kinds of clauses: independent (or main) and dependent (or subordinate) clauses.

12a INDEPENDENT CLAUSES

An **independent clause** (or **main clause**) can stand alone as a complete sentence. Even if the sentence in which it occurs contains other clauses, either independent or dependent, an independent clause can still be read alone as a complete sentence.

> The band began to play loudly. (independent clause)
>
> After it got warmed up, the band began to play loudly. (*The band began to play loudly* still makes sense as a complete sentence if you remove it from the larger sentence in which it occurs.)

12b DEPENDENT CLAUSES

A **dependent clause** is introduced by a subordinating word (a subordinating conjunction or a relative pronoun, adjective, or adverb) and must be attached to a main clause. It cannot stand alone as a complete sentence.

> After the game was over, the clean-up crew moved out onto the field. (*After the game was over* is a clause that has a subject, *game*, and a predicate, *was over*, but it begins with the subordinating conjunction *after*. Therefore, it must be joined to an independent clause to make a complete sentence.)

Noun clauses function as subjects, objects, or complements, just as single nouns and pronouns do. They are usually introduced by such words as *that, who, which, what, whom, whoever, whomever, whatever, whichever,* and *whether*.

> Whatever they decide will be all right by me. (The clause has a subject, *they*, and a predicate, *decide*. The entire clause is the subject of the sentence.)
>
> I know that you enjoy horror movies. (The clause has a subject, *you*, and a predicate, *enjoy*. The entire clause is the direct object of the verb *know*.)

Adjective clauses modify nouns, pronouns, and some word groups functioning as nouns. Adjective clauses are typically introduced by relative pronouns (*what, which, who, whom, that*), relative adjectives (*what, which, whose, whatever, whichever, whosever*), and relative adverbs (*where, why,* and *how*).

> The bed that I was in collapsed. (The clause modifies the noun *bed*.)
>
> This is the place where Al was born. (The clause modifies the noun *place*.)

Adverb clauses modify verbs, verb phrases, adjectives, adverbs, or entire clauses. They are usually introduced by subordinating conjunctions.

Vincent ran as fast <u>as he could</u>. (The clause modifies the adverb *fast*.)

<u>Until the Civil War began</u>, West Virginia was part of Virginia. (The dependent clause modifies the entire independent clause.)

12c ELLIPTICAL CLAUSES

Both independent and dependent clauses are called **elliptical clauses** when the subject or predicate has been left out and is understood only from the context.

Amy is bringing steaks and <u>Joan a salad and dessert</u>. (*Is bringing* is understood after *Joan*. This is an elliptical independent clause.)

<u>Although very well-mannered to adults</u>, the boy is a terror around other children. (*He is* is understood after *although*, and because that clause begins with a subordinating conjunction, the clause is an elliptical dependent clause.)

TROUBLESHOOTING

1. Do not write a dependent clause alone as a sentence. A dependent clause that is not attached to a main clause is called a *sentence fragment*.

INCORRECT	Because they wanted to take a look.
CORRECT	Because they wanted to take a look, they stayed behind.
INCORRECT	That he was coming with us.
CORRECT	Margie had not told anyone that he was coming with us.

2. Do not confuse noun clauses with adjective clauses. Both kinds of dependent clauses can begin with many of the same words, but the kind of clause it is depends entirely on its function within the sentence.

Harris did not know that Tetia had graduated. (*That Tetia had graduated* is a noun clause because it is the direct object, telling what it was that Harris did not know. *That* is a subordinating conjunction here.)

That was the jacket that his mother had given him. (*That his mother had given him* is a relative clause modifying *jacket*. *That* is a relative pronoun.)

3. Do not confuse clauses and phrases. A clause has both a subject and a predicate. Phrases may have infinitives, participles, or gerunds, but not full predicates.

CLAUSE	The church <u>that the tornado destroyed</u> will not be rebuilt. (The clause has a subject, *tornado*, and a predicate, *destroyed*.)
PHRASE	The church <u>destroyed by the tornado</u> will not be rebuilt. (The phrase has no subject.)

NAME _____ DATE _____

PART A

DIRECTIONS: In the blank after each italicized group of words, identify the italicized element as one of the following.

    NC not a clause   D-NO dependent noun clause

     I independent clause   D-ADV dependent adverb clause

   IE independent elliptical clause   D-ADJ dependent adjective clause

   DE dependent elliptical clause

> EXAMPLE: *That man waving and yelling to the construction crew* ____*NC*____ is the supervisor for this job, but *because of his hot temper and unpredictable moods* ____*NC*____, *all of the men really dislike him* ____*I*____.

1. Lou Ann could never decide *what to cook for dinner* _____: *each of her roommates liked a different kind of food* _____, and one of them refused to try anything *that she had not eaten as a child* _____, *much preferring pizza, hot dogs, and potato chips to meat and vegetables* _____.

2. *While shoveling the walk* _____, Gary found a half-frozen wren, which was completely revived after *spending the night indoors and feasting on some bread crumbs* _____.

3. *After she had talked Fred into auditioning for a part in the play* _____, Miriam, *who had never been in a play* _____, got cold feet and *convinced poor Fred to go alone to the audition* _____.

4. The new family *that moved into the old McCall house* _____ has not been eager to get acquainted with the neighbors; in fact, the husband leaves home at 8 a.m. each day, and *the wife and children at 9 a.m.* _____, and *no one returns home until nearly midnight* _____.

5. *In order for the entire committee to be there* _____, *the meeting had to be scheduled for a Friday night* _____, *an unpopular time with all the members* _____.

6. *Since their quarrel on Valentine's Day* _____, Frieda and Ed have not communicated at all, *in spite of their friends' efforts to get them together to talk over their differences* _____.

7. *Since they decided against selling the beach property to the industrial developer* _____, the Lentzes have learned *that many of their neighbors did sell* _____ *because the company offered to pay almost twice the appraised value of the property* _____.

8. *Because of the reputed side-effects of the drug* _____, Kelly was afraid to take it, *although her doctor assured her of its safety* _____.

9. *Suddenly the blackbirds came swarming into view* _____; they perched side by side along the utility lines like sitting ducks in a carnival game, and *as if by prearranged signal* _____, they abruptly flew off in unison, *forming a rapidly moving black cloud* _____.

10. *Even before the big blow-up in the office* _____, everyone knew *that something was going on* _____.

11. *Even before he had begun to speak* _____, Ellen had sensed that his message would not be pleasant, and *she was not wrong* _____, for *the essence of his remarks was clear* _____: *she had been disinherited by her father* _____.

12. *That the professor had had the nerve to assign a term paper over the Thanksgiving holidays* _____ really angered the class, *especially since he had not mentioned it until Thanksgiving week* _____.

13. *Before her beginner's course in auto mechanics* _____, Angela did not even know *what a spark plug is* _____ or *how often motor oil should be changed* _____.

PART B

DIRECTIONS: Write one sentence for each of the following specifications, and underline the specified element in your sentence.

> EXAMPLE: A sentence in which an adjective clause modifies the direct object.
>
> *Ruth wanted the rocking chair that had been her mother's.*

1. A sentence in which a noun clause is the direct object

_____

2. A sentence in which an adjective clause modifies the subject of the sentence

_____

3. A sentence that begins with an adverb clause

_____

4. A sentence with two independent clauses connected by a coordinating conjunction (with a comma before the coordinating conjunction)

_____

NAME _____ DATE _____

PART A

DIRECTIONS: In the blank following each group of italicized words in the following three passages, identify that group of words as a phrase (*P*), an independent clause (*IC*), or a dependent clause (*DC*).

> EXAMPLE: *After arriving home* ___P___, the old man, *who was tired from the long walk* ___DC___, brewed himself some coffee *and sat down to read the evening newspaper* ___P___.

1. *The typical comic book circa 1937-38* _____ measured about 7¼ by 10¼, averaged sixty-four pages in length, *was glisteningly processed in four colors on the cover and flatly and indifferently colored on the inside* _____, *if colored at all* _____. (For in the early days some stories were still in black and white; others in tones of sickly red on one page, sickly blue on another, *so that it was quite possible for a character to have a white face and blue clothing for the first two pages of a story and a pink face and red clothing for the rest* _____.) They didn't have the class of the daily strips but, to me, *this enhanced their value* _____. The daily strips, by their sleek professionalism, held an aloof quality which comic books, *being not quite professional* _____, easily avoided. They were closer to home, more comfortable to live with, less like grownups.

   —Jules Feiffer, *THE GREAT COMIC BOOK HEROES*

2. *When modern fliers think about Charles Lindbergh's flight across the ocean* _____, the picture *that probably comes into their minds* _____ is of a tiny silver monoplane, a speck in the limitless sky, *battling with the turbulent clouds tumbling against each other high above the Atlantic* _____. There were certainly periods in the flight when he had to fight the *Spirit of St. Louis* up to its maximum altitude *to pass over the storm and cloud conditions confronting him* _____, but in fact, for much of the way, he hugged so close to the sea *that he often had to remind himself of the danger of running into the masts of passing ships* _____. He had scoffed at reports that he used a periscope *for taking off and landing his plane* _____, but he had one aboard and used it for looking ahead *when he was airborne* _____. It was a simple affair run up for him by one of the workmen at the San Diego factory, two flat mirrors *set at the right angle in a tube* _____, which he could lower from the left side of the fuselage.

   —Leonard Mosley, *LINDBERGH: A BIOGRAPHY*

3. *In communicating emotions* _____, the dog's tail is the barometer of his ups and downs. And here again, in his emotional fluctuations, *there is a significant*

parallel with humans _____. *Through close association* _____, pets acquire many of their owners' likes and dislikes and personality traits. Unfortunately *some of these characteristics* _____ are undesirable. We are seeing more and more nervous and neurotic dogs in our veterinary clinics *as the human race becomes more neurosis-ridden* _____. I don't mean to imply *that all bad habits in the dog come from humans* _____. Canine playmates are often mischievous and bad-habit mates (*chasing cars, for instance, can be learned from a buddy* _____), and some dogs are emotionally disturbed *by heredity or from birth* _____. Nonetheless, *the main responsibility for each dog's behavior* _____ rests with his owner. Each dog expects his master to guide him through life in good health, and *in return he gives the ultimate in love, loyalty, and lifelong affection* _____.

Louis L. Vine, *YOUR DOG: HIS HEALTH AND HAPPINESS*

PART B

DIRECTIONS: For each word or group of words given, write two sentences, using the word or words first in a phrase and, second, in a clause (the clause may be dependent or independent). Indicate which sentence contains the phrase and which the clause.

EXAMPLE: *going*

Going to class, I fell and twisted my ankle. (Phrase)
As I was going to class, I fell and twisted my ankle. (Clause)

1. *hidden*

_____

_____

2. *running*

_____

_____

3. *a woman with red hair*

_____

_____

4. *a sunny day*

_____

_____

13/RESTRICTIVE AND NONRESTRICTIVE PHRASES AND CLAUSES

Phrases and clauses that modify (that is, phrases and clauses that function like adverbs or adjectives), are either *restrictive* or *nonrestrictive*, a distinction that is reflected in their punctuation.

Restrictive modifiers limit (or restrict) the meaning of the words they modify, and they are written without commas around them because they are essential to the understanding of the modified word or words.

Nonrestrictive modifiers, on the other hand, are usually set off with commas because they describe but do not limit the meaning of the words they modify.

In some cases, it is difficult for the reader to see much difference in meaning between the modifier set off by commas as a nonrestrictive modifier and the modifier written without punctuation as a restrictive one. In many cases, however, the difference is easy to see. It is important that you understand the difference in meaning of these two kinds of modifiers so that you, the writer, can make your meaning completely clear to your reader. If you fail to recognize the difference between the two kinds of modifiers and punctuate your sentences haphazardly, your reader will be given an imprecise account or a distorted version of what you wanted him or her to understand. The difference between the two kinds of modifiers is obvious in the following example.

| RESTRICTIVE | Men who are basically jolly seem to age gracefully. |
| NONRESTRICTIVE | Men, who are basically jolly, seem to age gracefully. |

The first sentence means that *only* those men who are basically jolly seem to age gracefully. The *who*-clause modifying *men* is essential to our understanding of *which* men it is who age gracefully. The second sentence, because of its punctuation, says something entirely different: it claims that *all* men are basically jolly. The *who*-clause here, punctuated as a nonrestrictive modifier, gives extra, nonessential information for the understanding of the main clause—that all men age gracefully.

Some additional examples should help clarify the differences.

RESTRICTIVE CLAUSE	All of the money which John left in his locker was stolen. (John may have had other money, but only that in the locker was stolen.)
NONRESTRICTIVE CLAUSE	All of the money, which John left in his locker, was stolen. (All of John's money was in the locker.)
RESTRICTIVE PHRASE	The little girls covered in mud were trying to repair their bicycles. (Only the little girls covered in mud were working on their bicycles.)
NONRESTRICTIVE PHRASE	The little girls, covered in mud, were trying to repair their bicycles. (All of the little girls on the scene were covered in mud.)

TROUBLESHOOTING

1. Clauses that begin with *that* are always restrictive modifiers and should never be enclosed in commas.

INCORRECT   The two albums, <u>that Wally's sister gave him for his birthday</u>, were dreadful.

CORRECT   The two albums <u>that Wally's sister gave him for his birthday</u> were dreadful.

INCORRECT   Jana said, <u>that we could not borrow her notes.</u>

CORRECT   Jana said <u>that we could not borrow her notes.</u>

2. Clauses in which the relative pronoun is omitted are also always restrictive modifiers and should never be set off by commas.

The woman (whom) I bought this sweater from runs a small yarn shop on Wickenden Street. (*Whom* can be omitted, so the clause is restrictive.)

Who sat on the peanut-butter sandwich (that) Reggie just made? (*That* can be omitted, so the clause is restrictive.)

NAME _____ DATE _____

PART A

DIRECTIONS: Indicate which of the following pairs of sentences contains a restrictive modifier (R) and which contains a nonrestrictive modifier (N) by writing *R* or *N* in the space provided before each sentence. Then write a sentence or two explaining the difference in meaning between the two sentences.

> EXAMPLE: __*R*__ The roses grown by Mr. Simpson are prize-winners.
> __*N*__ The roses, grown by Mr. Simpson, are prize-winners.

1. a. _____ All of the food which had been left in the open back of the station wagon had been eaten or scattered by the two bears.
   b. _____ All of the food, which had been left in the open back of the station wagon, had been eaten or scattered by the two bears.

_____

_____

_____

_____

2. a. _____ The stores which give trading stamps to their customers are popular.
   b. _____ The stores, which give trading stamps to their customers, are popular.

_____

_____

_____

_____

3. a. _____ The car scratched on the left front fender ran like a new one.
   b. _____ The car, scratched on the left front fender, ran like a new one.

_____

_____

_____

_____

4. a. _____ The monkeys grinning broadly swung to the top of the cage.
   b. _____ The monkeys, grinning broadly, swung to the top of the cage.

_____

_____

_____

_____

5. a. _____ The proctor who slept through the examination has been fired.
   b. _____ The proctor, who slept through the examination, has been fired.

_____

_____

_____

_____

6. a. _____ Alonzo went to visit his uncle, who lives in Boise.
   b. _____ Alonzo went to visit his uncle who lives in Boise.

_____

_____

_____

_____

NAME _____ DATE _____

PART B

DIRECTIONS: Use each phrase or clause given below in a pair of sentences. In the blank marked N, write a sentence using the phrase or clause as a *nonrestrictive* element; in the blank marked R, write a sentence using it as a *restrictive* element. Be sure that you punctuate the sentences correctly.

EXAMPLE: *found under the bed*

N *The red dress, found under the bed, needed buttons.*

R *The red dress found under the bed was dirty.*

1. *wearing the clown costume*

N _____

_____

R _____

_____

2. *which Jan had left in the closet*

N _____

_____

R _____

_____

3. *above the old-fashioned radiator*

N _____

_____

R _____

_____

4. *grinning sheepishly and blushing deeply*

N _____

_____

R _____

_____

5. *whom Dave's mother had never met*

N _____

_____

R _____

_____

6. *splashed by the bus's encounter with the mud puddle*

N _____

_____

R _____

_____

7. *whom Al had listed as a reference on his job application*

N _____

_____

R _____

_____

14/APPOSITIVES

Like modifiers, **appositives** refer to the same thing as the words, phrases, or clauses with which they are associated. But unlike other modifiers, appositives have the same grammatical function as the words or phrases to which they refer. That is, an appositive to a subject can also serve as subject, an appositive to a subject complement can also serve as subject complement, and so on. Appositives are most often nouns or noun substitutes, but they may also serve as adjectives, adverbs, or even predicates.

NOUN APPOSITIVE TO SUBJECT	The calf, a Holstein, became the family pet. (Note that you could substitute *a Holstein* for *the calf*: *A Holstein became the family pet.*)
ADJECTIVES APPOSITIVE TO SUBJECT COMPLEMENT	He was a real villain, dastardly and wicked. (You could also say *He was dastardly and wicked.*)
PREPOSITIONAL PHRASE APPOSITIVE TO PREPOSITIONAL PHRASE	We had to get up at daybreak—at 5:30 a.m. (You could also say *We had to get up at 5:30 a.m.*)

Most appositives are nonrestrictive and are thus set off by commas (sometimes by parentheses or dashes, as in the last example above). Noun appositives, however, are sometimes restrictive, especially if the appositive is a proper noun.

RESTRICTIVE APPOSITIVE	Their daughter Beth is a pilot.
NONRESTRICTIVE APPOSITIVE	Their daughter, Beth, is a pilot.

The punctuation in this last pair of sentences is important because it makes a difference in the meaning of the sentence. In the first, because *Beth* is a restrictive appositive (remember that *restrictive* means *essential* to understanding), the sentence means that, of the couple's daughters, Beth is the one who is a pilot. In the second sentence, however, because Beth is set off by commas as a nonrestrictive modifier, we understand that the couple has only one daughter, *Beth*, and she is a pilot. Her name is nonessential information.

NAME _____ DATE _____

PART A

DIRECTIONS: Underline and correctly punctuate all appositives in the following sentences.

> EXAMPLE: Mrs. Quarles, <u>my neighbor</u>, is just delightful, witty, kind, and helpful.

1. Lloyd's patience his most notable virtue was often sorely tried by his family of eight one shrieking wife, two sulky kids, an Irish setter, two canaries, and a pet goat.
2. Unfortunately Ginger's hobbies reading, needlework, and painting were all solitary pursuits, so the neighbors a gossipy lot called her "aloof."
3. Having been ordered to attend the meeting, Miss Jones the senior marketing director was furious with her boss a blustery, spineless fool.
4. Jill had made three requests of her parents to be able to take her car back to school, to open her own checking account, and to be permitted to work at the beach during the summer.
5. Sean an only child had been brought up by his mother an artistic woman who loved to travel.
6. Finally Lucy found the missing fifty dollars a birthday present from her grandparents in the most unlikely place in the back of her dresser drawer!
7. Unhappy or rather outraged at the new rules, the police officers all veterans of the force threatened a strike a move that would be applauded by other city employees.
8. The man who had been standing on the corner climbed into a car a blue sedan and drove off at breakneck speed at 70 or 80 miles an hour.
9. Beginning ballet students often have difficulty with *grands battements* the kicking up of a straight leg because they try to throw the leg too high at first.

PART B

DIRECTIONS: Write sentences using each of the following words or phrases as an appositive. Be sure to punctuate the appositives correctly.

> EXAMPLE: *a former roommate of mine*
>
> *I am going to meet Rose, a former roommate of mine, at the airport.*

1. *too late to get a good seat*

_____

_____

2. *a tattered rag doll, a yo-yo, and a red wagon*

_____

_____

3. *a tool used for pounding*

_____

_____

4. *one of the biggest he had ever seen*

_____

_____

5. *Meg, Jo, Beth, and Amy*

_____

_____

6. *tall, handsome, and clever*

_____

_____

15/NOMINALS, ADJECTIVALS, AND ADVERBIALS

An important characteristic of the English language is the ability of words to change grammatical function from sentence to sentence without changing form. If we say, for instance, "Landon went down the trail," *down* is a preposition; but if we write "down is the direction Landon went," *down* becomes the subject of the sentence; and we know that the subject of a sentence must be a noun or pronoun *or* a word or group of words functioning as a noun or pronoun. *Down*, which is usually an adverb or preposition, here has taken on the role of a noun, so we give it the name *nominal*.

Similarly, we normally think of *New York* as a proper noun, as in the sentence *I love New York*. But in the sentence *I love New York cheesecake*, *New York* modifies the noun *cheesecake*. Modifiers of nouns must be adjectives or words serving as adjectives. In this second sentence *New York* is a noun serving as an adjective so it is called an *adjectival*.

Finally, prepositional phrases are usually modifiers, but the kind of modifier they are depends on their function. In the sentence *Traffic was crawling along the expressway*, the prepositional phrase *along the expressway* modifies the verb *was crawling*; it is acting as an adverb and so is called an *adverbial*. (Compare *The traffic along the expressway was barely crawling*, where *along the expressway* modifies *traffic* and is thus an adjectival.)

The terms *nominal, adjectival*, and *adverbial* are particularly useful in describing the function of phrases and clauses, but individual parts of speech also serve as nominals, adjectivals, and adverbials.

15a NOMINALS

A **nominal** is a noun or any word or group of words that functions as a noun.

KIND OF NOMINAL	FUNCTION	EXAMPLE
Noun	Subject	The book is valuable.
Infinitive phrase	Direct object	Sarah chose to go home.
Gerund phrase	Object of preposition	Sean was in favor of going with them.
Participle phrase	Subject	Stuffed with food is Jon's favorite condition.
Prepositional phrase	Subject	Outside the police station is where Joan found herself.
Adjective	Direct object	He always bought the most expensive; we always bought the cheapest.
Adverb	Subject	There is a good place to picnic.
Dependent clause	Subject	Why they did that is a real puzzle.
Dependent clause	Object of a preposition	Give the package to whoever comes to pick it up.
Dependent clause	Direct object	Eric said that he does not care.

15b ADJECTIVALS

An **adjectival** is an adjective or a group of words that functions as an adjective. Adjectivals, like adjectives, modify nouns or pronouns.

KIND OF ADJECTIVAL	FUNCTION	EXAMPLE
Adjective	Modifies direct object	She wanted the <u>red</u> one.
Noun	Modifies subject complement	It was a <u>brick</u> wall.
Infinitive	Modifies subject	The urge <u>to peek</u> was too great to resist.
Participle	Modifies object of preposition	They escaped being hit by <u>shattered</u> glass.
Adverb	Modifies direct object	We could not believe the prices <u>there</u>.
Prepositional phrase	Modifies subject	The girl <u>with the freckles</u> is his sister.
Dependent clause	Modifies object of preposition	He gave the flowers to the girl <u>who was standing at the door</u>.

15c ADVERBIALS

An **adverbial** is an adverb or a group of words functioning as an adverb. Adverbials modify verbs, verbals (infinitives, participles, and gerunds), adjectives, and other adverbs.

ADVERBIAL	FUNCTION	EXAMPLE
Adverb	Modifies verb	She ran <u>quickly</u> from the scene.
Prepositional phrase	Modifies verbal (past participle)	The man fired <u>from that job</u> is a friend of mine.
Dependent clause	Modifies adverb	He spoke so rapidly <u>that I couldn't understand him</u>.
Infinitive	Modifies adjective	It is hard <u>to tell</u>.

NAME _____ DATE _____

PART A

DIRECTIONS: In the blank following each italicized word or group of words, identify that italicized element as one of the following:

NOM nominal   ADJ adjectival   ADV adverbial

EXAMPLE: *Playing* __*NOM*__ backgammon has become popular *among my friends* __*ADV*__.

1. *On the ledge* _____ was where the child, *frightened by the smoke* _____, had crawled.

2. For Andy, *decorating* _____ the cake was a rather comical exercise *in clumsiness* _____.

3. The man *decorating* _____ the cake obviously does not mind *getting* _____ everything in the kitchen sticky.

4. Paula, *looking* _____ down from her *lifeguard* _____ chair, saw *what looked like a shark* _____ *swimming* _____ fairly close *to the shore* _____.

5. *There* _____ is the place *where we were told to gather* _____ *when the directors came into the room* _____.

6. Keith was too young *to understand* _____ the agony *of the divorce* _____ *that his parents were going through* _____.

7. *That Jana was a great athlete* _____ came *as a complete surprise* _____ to everyone *except her* _____.

8. Phyllis's boss did not know *that she was going to school at night and on the weekends* _____.

9. In *stepping* _____ *out of the boat* _____, Walter dropped his binoculars *into the water* _____, and *stooping over* _____ to look for them, he felt his glasses slip *off his nose* _____, but he grabbed for them *in vain* _____ as they, too, splashed and disappeared *beneath the muddy water* _____.

10. *Cautioned* _____ *by his teacher* _____, Michael's parents tried *to give* _____ Michael a lot *of extra attention* _____ until he got over the trauma of the special tests _____.

11. *Decorated with Olympic medals* _____ is *how Ilsa sees herself in her daydreams* _____.

DIRECTIONS: In the space accompanying each item, write a sentence using the element specified. Underline the specified element in your sentence.

EXAMPLE: Use a present participle (adjectival) to modify the subject.

Shattering glass was falling all around them.

1. Use a nominal clause as the subject of the sentence.

_____

_____

2. Use a prepositional phrase as an adverbial modifying the verb.

_____

_____

3. Use a prepositional phrase as an adjectival modifying the subject complement.

_____

_____

4. Use a gerund (nominal) as the direct object.

_____

_____

5. Use a present participle (adjectival) to modify the direct object.

_____

_____

6. Use an adverb as a nominal.

_____

_____

16/CLASSIFICATION OF SENTENCES

In addition to describing sentences according to the elements they contain, sentences can also be classified by the types of clauses they contain, their function or purpose, and their affirmative or negative qualities.

16a CLASSIFICATION BY TYPES OF CLAUSES

Sometimes it is useful to classify sentences according to the number and kinds of clauses that they contain. There are four classifications of sentences according to structure.

1. **Simple sentences** consist of only one independent clause, though the subject, the predicate, or both subject and predicate may be compound (that is, may consist of at least two components joined by a coordinating conjunction.)

> Marvin is an excellent cook.
> Marvin and Fred are excellent cooks. (compound subject)
> Marvin and Fred are excellent cooks and enjoy having dinner guests. (compound subject and compound predicate)

2. **Compound sentences** consist of at least two, but perhaps more, independent clauses and no dependent clauses. The independent clauses are usually joined with a comma and a coordinating conjunction, though they may be linked by just a colon or a semicolon. (Independent clauses should *not* be joined with *only* a comma.)

> Marvin and Fred are excellent cooks, and they enjoy having dinner guests.
> Marvin and Fred are excellent cooks; they are, however, very messy in the kitchen.
> Marvin and Fred are excellent cooks: their appreciation of the color, taste, and texture of food means consistently delicious meals.

3. **Complex sentences** consist of only one independent clause and one or more dependent clauses.

> Because Marvin and Fred love to cook, they often invite guests to dinner.
> Marvin and Fred often invite guests to dinner because they love to cook.
> Although Marvin and Fred have a small apartment, they often have large dinner parties because they enjoy cooking for guests.

4. **Compound-complex sentences** consist of at least two independent clauses and at least one dependent clause.

> Marvin and Fred have a small apartment, but they often invite guests to dinner because they enjoy cooking for company.

16b CLASSIFICATION BY SYNTAX AND FUNCTION

Sentences may also be classified according to their function or purpose. Each of the four functional types has a typical word order.

1. **Declarative sentences** state a fact or opinion. The normal word order is subject + verb phrase + object or complement, if there are objects or complements.

> Mr. Besenbach admired the exhibit.
> The ducks had built nests along the creek.

2. **Interrogative sentences** ask questions. If the sentence begins with an interrogative word (*who, what, which, when, where, why,* or *how*), the word order is usually interrogative word + verb phrase + object or complement.

> Who was that fellow?

If the question is one to which the answer would be *yes* or *no*, the word order is auxiliary verb + subject + main verb + object or complement, if any.

> Has Anita been there before?
> Do toads cause warts?

3. **Imperative sentences** make requests or commands. Usually the subject is omitted, though it is understood to be *you*.

> Please give this report to Mr. Jenkins.
> Don't ever mention that again!

4. **Exclamatory sentences** express an attitude or strong emotion. They often begin with *what* or *how* and have inverted word order, but they may also have the same word order as declarative sentences.

> What a thrill that will be!
> How ridiculous he is about petty things!
> That will be a great thrill!

16c AFFIRMATIVE AND NEGATIVE SENTENCES

An affirmative sentence makes an assertion, and a negative sentence denies an assertion by means of a negating word such as *not, no,* or *never.*

AFFIRMATIVE	The bus is always on time.
NEGATIVE	The bus is never on time.
	No bus is ever on time.
	The bus is not on time.

NAME _____ DATE _____

PART A

DIRECTIONS: In the blank preceding each sentence, write the number from the list below that identifies the structure of the sentence and the letter from the second list below that identifies the function of the sentence.

1. Simple sentence
2. Compound sentence
3. Complex sentence
4. Compound-complex sentence

A. Declarative sentence
B. Interrogative sentence
C. Imperative sentence
D. Exclamatory sentence

EXAMPLE: __*3B*__ Are Bob and Anne coming, too, even if they were not invited?

_____ 1. Grocery shopping in America is an activity made up of frustration, entertainment, anger, and a certain amount of Yankee ingenuity.

_____ 2. In large cities many shoppers still frequent a bakery, a butcher shop, and a greengrocer's, where the shopkeepers know their customers' names; in small communities, on the other hand, shoppers are often at the mercy of a single entrepreneur who operates a dingy store filled with little more than overpriced staple goods.

_____ 3. Most grocery shoppers, however, make their purchases in regular forays to that great American institution—the supermarket.

_____ 4. And how super it is, this too fluorescently lit hybrid market for not only food but hardware, plants, toys, drugs, and even clothing!

_____ 5. Rolling a shiny cart down the endless aisles—valleys between mountains of paper towels, cookies, meats, and gadgets—is a trip through the cupboards of America; and your fellow shoppers are the tour guides who open cupboard after cupboard and life after life for your inspection and speculation.

_____ 6. Is that well-coiffured woman looking at the artichokes a lawyer, a professor, a business executive, or is she one of the idle rich, a well-to-do woman with nothing to do?

_____ 7. Do all five of those redheaded children really belong to that energetic couple who seems to be looking for new fast foods to try?

_____ 8. Check-out counters stand side by side across the front of the store, each counter lighted with a "this one's open" sign, and at these computerized cash registers, queues of customers listen with embarrassment or applause to various battles about whether yesterday's special is still special today, about whether this charge card or check is acceptable, or whether the bagger has put the eggs and bread underneath the canned goods.

_____ 9. At last your turn comes, and you read the computerized numbers and think what the people before you and the people after you have thought and will think: "I can't have spent this much money for two bags of things."

_____ 10. "Don't forget to come back soon."

PART B

DIRECTIONS: Write one sentence to fit each of the following specifications.

    EXAMPLE: A declarative compound sentence

I dislike grocery shopping, but I must shop at least twice a week.

1. An interrogative complex sentence

_____

_____

2. A declarative compound-complex sentence

_____

_____

3. An imperative compound sentence

_____

_____

4. A simple exclamatory sentence

_____

_____

17/PROBLEMS WITH VERBS AND VERB PHRASES

Because verbs require more inflections (changes in form) than any other parts of speech and because many verbs are irregular, grammatical problems with verbs are common.

17a FORMS OF VERBS

There are several types of problems involving the forms of verbs.

1. **Regular Verbs.** Some inflections of regular verbs, particularly the *-d* or *-ed* of the past tense and past participle and the *-s* or *-es* of the third-person singular present tense, are slurred over in speech or are simply difficult to hear. Remember to write these endings correctly.

| INCORRECT | They <u>attack</u> the chore with enthusiasm yesterday. |
| CORRECT | They <u>attacked</u> the chore with enthusiasm yesterday. |

| INCORRECT | Julie <u>test</u> her boyfriend's feelings on every possible occasion. |
| CORRECT | Julie <u>tests</u> her boyfriend's feelings on every possible occasion. |

The expressions *be supposed to* and *used to*, which are followed by the infinitive of the verb, are always written with the *-d* ending.

| INCORRECT | Gene <u>is suppose to</u> call his father. |
| CORRECT | Gene <u>is supposed to</u> call his father. |

| INCORRECT | Wanda <u>use to</u> teach horseback riding. |
| CORRECT | Wanda <u>used to</u> teach horseback riding. |

2. **Irregular Verbs.** Because speakers of English grow up learning the irregular principal parts of the 200 or so irregular verbs in English, you already know most of them and probably have only a few that cause you problems. Use your dictionary to double-check principal parts of irregular verbs.

Each of us has his or her own particularly annoying irregular verb—the one he or she can never seem to master—but seven irregular verbs present special problems for most students: *to lose, to loose, to lead, to lie, to lay, to sit*, and *to set*.

To lose, which means "to mislay, to be unable to find," is often confused with the verb *to loose*, which means "to release, undo." The principal parts of *to lose* are *lose, lost, lost*; the principal parts of *to loose* are *loose, loosed, loosed*. *To lead* is confusing because we often write its past tense as if it were the name of the metal *lead*. This verb does not, as we might expect, follow the pattern of *to read*, which has for its principal parts *read, read, read*—all spelled the same but pronounced in the past tense and past participle like the name of the color *red*. Both the past tense and past participle of *lead* are spelled *led*.

The most confusing irregular verbs, however, are the pairs *to lie/to lay* and *to sit/to set*. Here are the principal parts of these verbs:

| lie | lay | lain | sit | sat | sat |
| lay | laid | laid | set | set | set |

Although these verbs are frequently confused, even by well-educated people, the differences between the parts are not difficult to learn. *To lay* and *to set*, both of which mean basically "to put or to place something," are transitive (that is, they take direct objects). *To lie*, which means "to recline," and *to sit*, which means "to take a seat, to rest," are intransitive (that is, they do not take direct objects).

INCORRECT	Ernie wants <u>to lay</u> in the sun all afternoon.
CORRECT	Ernie wants <u>to lie</u> in the sun all afternoon.
INCORRECT	Ernie <u>laid</u> in the sun all afternoon.
CORRECT	Ernie <u>lay</u> in the sun all afternoon.
INCORRECT	Ernie <u>has laid</u> in the sun all afternoon.
CORRECT	Ernie <u>has lain</u> in the sun all afternoon.
INCORRECT	Ernie <u>lay</u> his blanket in the sun to dry.
CORRECT	Ernie <u>laid</u> his blanket in the sun to dry.
INCORRECT	I always <u>sit</u> the peanut butter in the refrigerator.
CORRECT	I always <u>set</u> the peanut butter in the refrigerator.
INCORRECT	Yesterday I <u>set</u> down to rest for half an hour.
CORRECT	Yesterday I <u>sat</u> down to rest for half an hour.
INCORRECT	Daniel <u>has</u> always <u>set</u> at the head of the table.
CORRECT	Daniel <u>has</u> always <u>sat</u> at the head of the table.

3. **Auxiliary Verbs.** Modal auxiliaries (*will, would, shall, should, can, could, may, might, dare, need, ought, must*) cause problems for some writers.

Shall-will. In American English, except for the most formal writing, *will* is used in all persons with the infinitive for forming the future tense. Some people, however, still prefer *shall* for first-person subjects and *will* for second- and third-person subjects in the future tense.

We <u>shall</u> write our senator tomorrow.
We <u>will</u> write our senator tomorrow.

Ought. Because no verb phrase should contain more than one modal auxiliary, it is incorrect to write such phrases as *should ought to, shouldn't ought to, had ought to,* and *hadn't ought to.*

INCORRECT	We <u>shouldn't ought to</u> keep these rooms so warm.
CORRECT	We <u>shouldn't</u> (*or* <u>should not</u>) keep these rooms so warm.
CORRECT	We <u>ought not</u> keep these rooms so warm.

Of for have. *Of* is not an auxiliary verb and should never be written as a substitute for *have*.

| INCORRECT | Dolores <u>should of</u> told him sooner. |
| CORRECT | Dolores <u>should have</u> told him sooner. |

Be going to. The semiauxiliary *be going to* should be used to form the future only in informal writing; it should be replaced with *will* in formal writing.

| INFORMAL | Mr. Diamond <u>is going to</u> enlarge his offices this spring. |
| FORMAL | Mr. Diamond <u>will</u> enlarge his offices this spring. |

17b TENSE OF VERBS

Most problems with verb tenses involve sequence of tenses. The term **sequence of tenses** refers to the relationship between the verb in the main clause of a sentence and the verb in a dependent clause or phrase. The following chart shows the correct sequence of tenses for dependent clauses according to the tense of the verb in the main clause.

VERB IN MAIN CLAUSE	VERB IN DEPENDENT CLAUSE
Any present tense (simple present, present progressive, present perfect, present-perfect progressive)	Any tense that expresses intended meaning
Any past tense (simple past, past progressive, past perfect, past-perfect progressive)	Also a past tense (unless the subordinate clause expresses a universal truth, in which case either a present or past tense is acceptable)
Any future tense (simple future, future progressive, future perfect, future-perfect progressive)	A present tense
A verb that implies future tense, such as the imperative	A present tense

MAIN VERB IN PRESENT TENSE	Chad <u>says</u> that he <u>is</u> frustrated by his job.
	Chad <u>has said</u> that he <u>is</u> frustrated by his job.
	Chad <u>says</u> that he <u>was</u> frustrated by his job.
	Chad <u>is saying</u> that he <u>is</u> frustrated by his job.
MAIN VERB IN PAST TENSE	Chad <u>said</u> that he <u>was</u> frustrated by his job.
	Chad <u>said</u> that he <u>had been frustrated</u> by his job.
	Chad <u>told</u> me that he <u>would be frustrated</u> by his job.
	Chad <u>had been telling</u> me that he <u>was frustrated</u> by his job.
UNIVERSAL TRUTH	Chad <u>knew</u> that a job <u>is</u> a necessity for most people.
	Chad <u>knew</u> that a job <u>was</u> a necessity for most people.
MAIN VERB IN FUTURE TENSE	Chad <u>will</u> <u>tell</u> <u>me</u> if he <u>is frustrated</u> by his job.
IMPERATIVE	<u>Tell</u> me if you <u>are frustrated</u> by your job.

The tenses in participle and infinitive phrases vary according to their relationship to the main verb.

Use a *present participle* or a *present infinitive* to express action simultaneous with that of the main verb. Also, use the *present infinitive* to express action later than that of the main verb.

<u>Driving</u> home, Larry <u>was</u> tired. (The driving and being tired occurred at the same time.)

Larry usually <u>likes</u> to <u>drive</u>. (The liking and the driving occur at the same time.)

Larry <u>agreed to drive</u>. (The driving occurred after the agreeing.)

Use a *perfect participle* or a *perfect infinitive* to express action that precedes the action of the main verb.

Having driven home, Larry ate his dinner. (The driving occurred before the eating.)

Larry would like to have driven across the country. (In the present, he would like to have driven in the past.)

In indirect discourse (a paraphrase of a speaker's words), the same sequence-of-tense rules apply as those that apply to other dependent clauses or verbal phrases.

She says that it is a difficult problem. (It is a difficult problem while she is speaking.)

She said that it was a difficult problem. (It was a difficult problem while she was speaking.)

17C MOOD OF VERBS

Of the three moods (indicative, imperative, and subjunctive) of English verbs, the subjunctive is the most troublesome.

In modern English, we use the subjunctive only in (1) certain kinds of clauses introduced by *that*, (2) subordinate clauses expressing unreal conditions, and (3) certain idioms.

That clauses with (a) verbs of requesting, ordering, and recommending (*ask, demand, command, suggest, recommend, order*, and *insist*, for example), (b) adjectives expressing urgency (*necessary, important, imperative, crucial, essential, urgent*), and (c) phrases such as *of great importance* require the present subjunctive. The present subjunctive has the same form as the infinitive of the verb.

It is urgent that he be present.

We suggest that they be prompt.

To express unreal conditions (that is, conditions contrary to fact) after the verb *wish* or in clauses beginning with *if*, the past subjunctive is used. It is identical in form to the plural past indicative of the verb (*were, had, saw*, for example).

If Jean were really dedicated, she would accept the assignment.

Jean wishes that she were really dedicated.

The past perfect form of the verb is used to express *actual* past time with the subjunctive.

If she had been more dedicated, Jean would have accepted the assignment.

Had she been more dedicated, Jean would have accepted the assignment.

The following idioms take the present subjunctive in an independent clause.

God help us   far be it from me
suffice it to say come what may
Heaven forbid   be that as it may
so be it

17d VOICE OF VERBS

The real problem with the voice of verbs tends to be stylistic, not grammatical: we often overuse the passive voice, creating wordy, ineffective prose.

WORDY   We had been misinformed by the contractor about how much it would cost for the basement to be remodeled by his workers.

IMPROVED   The contractor misinformed us about how much it would cost for his workers to remodel the basement.

In formal writing, avoid using *get* as an auxiliary for the passive voice.

ACTIVE   Lightning struck the barn.

COLLOQUIAL PASSIVE   The barn got struck by lightning.

FORMAL PASSIVE   The barn was struck by lightning.

17e INCOMPLETE VERB PHRASES

When a sentence has a compound predicate, we can often omit those parts of the verb phrases that are identical to those of the other verb phrase.

She promised to quit smoking but didn't really want to. (The second occurrence of *quit* can be omitted because it is identical to the first; both are infinitives.)

But do not omit parts of compound predicates that are not identical; the result is an incomplete verb phrase.

INCORRECT   She has not and will not tell us. (This is incorrect because the omitted verb is a past participle, *told*, and the other verb is an infinitive, *tell*.)

Similarly, do not omit the verb *to be* in a compound sentence when the omitted verb would have a different form in the two verb phrases.

QUESTIONABLE   The officer was annoyed and the motorists angry.

PREFERABLE   The officer was annoyed and the motorists were angry.

NAME _____ DATE _____

PART A

DIRECTIONS: Fill in the blank with the correct tense of the verb that is given in parentheses. Use your dictionary to be sure that you know the correct principal parts of these irregular verbs.

> EXAMPLE: The puppy really has ___*grown*___ (grow) since Joe
> ___*saw*___ (see) him a month ago.

1. Beginning March 1, Mark had faithfully _____ (lie) in the sun an hour each day, but by the first of June he still hadn't _____ (lose) his pasty white tone.

2. Alice _____ (loose) the dirt from around the jade tree's roots, _____ (set) the new pot on the counter, and _____ (begin) filling it with potting soil and sand.

3. Walt _____ (drink) what seemed like gallons of coffee as he _____ (sit) at his desk all day, double-checking the reports that members of his staff had _____ (write).

4. The boy, who had _____ (awake) when the birds first had _____ (begin) chirping, _____ (sit) straight up in bed, momentarily frightened because he had _____ (forget) that he _____ (be) at camp.

5. "What have you _____ (do) with that painting that _____ (hang) in your den for so long?" Kate's mother-in-law asked impatiently. "You wouldn't have _____ (give) it one of those garage sales or simply _____ (throw) it out, would you?"

6. The fabric _____ (weave) from that yarn had been _____ (mistake) for wool by traders from the East.

7. "That dress certainly is not what I would have _____ (choose)," Sally's mother said, "but I have never _____ (forbid) you to experiment with your wardrobe—within reason."

8. "If you hadn't _____ (freeze) the steaks, John, they would have _____ (be) much tenderer, and these salad greens, though they're not bad, would have _____ (have) a more delicate flavor if you had _____ (tear) them instead of chopping them," said Marvin, as he greedily _____ (eat) the last morsel on his neighbor's table.

9. The policeman _____ (lead) the photographer to the room where the robber had _____ (slay) the jeweler.

10. After they had _____ (*drive*) to the motel, Artie and Jack unpacked, _____ (*swim*) for an hour, _____ (*eat*) a hearty dinner, and _____ (*take*) a walk to the theater district.

11. Although the snow had _____ (*fell*) all night, by early morning it _____ (*begin*) to melt, and the girls _____ (*be*) able to get a cab to take them to the airport on time.

12. "I don't know if Aunt Adelaide has ever _____ (*forgive*) me," laughed Alison. "She has never quite _____ (*forget*) that I _____ (*break*) her best serving platter and _____ (*burn*) the fringe on her new oriental rug."

13. The black cat _____ (*creep*) through the house as if he had just _____ (*steal*) the crown jewels and had _____ (*begin*) a meticulously planned getaway.

14. After he had _____ (*read*) the last chapter of his history book, Michael _____ (*fling*) himself on the bed and _____ (*sleep*) so soundly that he almost missed the exam.

15. When she had _____ (*bring*) in the shopping bags and _____ (*set*) them on the kitchen counter, Marie _____ (*sit*) down to recover from her weekly ordeal at the grocery store.

PART B

DIRECTIONS: Write one complete sentence for each of the following often-confused verbs.

1. *lie*

_____

_____

2. *sit*

_____

_____

3. *led*

_____

_____

NAME _____ DATE _____

PART A

DIRECTIONS: In the following sentences, underline the verb forms that are inappropriate in formal English. On the lines following each sentence, rewrite the sentence, using the correct form. Write *C* on the line if the sentence contains no incorrect form.

> EXAMPLE: Now the child <u>rest</u> better than he <u>use</u> to.

Now the child rests better than he used to.
_____

1. Tomorrow we should ought to see about whether we are suppose to pay the apartment manager whenever we use the tennis courts.

   _____

   _____

2. If Joyce had not of been in such a hurry, she would of pack the alarm clock in her suitcase.

   _____

   _____

3. Yesterday Ernie jump off the high board for the first time.

   _____

   _____

4. Is the corporation going to buy up all the land on Portland Avenue?

   _____

   _____

5. Norma and Gilda use to say that their parents shouldn't ought to treat them like babies.

   _____

   _____

6. Tomorrow Henry shall tell us what we are suppose to do about getting our vacation pay.

   _____

   _____

7. Do you suppose that man could of been the same one who use to run the corner market in Greta's neighborhood?

_____

_____

8. She must of known that the boys were planning a surprise party for her.

_____

_____

9. All day Tuesday, while they might of been studying for the exam, Paul and Ethan bask in the sun at Folly Beach.

_____

_____

10. Joe has always talk a lot around his friends, but he shall never be very talkative around strangers.

_____

_____

PART B

DIRECTIONS: Write one sentence using each of the following words or phrases.

1. *attract* (use the past tense)

_____

2. *ought*

_____

3. *used to*

_____

4. *shall*

_____

5. *might*

_____

6. *could*

_____

NAME _____ DATE _____

PART A

DIRECTIONS: Fill in the blanks below with the appropriate form of the verb indicated in parentheses.

EXAMPLE: *Having read* for two hours, I fell asleep.
(*read*—participle)

1. By the time you leave tomorrow, Claude _____ reading your paper.
(*finish*)

2. _____ along the beach, Justin found the shell of a horseshoe crab.
(*walk*—participle)

_____ the shell in his knapsack, he continued his stroll.
(*put*—participle)

3. Bernice wanted to _____ five miles every day, but after she _____
(*run*—infinitive)   (*jog*)

less than two miles, she usually became too exhausted to _____ any
(*go*—infinitive)
farther.

4. I would have preferred to _____ the book before I saw the movie.
(*read*—infinitive)

5. His wife will be very annoyed when she _____ that he ____ all the deviled
(*discover*)   (*eat*)

eggs she _____ for her office picnic.
(*make*)

6. Gloria _____ that she has failed her history examination when she _____
(*discover*)   (*check*)

the bulletin board later this morning.

7. Jesse ____ in this town ever since he ___ born.
(*live*)   (*be*)

8. While Astrid ____ on the phone yesterday, the teakettle ____ dry.
(*talk*)   (*boil*)

9. We sat down to rest after _____ to the top of the mound. As we
   (*climb*—participle)

   were relaxing, we suddenly realized that we ___ on an anthill.
   (*sit*)

10. Wesley is too young to _____ in World War II.
    (*be*—infinitive)

PART B

DIRECTIONS: In the second, third, and fourth paragraphs below, underline the verb phrases, participles, and infinitives that violate correct sequence of tenses as established by the first paragraph. (The first paragraph is correct.) Above the underlined words, write the correct form of the verb.

Directing a play with amateur actors for a community theater tests the patience of even the most level-headed of directors. Zach Campbell had already experienced the frustrations of dealing with clerks and salespeople who wanted to be actors when he accepted an assignment to shepherd the cast of *The Front Page* at the Warehouse Theatre, a theater in a small mountain community.

The Front Page, which is first acted in New York in 1928, is a classic American comedy about the newspaper profession, but Campbell feared that the play will be more comic than classic when he views the crowd gathered to audition for the numerous roles. *The Front Page*, which is written by Charles MacArthur and Ben Hecht, painted newspapermen and politicians as a seedy lot. The authors would agree that Campbell's cast fit the bill. The director has individuals who can't read the script and some who could read but can't speak without having mumbled.

The first rehearsals were disasters. Even the dress rehearsal is a series of errors—missed cues, falling scenery, and blank actors. Never has Campbell been so distraught. He considered leaving town quietly but realizes that the old saying "the show must go on" meant hanging around at least until the curtain rises.

Opening night was better than Campbell could have believed. As the show had opened, his heart sinks, but early into the first act, he has discovered that not only is the audience laughing, but he himself was being well entertained.

NAME _____   DATE _____

PART A

DIRECTIONS: Rewrite the following sentences, putting all passives into the active voice and correcting errors in the use of the subjunctive mood.

> EXAMPLE: If I was in his place, I would refuse to let myself be intimidated by the rest of the team.

If I were in his place, I would refuse to let the rest of the team intimidate me.

1. Far is it from me to tell Lynn that she has been taken advantage of by her selfish roommates.

   _____

   _____

2. It is insisted on by Mr. Herron that we all are at our desks at 8:30 a.m. on the dot.

   _____

   _____

3. The council recommends that the sheriff's office is investigated by a special committee, although it is believed by the citizens that the sheriff's office has been discredited by the sheriff's political opponents.

   _____

   _____

4. If George was not dieting, all of the food on the buffet would have been wolfed down by him in his customary fashion.

   _____

   _____

5. Dr. Wanamaker got insulted by Pierre, the headwaiter at Chez Paul, when he got mistaken by Pierre for the wine salesman.

   _____

   _____

6. Ella wishes that she was in Hawaii, but if she was able to accept her parents' invitation to join them on their vacation, she would be deprived of a leisurely rest by her responsibilities at her office.

_____

_____

7. Even though Perry had been told by his lawyer that it was not necessary that Perry is in court for the hearing, it was ordered by the judge that he is there.

_____

_____

8. Maggie wishes she was able to understand why tests are always given by Professor Kinard on Monday morning, even though it is known to him that most of his students are beckoned from campus by the ski slopes every weekend.

_____

_____

9. It is of great importance that Willie comes with us so that he can be examined by the doctors before that long ordeal is undertaken by him.

_____

_____

PART B

DIRECTIONS: Use each group of words listed below in a sentence that is in the subjunctive mood.

> EXAMPLE: *Delia, wishes, Scotland*
>
> _Delia wishes that she were in Scotland._

1. *The commander, ordered that*

_____

2. *If, Fritz, scholarly, grades*

_____

3. *It is essential that Lois*

_____

4. *If she, aggressive*

_____

18/PROBLEMS WITH SUBJECT-VERB AGREEMENT

Agreement is the correspondence between grammatically related words whereby the use of one word requires the use of a specific form of another word. For example, if a writer chooses *she* for the subject and the verb *to be* in the present tense for the predicate, only the verb form *is* agrees with *she*.

The verb *to be* presents more problems with agreement than any other verb because it has three different forms in the simple present and two different forms in the simple past.

SIMPLE PRESENT	SIMPLE PAST
I am	I was
you are	you were
he, she, it is	he, she, it was
we, you, they are	we, you, they were

Most verbs, however, have the same form in all persons and numbers except in the third-person singular present, which typically ends in *-s* or *-es*. (First person refers to the speaker(s) or writer(s), second person refers to the person(s) being addressed, and third person refers to the person(s) or thing(s) being talked about.) Notice that although most nouns are made *plural* by adding *-s* or *-es* (*cats, babies*), third-person verbs are made *singular* by the *-s* or *-es* ending.

	SINGULAR	PLURAL
FIRST PERSON	I come	we come
SECOND PERSON	you come	you come
THIRD PERSON	he, she, it comes	they come

I and *you* in the singular take the same form as the plurals *we, you*, and *they*.

If we had only to learn to make the personal pronouns agree with the verb, the problem of agreement would be minor. All nouns and most pronouns, however, are third-person singular or plural, and deciding whether the subject is singular or plural causes problems with subject-verb agreement. Identifying the real subject may be difficult because of the word order of the sentence, because of compound elements, because of modifiers intervening between subject and verb, or because a whole phrase or clause is functioning as subject of the verb.

18a IDENTIFYING THE REAL SUBJECT

In most cases, the real agreement problem is not deciding whether the subject is singular or plural but deciding what the real subject is.

Three troublemakers that keep us from recognizing the real subject include:

1. **Intervening modifiers between subject and verb.** We often confuse a modifier with the subject, especially if the modifier includes a plural noun that comes between a singular subject and the verb, or if it includes a singular noun that comes between a plural noun and the verb.

INCORRECT	Mr. Jameson, a member of the Spartanburg Jaycees, are going to speak.
CORRECT	Mr. Jameson, a member of the Spartanburg Jaycees, is going to speak.

INCORRECT	The banjos, one of which belonged to my grandfather, <u>is</u> in excellent condition.
CORRECT	The banjos, one of which belonged to my grandfather, <u>are</u> in excellent condition.

2. Inverted order of subject and verb. If the sentence is inverted so that the verb precedes the subject, we often incorrectly make the verb agree with a noun that precedes the verb but is not the real subject.

INCORRECT	In the afternoon <u>comes</u> the advanced competitions.
CORRECT	In the afternoon <u>come</u> the advanced competitions.

INCORRECT	<u>Have</u> one of you seen the keys?
CORRECT	<u>Has</u> one of you seen the keys?

3. Subject and complement with different numbers. The number of the complement *never* affects the number of the verb: only the subject determines the number of the verb.

INCORRECT	Wild dogs <u>is</u> a problem in Harris County.
CORRECT	Wild dogs <u>are</u> a problem in Harris County.

INCORRECT	One problem in Harris County <u>are</u> wild dogs.
CORRECT	One problem in Harris County <u>is</u> wild dogs.

18b SPECIAL KINDS OF SUBJECTS

Even if we are certain what the subject is, we sometimes have trouble deciding whether it is singular or plural, particularly with the following kinds of subjects.

1. Collective nouns, which refer to groups, not individuals, normally take a singular verb but *may* take a plural verb if the individuals in the group, rather than the group itself, are being considered.

The team <u>has had</u> a great season. (The team is considered as a unit.)
The team <u>are</u> generally <u>impressed</u> with the new coach. (Team members are considered individually here.)

2. Proper nouns such as book titles and place names that are plural in form take a singular verb because they are considered a unit.

Dover Heights <u>is</u> a very nice neighborhood.
The Jeffersons <u>distorts</u> black culture in America.

3. Nouns with special forms can be deceptive because some that end in *-s* and *-ics* look plural but take a singular verb. Words like *mumps, news*, and *molasses* take singular verbs.

Mumps <u>is</u> a serious disease.
The news <u>is</u> good today.

Words like *ethics, politics*, and *genetics* take singular verbs when they refer to a general field but plural verbs when they refer to individual application.

Politics is interesting to study.
His politics are disreputable.

The meaning of the sentence determines whether nouns that have the same form in both singular and plural (such as *sheep, barracks, means,* and *fish*) take singular or plural verbs.

The sheep is in the corn.
The sheep are in the corn.

Some words—*clergy, clothes, cattle,* and *people,* for instance—have no singular form and take only plural verbs.

People certainly are strange.
The clergy are all opposed to rearmament.

If you are uncertain about whether your subject fits one of these categories, check your dictionary.

4. **Words as words** in citations take a singular verb, even if they are plural in form.

Unctions is the word Jack misspelled.

5. **Expressions of quantity** take either a singular or a plural verb in expressions of adding and multiplying. Expressions of subtraction and division take a singular verb.

Four and six is (*or* are) ten.
Four times six is (*or* are) twenty-four.
Six divided by three is two.
Six minus three is three.

As a subject, the phrase *the number* takes a singular verb, and the phrase *a number* takes a plural verb.

The number of entries is impressive.
A number of the entries are plagiarized.

Plural expressions of quantity take either a singular or a plural verb, depending on whether the expression is being considered a single unit or not.

Two weeks seems like an eternity to Frieda.
Two weeks are left before school begins.

18c COMPOUND SUBJECTS

Compound subjects joined with *and* always take a plural verb unless the two subjects are the same thing or unless they are so closely related that they are thought of as a single unit.

> Making money and having fun are Art's only goals.
>
> My colleague and friend has consented to address the group. (Here the colleague and the friend are the same person.)
>
> My colleague and my friend have consented to address the group. (Here two people are being discussed.)
>
> Bacon and eggs is my favorite breakfast. (*Bacon and eggs* is considered a single dish.)

When subjects are connected with the correlative conjunctions *neither . . . nor, either . . . or, not only . . . but*, or *not . . . but*, the verb agrees with the subject *nearest* the verb. (The same is true if *or* is used without *either*.)

> Either Mr. Mendoza or his sons plan to buy the land.
>
> Either Mr. Mendoza's sons or he plans to buy the land.
>
> The sons or the father plans to buy the land.

Nouns introduced in phrases beginning with (*along*) *with, as well as, rather than, more than*, or *as much as*, are not part of the subject, and do not affect the number of the verb, even when the phrase immediately follows the subject.

> The tenants, rather than the landlord, pay for utilities.
>
> Poor diet, more than overwork and nervous tension, was the cause of Nathan's collapse.
>
> Al, as well as Susan, is to blame.

18d PRONOUN SUBJECTS

The indefinite pronouns *either, neither, each, another, one*, and all pronouns ending in *-one, -body*, or *-thing* should always take a singular verb.

> One was cracked and another was broken in two.
>
> Either of them is acceptable, but neither is exactly what I want.

The indefinite pronouns *all, most, more*, and *some* take a singular verb if their antecedent is a mass or uncountable noun but a plural verb if their antecedent is a plural noun. *None* may take either a singular or plural verb.

> Before she went on vacation, Sally had lovely plants.
>
> All have died.   Most have died.
>
> None has died.   Some have died.
>
> None have died.   More have died.

> Returning from her vacation, Sally found uncollected garbage heaped in front of her apartment building.
>
> All of it has been there for at least a week.
>
> None has been collected.
>
> Most has not been collected.

Some <u>has</u> not been collected.

More <u>has</u> piled up than has ever been there before.

The expletive pronouns *it* and *there* do not share the same rule for agreement with their verbs. *It* always takes a singular verb. *There* takes either a singular or plural verb depending on the number of the noun or pronoun that follows the verb. Most grammarians consider the noun(s) or pronoun(s) that follow the verb to be the real subject of the sentence in this case. Therefore, the verb agrees with this following noun or pronoun, rather than with *there*, even though *there* is in the usual position of the subject.

It is <u>Bob</u> and Fred who made this mess.

There <u>is</u> a reason for this peace offering.

There <u>are</u> reasons for this peace offering.

When *relative pronouns* serve as subjects of clauses, their verbs agree with the antecedents of the relative pronouns.

Adolf is one of those actors who <u>are</u> appearing in the special performance. (*Actors* is the antecedent of *who* because the sentence implies that several actors are performing.)

Adolf is the only one of those actors who <u>is</u> appearing in the special performance. (*One* is the antecedent of *who* because the sense of the sentence would be the same if *of those actors* were omitted.)

Tamara gave me a jar of bean sprouts that <u>were</u> delicious. (The antecedent of *that* is *bean sprouts*.)

Tamara gave me the jar of bean sprouts that <u>was</u> in the refrigerator. (The antecedent of *that* is *jar*.)

18e PHRASES AND CLAUSES AS SUBJECTS

Phrases and clauses usually take a singular verb unless, of course, they are compound. *What*-clauses take a singular verb if the complement is regarded as a unit but a plural verb if the complement is regarded as several units.

Eating a big lunch <u>makes</u> Marty drowsy.

Eating a big lunch and having a martini <u>make</u> Marty drowsy. (compound phrases)

That he would refuse <u>is</u> what I expected.

That he would refuse and that he would criticize our efforts <u>are</u> what I expected. (compound clauses)

What he longs for <u>is</u> peace and quiet.

What were once treasures <u>are</u> now pieces of junk.

NAME _____ DATE _____

DIRECTIONS: Underline the subjects in the following sentences. If a sentence has more than one subject, underline each one. On the line after the sentence, write a revision of the sentence in which the subject(s) and verb(s) agree.

> EXAMPLE: The dreary <u>weather</u> and his <u>anxiety</u> over his new job has made Bob much less cheerful than <u>he</u> usually is.

> *The dreary weather and his anxiety over his new job have made Bob much less cheerful than he usually is.*

1. After the soup comes marinated artichoke hearts and London broil.

   _____

   _____

2. Riding carrousels and roller coasters delight the child.

   _____

   _____

3. Notepads is the only item on the list that haven't come yet.

   _____

   _____

4. Too much sleep and not enough exercise has made Jack flabby.

   _____

   _____

5. After Christmas comes two bleak months of sagging spirits and longing for spring.

   _____

   _____

6. Do any one of you three have any idea why Jack's checkbook and his address book is lying on the stairs?

_____

_____

7. The picket lines in front of the plant is not a welcome sight to the Clinton residents.

_____

_____

8. The display of Oriental prints have attracted many out-of-town visitors to the museum.

_____

_____

9. Tom, in addition to Jim and Chris, have signed up to play in the tennis tournament.

_____

_____

10. The necessary funding are $2,000 for office supplies and $30,000 for two salaries.

_____

_____

NAME _____ DATE _____

DIRECTIONS: Choose the correct verb given in parentheses and write it in the blank that precedes the parentheses. If both suggested forms are correct, write *either* in the blank.

EXAMPLE: Turnip greens _____*are*_____ (*is/are*) one of Jack's favorite foods.

1. The class _____ (*has/have*) complained about the reading assignments, and *Gulliver's Travels* _____ (*is/are*) high on the list of least favorite novels.

2. Marilyn never can remember what nine times eight _____ (*is/are*).

3. The six days _____ (*has/have*) dragged by for Tim.

4. A number of the faculty _____ (*believes/believe*) that a mandatory attendance policy should be established.

5. Suds _____ (*pours/pour*) out of the washing machine no matter how little detergent Bill puts in.

6. A gross of pencils _____ (*costs/cost*) much more now than at this same time last year.

7. Because Betty is extremely nearsighted, her glasses _____ (*is/are*) the

   first thing she reaches for when she gets out of bed.

8. Salmon _____ (*is/are*) plentiful in this area.

9. Although new, the scissors _____ (*was/were*) dull.

10. The press covering the meeting _____ (*is/are*) angry because the board

    _____ (*has/have*) voted to discuss the controversy in private session.

11. Rabies _____ (*is/are*) a problem in Valdosta County although the

    number of animals vaccinated against it _____ (*has/have*) increased

    since last year.

12. Ceramics _____ (*has/have*) always been Rodney's favorite form of

    art, but his own ceramics _____ (*has/have*) never turned out well.

13. The word *no* is clear, but *bicycles* _____ (*is/are*) hard to read.

14. Joe's trousers _____ (*is/are*) wrinkled, his socks _____ (*is/are*)

    mismatched, and his pajamas _____ (*is/are*) missing.

15. Hearts _____ (*is/are*) grandmother's favorite card game, and the

    family _____ (*has/have*) learned to enjoy playing with her.

NAME _____ DATE _____

DIRECTIONS: Choose the correct verb from those in parentheses, and write it in the blank preceding the parentheses.

> EXAMPLE: Not only the students but also the dean ___*is*___ (is/are) very angry over the incident.

1. Clifton, Edna, and the child, a lively five-year-old, _____ (spends/

    spend) their summer weekends hiking.

2. Neither Mr. McAfee nor his neighbors _____ (cares/care) whether the

    corporation buys up the land.

3. Not only Felicia and Daniel but also Juan _____ (agrees/agree) that

    the cost is too great.

4. Mrs. Hendrix, more than her daughters, _____ (is/are) looking forward

    to the annual family gathering.

5. Onion rolls and cream cheese _____ (tastes/taste) great at breakfast

    or for a snack.

6. Neither his parents nor his girlfriend _____ (has/have) noticed Mil-

    ton's sudden obsession with vegetarian meals.

7. This spring not only Mr. Burkhead but also his across-the-street neighbors

_____ (*has/have*) begun jogging at 5:30 a.m. every day.

8. Energy control and conservation _____ (*is/are*) the theme of Mr.

Bergstrom's speech.

9. Jordan, as well as her three roommates, _____ (*was/were*) thrilled at

the prospect of a week in Toronto.

10. Neither the United States nor the other three countries _____ (*wants/*

want) to get involved in the controversy over fishing rights.

11. Cowboys and Indians _____ (*was/were*) the favorite game of children

when Douglas was young.

12. In the camper _____ (*was/were*) the missing flashlight, along with the

backpack that Harold thought he had lost.

PART A

DIRECTIONS: Underline verbs that do not agree with their pronoun subjects, and write a correct form of the verb in the blank to the right of the sentence. Write *C* in the blank following a correct sentence.

> EXAMPLE: Everyone among the forty or so hikers <u>are</u> _____ *is* _____
> physically unfit for a walk of any real duration.

1. Although many of David's friends had come to the party _____

   as early as 7 p.m., most was still there at 3 a.m.   _____

2. Everyone driving up to the ski resorts say that Highway 14 _____
   is the shortest route.

3. There was a dog fight and a game of tag going on directly below _____
   my window.

4. Joyce is one of the doctors who is complaining about the _____
   emergency-call system.

5. Neither of the dogs have ever run loose on the beach before. _____

6. Each of the campers have brought her own pup tent.   _____

7. In the refrigerator there is cold turkey along with some left- _____
   over stuffing and pie.

8. Madeleine is the only one of the women who have any musical _____
   talent.

9. Even though Truman asks his roommates every week to _____

   refrain from eating his imported cheese, most disappear within _____
   a day or two after he buys it.

10. Thirty of Michael's prize roses were blooming yesterday, but _____ following the storm none was left.

11. Everyone from the three dorms are getting together to plan _____ the festivities.

12. Do either of the boys have permission to call their father at his _____ office at any time?

13. Another of the graduates are beginning that difficult search _____ for a good teaching job.

14. The merchandise—rugs, lamps, and chairs—was priced to sell _____

quickly, but more have been sold than even Mr. Clayton had _____ anticipated.

PART B

DIRECTIONS: Use each of the following words as the subject of a sentence using a verb in the present tense.

EXAMPLE: *each*

Each of these shingles is cut by hand.

1. *everything*

_____

2. *one*

_____

3. *either*

_____

4. *everyone*

_____

5. *neither*

_____

6. *all* (Write a compound sentence, giving the antecedent of *all* in the first clause.)

_____

7. *there* (Put *there* in the subject position before the verb, and put the real subject after the verb.)

_____

DIRECTIONS: Cross out those verbs in the following sentences that do not agree with their subjects. Above each verb that you have crossed out, write the correct form of the verb.

      EXAMPLE: After lunch Jack, accompanied by the other guys, ~~are~~ *is* going in

      search of glasses and a decanter, which ~~is~~ *are* what they want to

      give to Jack's sister.

1. Among the most interesting of human characteristics are the inclination of almost everyone to collect, store, and cherish everything from supermarket bags to the most bizarre kind of bric-a-brac.

2. Almost everybody, both young and old, have some items—old copies of *National Geographic*, antique bottles, rusted farm tools—which is known to neighbors and friends as his or her "collectibles."

3. A number of these personal treasures falls into the category of souvenirs: a china cup, suitably inscribed with the city visited (and likely made in Japan), is a favorite souvenir among some travelers, but plates, plaques, or figurines is also popular.

4. *We Love National Parks* say a slogan painted across a slab of redwood, a plaque carefully tucked amid twelve redwood cones from California, which is the owner's pride and joy.

5. Neither souvenirs nor bric-a-brac satisfy the acquisitive urge of some collectors: for one category of collector, the utility of the items are the foremost consideration.

6. On the other hand, there is, as might be expected, those collectors who, in spite of their overcrowded living quarters and empty purses, feels that all items, especially old, broken, and useless ones, are in need of a home.

7. This class of collectors haunt antique shops and garage sales and overbid at auctions only to arrive home with a dirty and worthless assortment of junk.

8. The number of collectors are astounding: nowadays not only the senior citizen and the young couple but also the college student and the young child seems to collect something.

9. To true collectors, their friends' approval of their treasures are of no importance.

10. A moth-eaten sampler with "Five minus two is two" embroidered in red is a wry bit of pleasure to an accountant, although his wife as well as his children make excuses to friends for his taste in decorative items.

11. Along the shelf in a child's room is jars of long-dead bugs captured during great adventures in the woods; in a dormitory room the word *tigers* leap out from a ten-year assortment of bumper stickers; and everywhere there is antique comic books, a popular treasure among those who loved comics when comics was the newest treat for children.

19/PROBLEMS WITH PRONOUNS

Pronouns are substitutes for nouns or nominals.

19a PRONOUN REFERENCE

The noun or nominal for which a pronoun substitutes is called its **antecedent**, and the relationship between a pronoun and its antecedent is called **reference**; we say that a pronoun *refers* to its antecedent.

Pronouns should always agree with their antecedents in gender (masculine, feminine, or neuter), number (singular, mass, or plural) and person (first, second, or third). A pronoun does *not*, however, necessarily agree in case (subject, object, or possessive) with its antecedent. The appropriate case of a pronoun is determined solely by its function in its own clause.

The antecedent of a pronoun should always be clear to the reader. Several kinds of reference present problems.

1. In referring to *collective nouns* (*group, team*), use the singular pronoun *it* if the unit is being considered as a whole, and use the plural pronoun *they* if individuals within the group are being considered.

> The staff is proud of its award. (The staff as a unified group got the award and is proud of it.)
>
> The staff are upset about their problems with the computer. (Individual members of the staff are upset.)

2. In speech the plural pronoun *they* is often used as a substitute for indefinite pronouns such as *anyone* and *everybody* and for indefinite nouns such as *individual, citizen, parent*, or *artist*, which can refer to either a male or a female. The use of *they* to refer to a singular antecedent is unacceptable in formal written English. The correct forms are *he* and *she*, and *he* has been traditionally used as the third-person substitute for indefinite pronouns and nouns. Many people, however, think that the exclusive use of *he* is sexist. If you do not want to offend these people, you may want to use *he or she*, although the use of both pronouns together throughout a paragraph becomes tedious to the reader. Instead, you can often rewrite the sentence, making the antecedent plural so that *they* may be correctly used as the pronoun.

> The citizen believes that he is not getting a fair return for his tax dollars. (sexist to some)
>
> The citizen believes that he or she is not getting a fair return for his or her tax dollars. (cumbersome to some)
>
> The citizens believe that they are not getting a fair return for their tax dollars.

3. The acceptable use of *you, they*, and *it* is very limited in correct writing, although these pronouns are widely used in speech to refer to people in general or to an unknown or irrelevant antecedent.

You is appropriate in imperative sentences (those that express a request, suggestion, or command) or in writing instructions.

> Check your dog regularly for ticks.

It is also appropriate in quoting proverbs or fixed expressions.

> You can't judge a book by its cover.

In informal writing, *you* may be used to make statements about human beings in general, but in formal writing *one* is preferred.

INFORMAL	When you have a positive attitude, positive things happen to you.
FORMAL	When one has a positive attitude, positive things happen to him or her.
HIGHLY FORMAL	When one has a positive attitude, positive things happen to one.

They is not appropriate as an indefinite pronoun in writing. Eliminate it by rewriting.

COLLOQUIAL	At the personnel office they said we have to have a birth certificate.
FORMAL	A birth certificate is required by the personnel office. *or* The personnel office requires us to have a birth certificate.

We is a somewhat less formal pronoun than *one* and can be used to avoid overworking the passive voice or to include the writer in a general statement.

PASSIVE	Costs can be expected to rise sharply.
REVISED	We can expect costs to rise sharply.
WRITER INCLUDED	We are all feeling the pinch of rising costs.

Although *one* is always correct as an indefinite personal pronoun, it may sometimes seem stilted. *He or she* can replace *one* after the first reference.

FORMAL	One would rather not admit that one is unprepared.
INFORMAL	One would rather not admit that he or she (*or* he) is unprepared.

The indefinite *it says* should not be used in formal writing to refer to printed matter.

UNACCEPTABLE	It says in the *Courier* that war has broken out.
REVISED	The *Courier* says that war has broken out.

4. Ambiguous reference should be corrected by rewriting the sentence or by repeating one of the nouns so that the antecedent is made clear to the reader.

AMBIGUOUS	As Jane and Marsha talked, she was visibly relieved to share her problem.
REVISED	As Jane and Marsha talked, Jane was visibly relieved to share her problem.
AMBIGUOUS	This skirt has a pocket in front. Do you want another one? (another skirt or another pocket?)
REVISED	This skirt has a pocket in front. Do you want another skirt?

5. If the pronoun is so far removed from its antecedent that the reader may be confused, rewrite the passage, renaming the antecedent or giving a synonym for it.

REMOTE REFERENCE	Harry's piano sounds wonderful now that it has been tuned. He gave a concert for friends, playing Chopin waltzes and Gershwin's *Rhapsody in Blue*. It has never sounded better.
REVISED	Harry's piano sounds wonderful now that it has been tuned. He gave a concert for friends, playing Chopin waltzes and Gershwin's *Rhapsody in Blue*. The piano has never sounded better.

6. Broad reference occurs when the pronouns *this, that, it*, and *which* refer to a whole preceding clause or sentence. Broad reference is widely used in speech and is acceptable in both speech and writing if the antecedent is completely clear.

UNCLEAR BROAD REFERENCE	Mrs. Imholtz came to visit and brought her dog, which was a shock.
REVISED	Mrs. Imholtz came to visit, and I was shocked that she brought her dog.
REVISED	That Mrs. Imholtz came to visit was a shock. She brought along her dog.

7. Implied reference occurs when a pronoun is used that has no antecedent or that refers to elements that are not nouns or nominals.

INCORRECT	The car has crushed velvet seats. This is harder to care for than vinyl.
REVISED	The car has crushed velvet seats, and crushed velvet is harder to care for than vinyl is.
INCORRECT	Tim dusted, which was futile as long as the furnace was smoking.
REVISED	Tim dusted, but dusting was a futile activity as long as the furnace was smoking.

8. Unnecessary reference occurs when both a noun and a pronoun are used as subject in the same phrase. One or the other should be eliminated.

INCORRECT	Those legislators they ought to do something!
CORRECT	Those legislators ought to do something!
CORRECT	They ought to do something!

19b PRONOUN CASE

The proper case of a pronoun—subject, object, or possessive—is determined solely by the pronoun's function in its own clause.

1. **Compound constructions.** In compound constructions (those joined by *and* or *or*), use the form of the pronoun that would be correct if it were not part of a compound.

INCORRECT	They gave the award to Jeffrey and I. (You would not say "They gave the award to I.")
CORRECT	They gave the award to Jeffrey and me.
INCORRECT	Eileen and me looked for an apartment. (You would not say "Me looked for an apartment.")
CORRECT	Eileen and I looked for an apartment.

Do not use the reflexive pronouns ending in *-self* as subjects. Do not use reflexive pronouns as objects unless the object refers to the same person or thing as the subject.

INCORRECT	Althea and <u>myself</u> were victims of circumstance.
CORRECT	Althea and I were victims of circumstance.
INCORRECT	Father made a toast to Carl and <u>myself</u>.
CORRECT	Father made a toast to Carl and me.

2. **Relative and interrogative constructions.** The relative and interrogative pronouns *who* and *whom* are troublesome to many writers. One reason is that *whom* is rapidly disappearing from speech, and because it seems strange to hear it, it also seems strange—even incorrect—to write it. However, in correct written English, the distinction between the cases of *who* should be made.

Who is the correct form for subjects; *whom* is the correct form for objects. The case of *who* is determined by its function within its own clause. In a *who*-clause, if there is no other subject for the verb, *who* must be the subject, but if there is another subject, then the pronoun is an object and its form should be *whom.*

He is the man <u>whom</u> I met at the party. (*I* is the subject of the relative clause, and *whom* is direct object.)

She is the woman <u>who</u> works in my office building. (*Who* is the subject of *works.*)

If a phrase or clause intervenes between the *who* or *whom* and the verb, determining the proper case becomes more difficult.

INCORRECT	<u>Whom</u> did you say is waiting? (This sounds correct, but if you take out the clause *did you say*, you are left with *whom is waiting*, which is obviously incorrect.)
CORRECT	<u>Who</u> did you say is waiting?
INCORRECT	Elsie is the one <u>whom</u> I believe should receive the award.
CORRECT	Elsie is the one <u>who</u> I believe should receive the award.

Remember that even the *who*-clause functions as the object of a preposition, the *who* takes its case from its *own* clause: it is not automatically an object. The entire clause—not the *who* or *whom*—is the object of the preposition.

INCORRECT	Give the tickets to <u>whomever</u> can use them. (*Whomever can use them* is the object of the preposition *to*, not the *whomever* alone. The subject of *can* must be the subject case of the pronoun.)
CORRECT	Give the tickets to <u>whoever</u> can use them.

3. **Possessive constructions.** *Whose* is the correct possessive form of *who* for both people and things, although many people prefer to use *of which* for things and *whose* for people. But if both *whose* and *of which* seem awkward, rewrite the sentence to avoid using either.

AWKWARD	Watergate was a scandal the real complexities of which we may never know.
IMPROVED	Watergate was a scandal whose real complexities we may never know.
IMPROVED	We may never know the real complexities of Watergate.

4. **Appositive constructions.** The case of a pronoun in apposition to a noun is not affected by that noun. It is in the same case as it would be if the noun were omitted.

INCORRECT   Us sunbathers are unhappy about the rainy spring. (You would not say "Us are unhappy.")

CORRECT   We sunbathers are unhappy about the rainy spring.

5. **Constructions with *than, as,* and *but*.** *Than* is a conjunction, not a preposition, and the appropriate case of the pronoun following *than* depends on the function of the pronoun in its own clause. Often *than*-clauses are elliptical; that is, the verb and the subject or object have been omitted. If you are unsure how the pronoun functions, furnish the missing words in your own mind, and you will know what the case of the pronoun should be.

Mrs. Rutkowski always relied on Harry more than me. (This sentence means that she always relied on Harry more than she relied on me.)

Mrs. Rutkowski always relied on Harry more than I. (This sentence means that she always relied on Harry more than I relied on Harry.)

As ... as constructions are also often elliptical, and the writer must mentally supply the missing words in order to determine the proper case of the pronoun.

Gordon complains to Theresa as much as her. (This means that Gordon complains to Theresa as much as Gordon complains to her.)

Gordon complains to Theresa as much as I. (This means that Gordon complains to Theresa as much as I complain to Theresa.)

In the meaning "except," *but* is a preposition and always requires the object case of the pronoun.

Everyone but him had written to Carter.

Carter heard from all of his friends but him.

6. **After the verb *to be*.** In speech we usually find it awkward to say "It was she" or "That was I" or "Those were they," although these are the correct forms for formal English. In writing, if the sentence seems stilted, rewrite to avoid the problem.

AWKWARD TO SOME   Grandmother did not know it was I who sent the flowers.

REVISED   Grandmother did not know that I was the one who sent the flowers.

NAME _____ DATE _____

DIRECTIONS: Rewrite each of the following sentences, correcting all errors in pronoun reference. Write *C* in the space after correct sentences.

EXAMPLE: Every time Tom and Bill meet, he asks to borrow money.

Every time Tom and Bill meet, Tom asks to borrow money.

1. Every artist at the exhibit is demanding more space for their paintings.

_____

_____

2. The team congratulated itself on winning the bowl game, and they drank champagne in their locker room and talked over the entire season.

_____

_____

_____

3. When Bernadette was going to grade school, the many small, personal things that happened, they didn't mean much; now that she is much older, they do.

_____

_____

_____

4. Gilda had begun reading *War and Peace* when she decided to study a little Russian history and language, and all of her efforts have made it more meaningful.

_____

_____

_____

5. When Nora confronted Alice with the evidence, she was very indignant.

_____

_____

6. Dr. Jarvis admitted that he had once failed a basic chemistry course, which amazed Lewis.

_____

_____

7. Anyone who signs up beforehand can take whatever mini-courses they want to take.

_____

_____

_____

8. "This layer cake has that awful hole on one side," said George. "Shall we make another?"

_____

_____

9. Everybody always brings his own linens and food to the beach house.

_____

_____

10. It says in the *Times* that flight crews for three airlines may strike.

_____

_____

NAME _____ DATE _____

PART A

DIRECTIONS: In the following sentences, underline each pronoun that is in the incorrect case and write the correct form in the blank on the right. If a sentence is correct, write *C* in the blank.

      EXAMPLE: The Downings and <u>them</u> have gone to Arizona   *they*
                   camping.

1. Us two simply had not realized what a tornado is like.   _____

2. Jeff liked split pea soup much more than me.   _____

3. Millie and them rented the apartment in June.   _____

4. Frank and myself never were very dedicated joggers.   _____

5. It does not seem fair that Jeanne and her should do all of that _____
   work.

6. If you are looking for the old comic books, these are they. _____

7. Kenny sent Carol and I some plants for the new apartment. _____

8. Whom did the doctor think was responsible for the accident? _____

9. Everyone but she was willing to chip in a dollar toward a gift _____
   for Mr. Pyron.

10. Hettie lends her sailboat to whomever she thinks will take _____
    good care of it.

11. Disco music is usually too loud for Carla and he.   _____

12. Joseph and Marilyn are the couple the poems of whom have _____
    been published in three magazines.

PART B

DIRECTIONS: Use each of the following pronouns in a sentence.

1. *whom*

_____

_____

2. *they*

_____

_____

3. *them*

_____

_____

4. *he*

_____

_____

5. *her*

_____

_____

6. *whoever*

_____

_____

NAME _____ DATE _____

DIRECTIONS: Underline incorrectly used pronouns or those that are especially awkward. Rewrite the sentences, using the correct form of the pronoun and making any necessary changes in the number of the verb.

EXAMPLE: Everyone will have to buy <u>their</u> own materials for the art course.

Everyone will have to buy his or her own materials for the art course.

1. When he or she hears the term *Wild, Wild West*, many Americans think immediately of his or her favorite western hero who they may have come to know on the radio, but whom they most likely became acquainted with in the movies of the 1940s and 1950s or in the television programs of the 1950s and 1960s.

_____

_____

_____

_____

2. Although they brought to life many heroes of the West, the movie or television western offered a distorted view of how the West was really won and whom the real heroes and villains were.

_____

_____

_____

3. Indeed, the Lone Ranger, astride his magnificent horse, Silver, he was something like a medieval knight, always ready to save whomever was in distress.

_____

_____

4. His faithful Indian companion, Tonto, and him could bring the worst of cattle thieves or bank robbers to justice, and Tonto and himself could keep peace between the settlers and the Indians, who they knew well and who trusted them.

_____

_____

_____

5. Even though the Lone Ranger and Tonto shot plenty of crooks, they never died in the bloody mode of latter-day television characters, although they usually suffered severe powder burns or minor shoulder wounds.

_____

_____

_____

6. Neither of them two had any trouble fighting ten or twelve men, though it was an impossible task for anyone but they.

_____

_____

_____

7. It is him, the romantic and uplifting exploits of whom captivated us viewers, who most resembles the heroes of escapist movies in the 1970s—Batman, Superman, Wonder Woman, and Luke Skywalker.

_____

_____

_____

8. Roy Rogers and Gene Autrey were very similar to the Lone Ranger in their quest for good and his devotion to the fight against evil, but the difference between them and he is that they were singing cowboys and they were more closely tied to ranch settings than him.

_____

_____

_____

9. Even the cattle itself perked up their ears to the strumming guitars and the melodious voices of these cowboys.

_____

_____

_____

10. Although the early television shows and films they depicted Indians as ruthless beasts who must be overcome and women as either shrinking flowers or too-rough types, several minority heroes emerged who the audiences adored—Annie Oakley, a female sharpshooter, and the Cisco Kid and Zorro, Mexican cowboys.

_____

_____

_____

_____

11. Annie Oakley was, of course, a real person, the life of which inspired the movie and stage play *Annie Get Your Gun* and TV series about her. It was her, more than any other western woman, after who every little girl in America patterned their make-believe cowgirl personality and costume.

_____

_____

_____

_____

12. In retrospect, however, Annie Oakley was not the liberated woman who the modern woman might applaud as a real western heroine and symbol of the freedom afforded women by the West; she was rather a woman who was much less free than us women today because the very fact that a woman could be as talented as her was something odd, interesting, and almost freakish, but certainly not normal.

_____

_____

_____

_____

13. Even the bad guys like Billy the Kid and Jesse James they were whitewashed into stock types, villainous enough to be interesting but not as vicious, cunning, and complex as them two likely were in real life or as horrible as those criminals and terrorists are who, in our age, people fear on every hand.

_____

_____

_____

_____

14. It is them—Tom Mix, Lash Larue, Johnny Mack Brown, Marshal Dillon, the Rifleman, Paladin, Buffalo Bill, Ben Cartwright, and all the rest (even Rin Tin Tin)—who we looked to for portrayals of the Wild West, but everybody who peopled those shows and movies, each with their own distinctive trademark, helped we Americans to form, not a picture of the real West, but a romantic view of they and their era.

_____

_____

_____

_____

_____

_____

20/PROBLEMS WITH MODIFIERS

Modifiers are words that describe or limit the meaning of other words. Modifiers may be either adjectival or adverbial and may consist of a single word, a phrase, or an entire clause.

20a ADJECTIVES

1. **Predicate Adjectives.** An adjective that serves as a subject complement is called a **predicate adjective.** Predicate adjectives are used only after linking verbs. Linking verbs include verbs of sensation (*feel, look, smell, sound, taste*) and verbs expressing existence (*be, act, appear, become, continue, grow, prove, remain, seem, sit, stand*, and *turn*, for example).

> Your plan sounds <u>reasonable</u>.
>
> The sky became <u>dark</u> and the air seemed <u>oppressive</u>.

Confusion often occurs because many linking verbs can also be used as ordinary verbs and be followed by adverbs. Remember that if the modifier following a linking verb describes the subject, the modifier should be an adjective. If the modifier describes the verb, the modifier should be an adverb.

PREDICATE ADJECTIVE	Ginny's boyfriend appeared <u>nervous</u>. (*Nervous* describes the subject, *boyfriend*.)
ADVERB	Ginny's boyfriend appeared <u>suddenly</u>. (*Suddenly* describes the verb, telling how he appeared.)
PREDICATE ADJECTIVE	The milk turned <u>sour</u>. (*Sour* describes the milk.)
ADVERB	The key turned <u>easily</u>. (*Easily* describes the action of the verb *turned*.)

2. **Possessives.** Words are made into possessive modifiers either by adding -'s or by using *of*. Problems sometimes arise in knowing when to use -'s and when to use *of*. Some indefinite pronouns are made into possessive modifiers by adding -'s. These include, for example, *neither, someone, everybody else*, and *one*.

> <u>One's</u> own dirt never seems as dirty as <u>somebody else's</u> dirt.

Other indefinite pronouns form their possessives only with *of* (*any, each, both, few, many, several, all*, and *much*, for example).

INCORRECT	Reuben and Hugh entered the tiddlywinks tournament, but <u>both's</u> performance was disappointing.
CORRECT	Reuben and Hugh entered the tiddlywinks tournament, but the performance <u>of both</u> was disappointing.

3. **Group Possessives.** When we speak, we often put the -'s of a possessive at the end of an entire noun phrase, that is, after all the modifiers of the noun. Such constructions are called **group possessives.**

> Our TV with the <u>remote control's</u> antenna is broken.
>
> Check <u>the bus leaving from Detroit's</u> schedule.

In writing, a group possessive is usually awkward. Rewrite the sentence to avoid it.

The antenna is broken on our TV with the remote control.
Check the schedule of the bus leaving from Detroit.

4. **Gerunds. Gerunds** are nouns made from verbs by adding *-ing*. Like other nouns, gerunds should be modified by the possessive form of nouns and pronouns.

Rodney said that no one liked <u>his</u> singing.
<u>Claudine's</u> cooking has improved greatly.

It is sometimes hard to tell whether a word is a gerund or a present participle because both end in *-ing*. If the *-ing* word is a subject or object in the sentence, it is a gerund and the preceding noun or pronoun should be possessive.

I was kept awake by Maggie's typing. (It was the typing that kept me awake; *typing* is the object of the preposition, so *Maggie* is a modifier and should be possessive.)

His refusing to eat vegetables disturbs his wife. (It is the *refusing* that disturbs his wife; *refusing* is the subject.)

If the noun or pronoun preceding an *-ing* word is a subject or object, the *-ing* word is a present participle and a modifier, and the noun or pronoun should not be possessive.

I was surprised to see Maggie typing so late at night. (It was *Maggie* that you saw; *Maggie* is the object, and *typing* is a present participle modifying *Maggie*.)

His wife watched him eating potato chips. (His wife watched *him*, not the *eating; him* is the object.)

20b ADVERBS

Adverbs can cause a number of problems in writing.

1. **Adjectives as adverbials.** Adjectives such as *real, sure, awful, pretty, bad,* and *good* are often used to modify verbs in spoken English, but in written English, only adverbs should modify verbs. Check your dictionary if you are not sure whether a word is an adjective or an adverb.

INCORRECT	The new car handles <u>good</u>.
CORRECT	The new car handles <u>well</u>.
INCORRECT	He seemed <u>real</u> tired.
CORRECT	He seemed <u>really</u> tired.

2. **Double negatives.** Unacceptable double negatives occur when a negative adverb appears in the same clause with another negative word that serves only to intensify the meaning of the negative. To correct a double negative, eliminate all but one of the negative words.

INCORRECT	He had <u>not</u> <u>hardly</u> had time to eat.
REVISED	He had <u>hardly</u> had time to eat.
REVISED	He had <u>not</u> had time to eat.

INCORRECT	Scarcely nobody ate nothing.
REVISED	Scarcely anyone ate anything.
REVISED	Almost nobody ate anything.

3. *So, such,* and *too.* Although these adverbs are used to intensify statements made in speech, they should not be used in writing without a following clause or phrase that completes the meaning.

COLLOQUIAL	I like Edith's dress so much.
REVISED	I like Edith's dress so much that I am going to buy one like it.
REVISED	I like Edith's dress very much.
COLLOQUIAL	It is such a pleasant day!
REVISED	It is such a pleasant day that Herb is going fishing.
REVISED	It is a particularly pleasant day.
COLLOQUIAL	The party was simply too exciting!
REVISED	The party was simply too exciting to be described!
REVISED	The party was indescribably exciting!

20c PLACEMENT OF MODIFIERS

A **misplaced modifier** is one that appears to modify the wrong word or words because of its position in the sentence. Misplaced modifiers can be one-word modifiers, phrases, or clauses. Single adjectives usually precede the words they modify, and although adverbs are more flexible in their placement, they should be placed as close as is grammatically possible to the words they modify. Sentences with a misplaced modifier should be rewritten to put the modifier closer to the word or words it is meant to modify.

MISPLACED	Fred told us about an avalanche that only happened a week ago. (misplaced adverb)
REVISED	Fred told us about an avalanche that happened only a week ago.
MISPLACED	Flying across the dark sky, Mr. Chappelear showed us the shooting star. (misplaced participle phrase)
REVISED	Mr. Chappelear showed us the shooting star flying across the dark sky.
MISPLACED	Mrs. Bonds took the letter out of her purse that she wanted to send special delivery to California. (misplaced dependent clause)
REVISED	Mrs. Bonds took out of her purse the letter that she wanted to send special delivery to California.

Misplaced modifiers can be of several kinds.

1. **Dangling modifiers** either seem to modify the wrong words or seem to have nothing to modify. They are usually participle phrases, infinitive phrases, gerund phrases, or elliptical clauses. (An elliptical clause is one in which words have been omitted because they are understood from the context.)

DANGLING PRESENT PARTICIPLE	Hiding behind the mayonnaise on the third shelf of the refrigerator, Marian found the olives. (Is Marian in the refrigerator?)

REVISED	Marian found the olives hiding behind the mayonnaise on the third shelf of the refrigerator.
DANGLING PAST PARTICIPLE	Confronted with the evidence, the police listened to the robber's confession. (Who is being confronted with evidence?)
REVISED	After the robber had been confronted with the evidence, the police listened to his confession.
DANGLING INFINITIVE	To get into the house without breaking a window, great skill was required. (Who wants to get into the house?)
REVISED	To get into the house without breaking a window, John had to exercise great skill.
DANGLING GERUND PHRASE	After searching all night, the keys were found in Ann's purse. (Who did the searching?)
REVISED	After Ann had searched all night, she found the keys in her purse.
DANGLING ELLIPTICAL CLAUSE	A magnificent dog, all of the top awards at the dog show went to Grendel.
REVISED	Because she is a magnificent dog, Grendel took all of the top awards at the dog show.

2. **Squinting modifiers** are modifiers that cause ambiguity because they can refer either to what precedes or to what follows them. Correct them by placing them so that they clearly modify only the intended words.

SQUINTING	The teacher reminded the first-graders often to wash their hands.
REVISED	The teacher often reminded the first-graders to wash their hands.
REVISED	The teacher reminded the first-graders to wash their hands often.

3. **Split infinitives** occur when a modifier comes between the word *to* and the present infinitive form of the verb. (*To cautiously move* is a split infinitive. *To have cautiously moved* is not a split infinitive because *to have moved* is the perfect form of the infinitive.) Some people do not consider split infinitives incorrect, but others disapprove of them, partly because they are often awkward. Infinitives should be split only to improve clarity or to avoid awkwardness.

An infinitive should never be split with a modifier that is several words long.

SPLIT	To <u>completely</u> master chess is what John wants.
REVISED	To master chess <u>completely</u> is what John wants.
AWKWARD	<u>Actually</u> to own a car was Laura's dream.
AWKWARD	To own <u>actually</u> a car was Laura's dream.
REVISED	To <u>actually</u> own a car was Laura's dream.
AWKWARD	The rusty old crank started to <u>slowly and with a creaking sound</u> turn.
REVISED	The rusty old crank started to turn <u>slowly and with a creaking sound</u>.
REVISED	<u>Slowly and with a creaking sound</u>, the rusty old crank started to turn.

4. **Unidiomatic modifiers** are modifiers whose placement in the sentence makes the sentence sound unnatural to English. Reading sentences aloud is a way of catching these misplaced modifiers.

As a general rule, adverbials of place (*here, in the cupboard, upstairs*) precede adverbials of time (*later, last week, in the evening*), and both follow the rest of the predicate. Adverbials of manner (*quickly, carefully, in a solemn voice*) usually come before the main verb or after the entire predicate. If this normal order is rearranged, the sentence will often be unidiomatic.

UNIDIOMATIC	Jack on Thursday met Fred in Toledo.
REVISED	On Thursday Jack met Fred in Toledo.
REVISED	Jack met Fred in Toledo on Thursday.
UNIDIOMATIC	Miranda slammed suddenly the door.
REVISED	Suddenly Miranda slammed the door.
REVISED	Miranda slammed the door suddenly.

20d RESTRICTIVE AND NONRESTRICTIVE MODIFIERS

Modifiers that are essential to the identification of the word or group of words being modified are restrictive modifiers. They are never set off with commas or other punctuation.

Modifiers that provide additional information that is not essential to the identification of the word or words being modified are called nonrestrictive modifiers. They are usually enclosed in commas, though they may be set off with parentheses or dashes.

If restrictive or nonrestrictive modifiers are improperly punctuated, the reader may be confused or even completely misunderstand the sentence.

Children who grow up having everything they want often become unambitious, complaisant adults.

Children, who grow up having everything they want, often become unambitious, complaisant adults.

In the first sentence, the writer—by omitting the commas after *children* and *want*—indicates that it is those children who grow up having everything they want who often become unambitious and complaisant. In the second sentence, the writer indicates, by using commas, that children in general grow up having everything they want and become unambitious and complaisant.

NAME _____ DATE _____

PART A

DIRECTIONS: Underline all one-word modifiers and group possessives that are misused or awkward. In the space following each sentence, write a revision correcting the problem. Write a *C* after correct sentences.

EXAMPLE: They ran <u>real</u> hard for the first mile.

They ran really hard for the first mile.

1. Barbara's attitude is so atypical for a girl in her situation.

   _____

2. When he showered this morning, Lewis sang so good that his next-door neighbor telephoned his compliments.

   _____

3. At least fifteen members made fund-raising suggestions, and several's were quite good.

   _____

4. Tom failing chemistry for the second time was a major setback for his G.P.R.

   _____

5. That tiny, blond-haired girl swimming there is the minister of Pat's church's daughter.

   _____

6. Him not being able to get home for the wedding was sure a disappointment to Jeff's sister.

   _____

7. Lennie was not hardly ever able to keep his buddies from raiding his refrigerator when they came over to study.

   _____

   _____

8. After exams Lucy looked pretty awful, but plenty of sleep and some good meals soon brought back her energy and cheerfulness.

_____

_____

9. It wasn't but seldom that Ernie could get a ride home for the weekend.

_____

10. Nothing further was ever mentioned about anyone else's moving into the house with Dave and Chad.

_____

PART B

DIRECTIONS: Write two sentences using each of the following verbs. In the first sentence, follow the verb with a predicate adjective; in the second, follow the verb with an adverbial.

EXAMPLE: *smell*

The pie smelled good.

The tent smelled suspiciously of skunk.

1. *look*

_____

_____

2. *act*

_____

_____

3. *grow*

_____

_____

4. *sit*

_____

_____

NAME _____ DATE _____

PART A

DIRECTIONS: On a separate sheet of paper, revise the following sentences, correcting all dangling and misplaced modifiers. Label correct sentences with a *C*.

EXAMPLE: To fry an egg, a little butter or margarine helps.

To fry an egg, you will find a little butter or margarine helps.

1. Stalking a bird through the tall grass, a tree limb suddenly fell, scratching the hind leg of the startled cat.

2. To learn to sail, some basic knowledge of math is essential.

3. A child was found wandering in a state of amnesia on Oak Avenue that had been considered missing by the police.

4. An unusual specimen, the scientist arranged for her colleagues to see the plant.

5. Complicated by her stock dividends, Anna found that she needed more information before computing her income tax.

6. The Little Leaguers were warned about showing poor sportsmanship on the bus heading for the championship game.

7. Although not a bad dish, Lisa preferred her own chicken casserole to the one José had served her.

8. By doing word puzzles, many interesting and stimulating trivia come to light.

9. While jogging, the elastic in Andy's shorts broke.

10. Terribly frightened of all spiders, an old newspaper was the only weapon that Wilbur could find to do battle with the one creeping up his bedspread.

11. Recuperating from a fall down the cellar stairs, the big, overstuffed armchair was the most comfortable place for James to sit.

12. After cramming all night for the exam, Jan's back and neck were sore.

13. Mr. Stracke took the steaks out of the freezer that he meant to grill for dinner.

14. Confined to bed for three weeks with the mumps, television and books were the only company Alex had.

15. To stop smoking, chewing gum and worry beads relieve the tension and the need for something to do with the hands.

16. Stopped for driving twenty miles an hour over the speed limit, the policeman strongly admonished Joe.

DIRECTIONS: In the blank before each sentence, identify the error in the sentence as *SQ* (squinting modifier), *UN* (unidiomatic modifier), or *SI* (split infinitive). Then, on a separate sheet of paper, rewrite the sentence, correcting the error. If the error is a split infinitive that is better split than not, write *same* instead of a revision.

EXAMPLE: ___*UN*___ Harris was frightened in the dark room suddenly.

Suddenly Harris was frightened in the dark room.

_____ 1. Every employee was given the mandate to earnestly strive to improve the company's image.

_____ 2. Mr. Romanstine told his daughter sometimes to be less sarcastic to her mother.

_____ 3. We were scheduled to arrive on the dot at 9 a.m. in London.

_____ 4. The piano teacher instructed Leonard regularly to practice.

_____ 5. It took Andrea months to meticulously stitch the crewel work that hangs over the fireplace.

_____ 6. Mrs. Hebrack warned the neighborhood kids kindly to refrain from riding bicycles on her lawn.

_____ 7. The sergeant ordered the recruits quickly to march.

_____ 8. Andrew was very angry about the insult, but all he really could do was to patiently endure it.

_____ 9. Cynthia on Friday severed her ties with the company.

_____ 10. They all love to play backgammon because there is just no way to accurately predict the outcome of the game.

_____ 11. Dolly picked up the broken cup and with glue mended it.

_____ 12. You must really in the future be more careful.

21 / PROBLEMS WITH COMPARISONS

The change in form of adjectives and adverbs to indicate differences in degree is called **comparison**. The three degrees of comparison are **positive** (*early, recent*), **comparative** (*earlier, more recent*), and **superlative** (*the earliest, the most recent*). See also section 5.

21a DOUBLE COMPARISONS

Do not use both *more* and *-er* to make a single adjective or adverb comparative, and do not use both *most* and *-est* to make a single adjective or adverb superlative.

INCORRECT   He is <u>much more handsomer</u> than his brother is.

REVISED   He is <u>much handsomer</u> than his brother is.

REVISED   He is <u>much more handsome</u> than his brother is.

INCORRECT   Fran was <u>the most happiest</u> of all those at the wedding.

REVISED   Fran was <u>the happiest</u> of all those at the wedding.

21b COMPARISON OF ABSOLUTES

Such words as *complete, perfect, dead*, and *round* are logically already superlative and thus should not be compared. However, we often wish to express a comparison between two things that have qualities of roundness or perfection, even though we know that nothing can ever be wholly round or perfect. The formal way to express comparison with absolute terms like these is to use *more nearly* rather than *more*, and *most nearly* rather than *most*.

INFORMAL   One actor seemed <u>more dead</u> than the other.

FORMAL   One actor seemed <u>more nearly dead</u> than the other.

INFORMAL   The figure on the left seems <u>the most round</u>.

FORMAL   The figure on the left seems <u>the most nearly round</u>.

21c MISUSE OF THE SUPERLATIVE

Do not use a superlative where a comparative is appropriate. In comparing two items, use the comparative, but in comparing three or more items, use the superlative.

COLLOQUIAL   Of the two rabbits, Jackson is the fastest.

REVISED   Of the two rabbits, Jackson is the faster.

REVISED   Of the three rabbits, Jackson is the fastest.

Do not use a superlative as an intensifier to emphasize an adjective when a comparison is not intended. For that kind of emphasis use an adverb instead of the superlative.

COLLOQUIAL   They met <u>the wittiest</u> man last night.

REVISED   They met a <u>very witty</u> man last night.

21d ILLOGICAL COMPARISONS

Illogical comparisons imply a comparison between things that the writer does not mean to compare or things that cannot be compared. Sentences containing illogical comparisons should be revised.

ILLOGICAL   Harry wears a shoe bigger than his brother. (Is the shoe bigger than the brother?)

REVISED   Harry wears a shoe bigger than his brother's.

ILLOGICAL   Dorothy's mood is more cheerful than last week.

REVISED   Dorothy's mood is more cheerful than it was last week.

21e AMBIGUOUS COMPARISONS

Comparisons of equality or superiority can be troublesome when the second part of the comparison is elliptical; that is, when some words in the second part of the comparison have been left out because they are understood from the context. Many elliptical comparisons are clear, but, in some cases, it is not clear whether the second part of the comparison is intended as subject or object. Include as many words as are necessary to ensure clarity.

AMBIGUOUS   They like Ferenc better than Karl.

REVISED   They like Ferenc better than Karl does.

REVISED   They like Ferenc better than they like Karl.

21f INCOMPLETE COMPARISONS

Do not make a comparison unless you state clearly what two things you are comparing.

INCOMPLETE   Peanut butter gives you more protein.

REVISED   Peanut butter gives you more protein than potato chips do.

INCOMPLETE   Mei-ling has the fattest dog.

REVISED   Mei-ling has the fattest dog that I have ever seen.

21g THE IDIOM OF COMPARISON

Introduce a comparative clause with the subordinating conjunctions *as* or *as if* and a comparative phrase with the preposition *like*.

CLAUSE   That sofa looks as if its previous home had been the dump.

PHRASE   That sofa looks like a piece of junk.

Use *other* or *any other* to compare members of the same class, and use *any* to compare members of different classes.

Diamonds are more popular than other precious stones. (Diamonds belong to the class of precious stones.)

A diamond is more popular than any other precious stone.

Diamonds are more popular than any costume jewelry. (Diamonds do not belong to the class of costume jewelry.)

If you use *more* (or *less*) in the first part of a comparison, do not use *rather than* to introduce the second part of the comparison.

INCORRECT   The painting looks <u>more like</u> an Impressionist <u>rather than</u> an Expressionist work.

REVISED   The painting looks <u>more like</u> an Impressionist <u>than</u> an Expressionist work.

It is always correct to write *different from*; but *different than*, although widely disapproved of until recently, is gaining acceptance, especially if the object of *than* is a clause. *Different to* is not acceptable.

INCORRECT   The price was <u>different to</u> last year's.

ACCEPTABLE   The price was <u>different than</u> last year's.

CORRECT   The price was <u>different from</u> last year's.

Use *fewer* in comparing plural nouns and *less* in comparing mass nouns.

INCORRECT   Hilda had <u>less</u> natural <u>talents</u> than her sister did. (*Less natural talents* is incorrect because *talents* is a plural noun.)

REVISED   Hilda had <u>fewer</u> natural talents than her sister did.

INCORRECT   The room would have looked better with <u>less</u> furniture and pictures. (Even though *less furniture* is correct, *pictures* is a plural noun and should be modified by *fewer*.)

REVISED   The room would have looked better with <u>less</u> furniture and <u>fewer</u> pictures.

A comparison of equality states that two things share an equal degree of some quality: *Minnesota is as cold as North Dakota.* When using a comparison of equality and a regular comparative in the same clause, do not omit the *as* after the first adjective or adverb.

INCORRECT   Snapdragons are <u>as hardy</u> or <u>hardier than</u> petunias.

CORRECT   Snapdragons are <u>as hardy as</u> or <u>hardier than</u> petunias.

INCORRECT   Enamel paint takes <u>as long</u> or <u>longer than</u> latex to dry.

CORRECT   Enamel paint takes <u>as long as</u> or <u>longer than</u> latex to dry.

NAME _____ DATE _____

DIRECTIONS: Revise the following sentences, correcting incorrect or illogical comparisons.

> EXAMPLE: That monument is as tall or taller than the one we saw in Detroit.
>
> *That monument is as tall as or taller than the one we saw in Detroit.*

1. Terry has a dog bigger than her brother.

   _____

2. Mr. Bruce has better rapport with his son than his wife.

   _____

3. Sidney's dancing is better than last year.

   _____

4. The kind of animation used in the film was different to any that Jessica had ever seen.

   _____

5. That car is supposed to give better gas mileage.

   _____

6. Billboard advertising is as effective or more effective than circulars or brochures.

   _____

7. The South has less noise and air pollution and less problems keeping rivers and lakes clean than do other parts of the country.

   _____

   _____

8. Today Chris looks more prettier than ever before.

_____

_____

9. Gunnar got a higher grade than Ahmed did because the professor judged Gunnar's project more complete than Ahmed.

_____

_____

10. Of the two photographers, Sara was the most knowledgeable.

_____

11. The Bertlands witnessed the most embarrassing scene in the restaurant last night.

_____

12. Roses are traditionally more symbolic than any flower.

_____

13. When Alison came in, she looked like she had seen a ghost.

_____

14. Bob's friends taught him the most fascinating game, which is played with pebbles and sticks.

_____

22/PROBLEMS WITH PREPOSITIONS

Prepositions are words used before nouns or pronouns to form phrases that modify some part of a sentence.

22a PLACEMENT OF PREPOSITIONS

In speech and in informal writing, prepositions often follow their objects and appear at the end of a clause or sentence. Some people, however, disapprove of ending a sentence or a clause with a preposition. In very formal writing, prepositions should precede their objects unless this word order is extremely awkward.

INFORMAL	What course is he asking <u>about</u>?
FORMAL	<u>About</u> what course is he asking?
INFORMAL	Which novel did the essay refer <u>to</u>?
FORMAL	<u>To</u> which novel did the essay refer?

22b REPETITION OF PREPOSITIONS

Do not repeat a preposition that has already appeared with its object earlier in the sentence.

INCORRECT	<u>On</u> which poems was Professor Eimas lecturing <u>on</u> today?
CORRECT	Which poems was Professor Eimas lecturing <u>on</u> today?
CORRECT	<u>On</u> which poems was Professor Eimas lecturing today?
INCORRECT	Taxidermy is a subject <u>about</u> which I have always had a great deal of curiosity <u>about</u>.
CORRECT	Taxidermy is a subject which I have always had a great deal of curiosity <u>about</u>.
CORRECT	Taxidermy is a subject <u>about</u> which I have always had a great deal of curiosity.

22c IDIOMATIC USE OF PREPOSITIONS

Many nouns, verbs, adjectives, and phrases are associated with specific prepositions in such a way that the use of any other preposition is unidiomatic and therefore awkward to native speakers of English. If you are uncertain which preposition is generally used in a phrase or with a particular word, check your dictionary under the noun or verb or other part of speech that you believe to be part of such an idiom. Here are some of the most troublesome phrases.

according to	border on
amazed at *or* by	capable of
annoyed at *or* by	coincide with
astonished at *or* by	compatible with
attached to	conform to
aware of	consist of
beneficial to	consistent with
beware of	convince (someone) of something

critical of

deprive of

despair of (+ gerund)

differ with (someone) about (something)

differ from (something else)

disapprove of

distinct from

eager for

envious of

familiar to (someone)

familiar with (something)

identical to

in accordance with

in search of

inferior to

intent on

married to

overcome by *or* with

prior to

refrain from

responsible to (someone) for (something)

result from (a cause)

result in (an effect)

speak to (someone) about (something)

succeed in

surprised at

take charge of

NAME _____ DATE _____

DIRECTIONS: Revise the following sentences, correcting errors in the placement, repetition, and unidiomatic use of prepositions. The sentences should be written in very formal English. Write *C* after correct sentences.

EXAMPLE: The major will take charge over the situation.

The major will take charge of the situation.

1. Jan wondered through which cities Jody would drive through on his way to Chicago.

_____

2. It was a perfect day to hold a demonstration on.

_____

3. You will find that our services coincide to all your expectations.

_____

4. Luella asked the guide how many bridges she would go over before she reached the street on which the museum was located on.

_____

_____

5. If only Mr. Costanza would refrain in asking impertinent questions about affairs in which he is not concerned in, he would not be a bad neighbor.

_____

_____

6. Muriel is very critical toward activities with which she is not involved in.

_____

7. The scientists were uncertain under what kind of schedule they were laboring under to develop the vaccine.

_____

_____

8. The garage recommended to Adolph was the one which he had had several bad experiences at.

_____

_____

9. The workshop had not been consistent to Frank's expectations, and the entire convention had been unproductive and overrated.

_____

_____

10. When they saw the condition that the cabin was in, the family could not decide to whom they should complain to first.

_____

_____

11. Eleanor of Aquitaine, with whom Louis VII had been married with for fifteen years, later became the wife of Henry II of England.

_____

_____

12. The circus tent which the child stood in front of was a marvelous, multicolored wonder.

_____

_____

13. The quarrel resulted over Jackson's talking to reporters without informing his superiors.

_____

_____

14. Fran found that, according to state law, her car registration, which she had been very careless with, had to be in her possession at all times.

_____

_____

23/PROBLEMS WITH SENTENCE FORM

Problems with sentence form include sentence fragments, shifted constructions, comma splices and fused sentences, mixed constructions, faulty complements and appositives, and improper parallelism.

23a SENTENCE FRAGMENTS

Sentence fragments are incomplete sentences—constructions that have no independent clause. Although they occur frequently in speech, sentence fragments are rarely acceptable in written English.

Dependent clauses are one of the most common forms of sentence fragment. Although a dependent clause does have a subject and a predicate, it is always introduced by a subordinating conjunction or a relative pronoun, words that never introduce independent clauses. To correct a sentence fragment consisting of a dependent clause, either join it to the preceding sentence or make the dependent clause into an independent clause.

FRAGMENT   Traffic was stalled for ten miles on the freeway. <u>Because repairs were being made on potholes.</u>

REVISED   Traffic was stalled for ten miles on the freeway because repairs were being made on potholes.

FRAGMENT   The manager of the building had seemed unwilling to rent an apartment to Jim and Chuck. <u>Until they offered to pay six months' rent in advance.</u>

REVISED   The manager of the building had seemed unwilling to rent an apartment to Jim and Chuck until they offered to pay six months' rent in advance.

REVISED   The manager of the building had seemed unwilling to rent an apartment to Jim and Chuck. However, he changed his mind when they offered to pay six months' rent in advance.

Incomplete clauses are sometimes mistakenly written as sentences, especially when the sentence contains lengthy modifiers. Sometimes writers begin a sentence with the subject and modify it with such long phrases or subordinate clauses that, by the time they reach the end of the modifiers, they do not notice that there is no verb to complete the main clause. These sentence fragments must be rewritten to include the missing elements.

FRAGMENT   The two girls next door, although they mean well and do not realize that their constant borrowing of sugar, eggs, and milk and their inquisitiveness about everyone else in the apartment complex.

REVISED   The two girls next door, although they mean well and do not realize that their constant borrowing of sugar, eggs, and milk and their inquisitiveness about everyone else in the apartment complex are annoying, are, fortunately, quiet.

FRAGMENT   Although the foreman had signaled for the convoy, made up of sixteen trucks and three bulldozers, to move out of the area.

REVISED   Although the foreman had signaled for the convoy, made up of sixteen trucks and three bulldozers, to move out of the area, some kind of delay kept the convoy waiting for another hour.

153

Detached compound predicates are fragments that consist of the second part of a predicate that should be attached to the preceding sentence.

FRAGMENT	Miranda was excited about the internship in Washington. But was also a little afraid.
REVISED	Miranda was excited about the internship in Washington but was also a little afraid.
FRAGMENT	On Saturday mornings, Quentin likes to putter around the house. Or simply sleep late.
REVISED	On Saturday mornings, Quentin likes to putter around the house or simply sleep late.

Modifying phrases are often written as fragments and usually should be attached to the preceding sentence. Prepositional phrases, appositives, participle phrases, and infinitive phrases are often mistakenly punctuated as sentences.

PREPOSITIONAL PHRASE	Gina was extremely irritable. Because of all the confusion.
REVISED	Gina was extremely irritable because of all the confusion.
APPOSITIVE	The plant Alice gave George is a *Crassula argentea*. Or jade plant.
REVISED	The plant Alice gave George is a *Crassula argentea*, or jade plant.
PARTICIPLE PHRASE	The clouds were simply beautiful. Drifting across the sky.
REVISED	The clouds were simply beautiful drifting across the sky.
INFINITIVE PHRASE	After exams were over, Alex was very concerned when he met Tricia. To see that lack of sleep and nervousness had made her quite ill.
REVISED	After exams were over, Alex was very concerned when he met Tricia to see that lack of sleep and nervousness had made her quite ill.

Explanatory phrases introduced by such words as *such as, namely*, and *for example* are often mistakenly written as sentences. These fragments should be incorporated into the preceding sentence.

FRAGMENT	As a ten-year old, Philip enjoyed reading only about unusual subjects. Such as alchemy, hypnosis, and cuneiform writing.
REVISED	As a ten-year-old, Philip enjoyed reading only about unusual subjects such as alchemy, hypnosis, and cuneiform writing.
FRAGMENT	The senator's speech was very provocative. That is, her address on the Year of the Child.
REVISED	The senator's speech, that is, her address on the Year of the Child, was very provocative.

Although some people think that sentences beginning with a coordinating conjunction are fragments, they are not. (Do not, however, fall into the habit of beginning many sentences with coordinating conjunctions because your style will become choppy and monotonous.) On the other hand, remember that a clause introduced by a subordinating conjunction is always a fragment unless it is attached to an independent clause.

FRAGMENT	My sister enjoys making pottery. <u>Although I do not.</u>
CORRECT	My sister enjoys making pottery. <u>But I do not.</u>
FRAGMENT	Jessica didn't call her friends while she was at work because her supervisor objected to the practice. <u>Even when business was slow.</u>
CORRECT	Jessica didn't call her friends while she was at work because her supervisor objected to the practice. <u>And her supervisor somehow seemed to know everything she did.</u>

23b SHIFTED CONSTRUCTIONS

Shifted constructions occur when the writer illogically or unnecessarily changes tense, voice, person, number, or mood within a sentence.

1. **Shifted tense.** Do not shift from a past to a present tense, or vice versa, unless you intend to express a change in the time of action.

SHIFTED TENSE	The salesperson <u>brought</u> me twenty pairs of shoes to try on, but he <u>seems</u> very annoyed when I <u>do</u> not buy any of them. (unnecessary shift from past to present)
REVISED	The salesperson <u>brought</u> me twenty pairs of shoes to try on, but he <u>seemed</u> annoyed when I <u>did</u> not buy any of them.

2. **Shifted voice.** Do not shift from the active to the passive voice, or vice versa, within one sentence.

SHIFTED VOICE	After the pan <u>had been greased and floured</u>, Bert <u>filled</u> it carefully with the cake batter. (unnecessary shift from passive to active)
REVISED	After he <u>had greased and floured</u> the pan, Bert <u>filled</u> it carefully with the cake batter.

3. **Shifted person.** Do not shift from third person (*one, he*) to second person (*you*), or vice versa, when you are addressing or talking about the same person.

SHIFTED PERSON	If <u>one</u> wants to soar to the highest achievements, <u>you</u> should not spend all of <u>your</u> time gazing at the stars. (unnecessary shift from third person to second person)
REVISED	If <u>one</u> wants to soar to the highest achievements, one (*or* <u>he or she</u>) should not spend all of <u>his</u> (*or* <u>or her</u>) time gazing at the stars.

4. **Shifted number.** Do not shift unnecessarily from singular to plural, or vice versa.

SHIFTED NUMBER	When <u>someone</u> talks constantly about dieting, <u>they</u> not only become boring but usually remain fat. (unnecessary shift from singular *someone* to plural *they*)
REVISED	When <u>someone</u> talks constantly about dieting, <u>that person</u> (*or* <u>he or she</u>) not only becomes boring but usually remains fat.
REVISED	When <u>people</u> talk constantly about dieting, <u>they</u> not only become boring but usually remain fat.

5. **Shifted mood.** Do not shift unnecessarily from indicative to imperative, or vice versa.

SHIFTED MOOD
While we are away, please <u>feed</u> the dog twice a day, and you <u>should water</u> the plants on the porch weekly. (unnecessary shift from imperative *feed* to indicative *should water*)

REVISED
While we are away, please <u>feed</u> the dog twice a day and <u>water</u> the plants on the porch weekly.

REVISED
While we are away, you <u>should feed</u> the dog twice a day and <u>you should</u> water the plants on the porch weekly.

23c COMMA SPLICES AND FUSED SENTENCES

Comma splices and fused sentences are very serious errors that tell the reader that the writer cannot punctuate properly or identify correct sentence form.

The **comma splice** (sometimes called a **comma fault**)—the splicing, or linking together, of two independent clauses (along with any subordinate clauses that they may have) with *only* a comma—is not only a matter of improper punctuation but of inability to distinguish one complete sentence from another. Remember that independent clauses should be linked by a comma *only* when the comma is used with a coordinating conjunction. Never patch two sentences together with only a comma.

COMMA SPLICE
The new car was very economical, the old one was more comfortable.

You can usually revise a comma splice in one of four ways. You can (1) insert a coordinating conjunction to be used with the comma, (2) replace the comma with a semicolon, (3) make two sentences, or (4) subordinate one of the independent clauses.

USE COORDINATING CONJUNCTION
The new car was very economical, <u>but</u> the old one was more comfortable.

USE SEMICOLON
The new car was very economical; the old one was more comfortable.

MAKE TWO SENTENCES
The new car was very economical. The old one was more comfortable.

SUBORDINATE ONE CLAUSE
Although the new car was very economical, the old one was more comfortable.

COMMA SPLICE
David and Sarah had dinner with us, then we all went to a play.

REVISED
David and Sarah had dinner with us, and then we all went to a play.

REVISED
David and Sarah had dinner with us; then we all went to a play.

REVISED
David and Sarah had dinner with us. Then we all went to a play.

REVISED
After David and Sarah had dinner with us, we all went to a play.

The **fused sentence** (sometimes called a **run-on sentence**) occurs when two sentences are jammed together with *no* punctuation dividing one from the other.

FUSED SENTENCE
The turtle inched its way toward the highway it seemed oblivious to the oncoming cars.

Fused sentences may be revised in the same ways as comma splices.

USE COMMA AND COORDINATING CONJUNCTION	The turtle inched its way toward the highway, and it seemd oblivious to the oncoming cars.
USE A SEMICOLON	The turtle inched its way toward the highway; it seemed oblivious to the oncoming cars.
MAKE TWO SENTENCES	The turtle inched its way toward the highway. It seemed oblivious to the oncoming cars.
SUBORDINATE ONE CLAUSE	As the turtle inched its way toward the highway, it seemed oblivious to the oncoming cars.

TROUBLESHOOTING

1. Comma splices often occur in sentences where adverbial conjunctions (*thus, therefore, however, nevertheless, on the other hand, in addition*, and the like) appear between main clauses. When an adverbial conjunction appears *within* a single main clause, it is usually set off by commas; but when it appears *between* main clauses, it must be preceded by a semicolon (it is often followed by a comma).

COMMA SPLICE	Jennifer and Estelle were close friends at school, however, they rarely see each other now that they have graduated.
CORRECT	Jennifer and Estelle were close friends at school; however, they rarely see each other now that they have graduated.
COMMA SPLICE	Carl and Maria had thought that they could push the car out of the rut, nevertheless, an hour's efforts brought no success.
CORRECT	Carl and Maria had thought that they could push the car out of the rut; nevertheless, an hour's efforts brought no success.

2. Fused sentences often occur when the second sentence begins with such words as *then, still, afterwards, often, sometimes*, and other words expressing duration or frequency of time. Remember that these words are not coordinating conjunctions and must be preceded by either a semicolon or a coordinating conjunction and comma when they appear between sentences.

FUSED SENTENCE	Mrs. Hammersla was at first quite jovial afterwards she became very irritable.
REVISED	Mrs. Hammersla was at first quite jovial; afterwards, she became very irritable.
REVISED	Mrs. Hammersla was at first quite jovial, but afterwards she became very irritable.
REVISED	Mrs. Hammersla was at first quite jovial. Afterwards she became very irritable.
FUSED SENTENCE	Curt's family move a lot sometimes they move two or three times a year.
REVISED	Curt's family move a lot; sometimes they move two or three times a year.
REVISED	Curt's family move a lot. Sometimes they move two or three times a year.

23d MIXED CONSTRUCTIONS

Mixed constructions occur when the writer begins a phrase, clause, or sentence with one type of construction and then changes to another type without completing the first construction. Several kinds of mixed constructions are especially common.

1. Do not mix a direct and an indirect quotation or question.

MIXED	She said I am unrivaled in the art of forgetfulness.
REVISED	She said that she is unrivaled in the art of forgetfulness.
REVISED	She said, "I am unrivaled in the art of forgetfulness."

MIXED	I am curious why has the smog over the city not lifted.
REVISED	I am curious why the smog over the city has not lifted.
REVISED	I am curious. Why has the smog over the city not lifted?

2. Do not use an adverbial clause or phrase as a subject or complement.

MIXED	Because Jamie sat on her glasses was how they were broken.
REVISED	Jamie broke her glasses by sitting on them.
REVISED	Jamie's glasses were broken because she sat on them.

MIXED	After watching the documentary on Egyptian history was when Sheila became interested in the pyramids.
REVISED	After watching the documentary on Egyptian history, Sheila became interested in the pyramids.
REVISED	Watching the documentary on Egyptian history spurred Sheila's interest in the pyramids.

3. Do not mix a subject and an object.

MIXED	The bright carnival lights, we saw them from two miles away. (*The bright carnival lights* looks like the subject because it begins the sentence. But then the writer starts again with a new subject, *we*, and uses *them* as a new direct object.)
REVISED	We saw the bright carnival lights from two miles away.
REVISED	The bright carnival lights were visible from two miles away.

MIXED	The old coin Frank found in the attic, he is going to have it appraised.
REVISED	Frank is going to have the old coin, which he found in the attic, appraised.

4. Do not improperly use a clause as the subject of a sentence. Only nominal clauses should be subjects.

MIXED	Since Marilyn has never lost a contest explains why she is so self-confident about the approaching competition.
REVISED	Since Marilyn has never lost a contest, she is very self-confident about the approaching competition.

MIXED	The youth's manner was so polite was what charmed the staff.
REVISED	The youth's polite manner charmed the staff.

23e FAULTY COMPLEMENTS AND APPOSITIVES

When a linking verb is used to equate a subject and its complement, the subject and the complement should be logically and grammatically equivalent. Not all nouns can be grammatically and logically connected by the verb *to be* (and other linking verbs).

FAULTY	Finger-picking is the strings of a guitar being plucked by fingers instead of a pick. (*Strings* are not *finger picking*.)
REVISED	Finger-picking is plucking the strings of a guitar with one's fingers instead of a pick.
FAULTY	Her indigestion was cold pizza and mocha ice cream for breakfast. (*Pizza* and *ice cream* are not *indigestion*.)
REVISED	Her indigestion was brought on by eating cold pizza and mocha ice cream for breakfast.

Faulty appositives are faulty complements in which the verb *to be* has been omitted.

FAULTY	Many people prefer to read about violence—murderers, terrorists, and arsonists, for example. (*Murderers, terrorists,* and *arsonists* are not *violence*.)
REVISED	Many people prefer to read about violence—murder, terrorism, and arson, for example.

23f PARALLELISM

Parallelism means using the same grammatical structure for all items that have the same function. **Faulty parallelism** occurs when the second idea or successive ideas in a sentence do not fit the pattern you have established for the first idea. Faulty parallelism is especially common in series, where items are connected by coordinating or correlative conjunctions. Correct faulty parallelism by putting all the related ideas into the same grammatical form.

FAULTY	For a child, stamp collecting can be entertaining, inexpensive, and it can teach him or her a great deal. (*Entertaining* and *inexpensive* are adjectives, but *it can teach him or her a great deal* is a clause.)
REVISED	For a child, stamp collecting can be entertaining, inexpensive, and educational.
FAULTY	I ride a bicycle for enjoyment and to get exercise. (*For enjoyment* is a prepositional phrase and *to get exercise* is an infinitive phrase.)
REVISED	I ride a bicycle for enjoyment and for exercise.
FAULTY	They couldn't agree on whether Sheldon was a carpenter or did electrical work. (*Was a carpenter* is a linking verb plus a complement, and *did electrical work* is a verb plus a direct object.)
REVISED	They couldn't agree on whether Sheldon was a carpenter or an electrician.

    False parallelism occurs when ideas that are not parallel in grammatical function or meaning are put into parallel or seemingly parallel form. Correct false parallelism by rewriting to eliminate the parallelism.

FALSE PARALLELISM	On our picnic we had chicken, sandwiches, pickles, cake, cookies, and desserts. (*Desserts* is a general term that includes *cake* and *cookies*.)
REVISED	On our picnic we had chicken, sandwiches, pickles, cake, cookies, and other desserts.
FALSE PARALLELISM	Jonas will be shocked at hearing the truth at his vacation retreat at this unexpected time. (The repetition of the preposition *at* leads the reader to expect the objects of *at* to be parallel.)
REVISED	Jonas will be shocked to hear the truth at this unexpected time during his vacation.
FALSE PARALLELISM	They enjoy taking long walks along the river, looking for wildflower specimens, and which the rest of the group finds boring. (The first two phrases are direct objects of *enjoy*, and the rest of the sentence [*which the rest of the group finds boring*] is a modifier of those objects, but the *and* leads the reader to expect a third object of *enjoy*.)
REVISED	They enjoy taking long walks along the river and looking for wildflower specimens, activities that the rest of the group finds boring.

    Repetition of words common to all parallel elements is a device that helps identify and clarify parallel structures. However, if you repeat a common word, you should repeat it before all the elements.

FAULTY	Fritz looked for the new brand of glue in the supermarket, the drugstore, in the hardware store, and the builders' supply company.
REVISED	Fritz looked for the new brand of glue in the supermarket, in the drugstore, in the hardware store, and in the builders' supply company.
REVISED	Fritz looked for the new brand of glue in the supermarket, the drugstore, the hardware store, and the builders' supply company.

NAME _____ DATE _____

DIRECTIONS: Underline all sentence fragments. On the lines following each group of words, write a revision of each fragment, incorporating it into the preceding sentence, if it is logical to do so, or making a correct sentence out of it. If a numbered group of words contains no fragments, write *C* in the space.

    EXAMPLE: Aubrey is particularly fond of fattening foods. <u>Such as spareribs, fried potatoes, and desserts.</u>

       Aubrey is particularly fond of fattening foods such as spareribs, fried potatoes, and desserts.

1. Good food is near and dear to the minds and stomachs of all Americans. Although American cuisine is ridiculed around the world.

_____

_____

2. Much may be said, however, in defense of the diversity of foods found in American restaurants. If not in defense of the quality.

_____

_____

3. Almost every town of any size in the United States has a strip of highway. Ablaze with neon signs inviting the American family to eat everything from tacos and pizza to egg rolls and bagels.

_____

_____

_____

4. Indeed, the large national chains win many adult customers through children. Whom they entice with catchy television commercials, the personal appearances of talking animals and other entertainers, and special hats or games inscribed with the restaurant's name.

_____

_____

_____

_____

5. The popularity of the automobile helped bring about the drive-in restaurant of a few decades ago, the place where uniformed curb-boys or waitresses on roller skates rushed to take the order of the passengers. And brought it out to them on a tray, which was then neatly attached to the car at the driver's rolled-down window.

_____

_____

_____

6. But Americans, always increasing their pace of life, traded the drive-in for the drive-through restaurant, where they read an elaborate outdoor menu printed on a large speaker that takes the order and informs the driver how much the meal costs.

_____

_____

_____

7. Then the motorist drives up to a window. Where he pays, collects his food, and goes on his merry way.

_____

_____

8. On the other hand, many Americans scorn the fast-food restaurants. Because they believe them to be nutritionally unsound and because they find the food boring.

_____

_____

9. Establishments that serve soup and salad or vegetarian meals are becoming more and more popular. Especially among young people who often cannot afford the high cost of meat and among people of all ages who want to consume less meat for the well-being of their bodies.

_____

_____

_____

NAME _____ DATE _____

DIRECTIONS: In the blank at the left of each group of words, identify that group of words as *C* (correct sentence) or *CS* (comma splice). Revise each comma splice in each of four ways: (1) make two sentences, (2) use a comma and a coordinating conjunction, (3) use a semicolon, and (4) subordinate one of the main clauses.

EXAMPLE: __*CS*__   Stan is extraordinarily fond of zoos, every week he spends all of his free time at the Central Park Zoo.

a. two sentences

Stan is extraordinarily fond of zoos. Every week he spends all of his free time at the Central Park Zoo.

b. comma and coordinating conjunction

Stan is extraordinarily fond of zoos, and every week he spends all of his free time at the Central Park Zoo.

c. semicolon

Stan is extraordinarily fond of zoos; every week he spends all of his free time at the Central Park Zoo.

d. one clause subordinated

Because Stan is extraordinarily fond of zoos, he spends all of his free time at the Central Park Zoo.

_____ 1. One type of playing card is found in Spain and Italy, where the first European cards seem to have appeared, this type has as the emblems of its suits money, swords, cups, and batons.

a. two sentences

_____

_____

_____

b. comma and coordinating conjunction

_____

_____

_____

c. semicolon

_____

_____

_____

d. one clause subordinated

_____

_____

_____

_____ 2. Suits in cards of Germany and Central Europe have as emblems hearts, bells, leaves, and acorns, except in Switzerland, where shields and flowers replace hearts and leaves.

a. two sentences

_____

_____

b. comma and coordinating conjunction

_____

_____

c. semicolon

_____

_____

d. one clause subordinated

_____

_____

NAME _____ DATE _____

_____ 3. Spanish playing cards were the first to arrive in America, nevertheless, the English playing cards were the ones adopted by the Americans.

a. two sentences

_____

_____

b. comma and coordinating conjunction

_____

_____

c. semicolon

_____

_____

d. one clause subordinated

_____

_____

_____ 4. Playing cards were no more acceptable in the New World, however, than they were in Europe, for American records from the early seventeenth century record fines given to cardplayers.

a. two sentences

_____

_____

b. comma and coordinating conjunction

_____

_____

c. semicolon

_____

_____

d. one clause subordinated

_____

_____

_____ 5. By the mid-eighteenth century, cards were being made in America, in fact, Americans made a notable addition to the deck, the joker, a card that was then adopted by cardplayers in Great Britain and many other countries.

a. two sentences

_____

_____

_____

b. comma and coordinating conjunction

_____

_____

_____

c. semicolon

_____

_____

_____

d. one clause subordinated

_____

_____

_____

NAME _____ DATE _____

DIRECTIONS: In the blank to the left of each group of words, identify that group
of words as *FS* (fused sentence) or *C* (correct sentence). Revise each *FS* in each
of these four ways: (1) make two sentences, (2) use a comma and a coordinating
conjunction, (3) use a semicolon, and (4) subordinate one of the main clauses.

EXAMPLE: ___*FS*___ The snow began to fall soon the roads became impassable.

a. two sentences

*The snow began to fall. Soon the roads became
impassable.*

b. comma and coordinating conjunction

*The snow began to fall, and soon the roads became
impassable.*

c. semicolon

*The snow began to fall; soon the roads became
impassable.*

d. one clause subordinated

*Soon after the snow began to fall, the roads became
impassable.*

_____ 1. No matter what their interests, talents, and economic positions, most
adults have in common one of life's most trying ventures they have
all undergone that frustrating process known as job-hunting.

a. two sentences

_____

_____

_____

b. comma and coordinating conjunction

_____

_____

_____

c. semicolon

_____

_____

_____

d. one clause subordinated

_____

_____

_____

_____ 2. A job is, of course, the foremost goal of the search, although the job-hunting process often results in much more than regular hours and a regular paycheck.

a. two sentences

_____

_____

b. comma and coordinating conjunction

_____

_____

c. semicolon

_____

_____

d. one clause subordinated

_____

_____

NAME _____ DATE _____

_____ 3. Many job-hunters, particularly those with specialized skills, prefer to market their abilities with the help of professional employment agencies such agencies often retain as permanent clients large firms that frequently need new employees.

a. two sentences

_____

_____

_____

b. comma and coordinating conjunction

_____

_____

_____

c. semicolon

_____

_____

_____

d. one clause subordinated

_____

_____

_____

_____ 4. It's finally your turn to be shown into the plush office at the end of the hall your chance has come to prove to the interviewer that you are the right person for one of the numerous career opportunities listed in the agency's advertisements.

a. two sentences

_____

_____

b. comma and coordinating conjunction

_____

_____

_____

c. semicolon

_____

_____

_____

d. one clause subordinated

_____

_____

_____

_____ 5. Your whole life passes before your eyes then, after an eternity of two-way scrutiny, the interviewer shows you out with a promise to call you the minute he or she has "just the right thing."

a. two sentences

_____

_____

b. comma and coordinating conjunction

_____

_____

c. semicolon

_____

_____

d. one clause subordinated

_____

_____

NAME _____ DATE _____

DIRECTIONS: Revise the following sentences, correcting shifted and mixed constructions and faulty parallelism.

> EXAMPLE: If anyone had stopped to help, they would have been handsomely rewarded by the stranded millionaire.

If anyone had stopped to help, that person would have been handsomely rewarded by the stranded millionaire.

1. If a person wants to get ahead in the business world, you have to keep abreast of economic developments in the country and technological advances in your field.

   _____

   _____

   _____

2. "Just turn the bags over to make them fit will be fine," the woman instructed the clerk who was trying to fit six grocery bags into the small trunk of her foreign car.

   _____

   _____

   _____

3. "That skateboard, I'm going to kill myself on it one of these days," Herbie's father muttered to himself as he trips over it on his way out the door.

   _____

   _____

4. After jogging for the first time was how Linda realized what poor physical condition she was in.

   _____

   _____

5. Myron is allergic to cats, to certain kinds of pollen, and also bee stings make him break out in a rash.

_____

_____

6. That particular airline serves good food, has friendly crew members, and it offers excellent cut-rate fares.

_____

_____

7. "Please tell me the truth about my painting," the art student said to her instructor, "and you should not worry about hurting my feelings."

_____

_____

8. John has always longed to visit foreign countries, especially the Japanese, the Chinese, and the Russians.

_____

_____

9. He asked do you care to wait until Mr. Hinson returns.

_____

10. In tasting buttermilk for the first time was one of the most awful experiences Mark had ever had with food.

_____

_____

11. The town's recreation office was six men and seven women.

_____

12. Joanna planned to visit her parents for two weeks, camping in the Great Smoky Mountains for a week, and she wanted to attend the second session of summer school at Stanford.

_____

_____

_____

24/PERIODS

The **period** has a number of uses, but its most important role is to separate one sentence from another.

24a AS ENDING PUNCTUATION

The period is the most frequently used mark of punctuation for ending sentences. Use it to end declarative sentences, indirect questions, and polite commands (even if such a command has the word order of a question). An indirect question paraphrases the speaker's words without quoting them exactly and usually takes the form of a subordinate clause.

DECLARATIVE SENTENCE	Jeannie tried to repair the radio herself.
INDIRECT QUESTION	The new girl in the dorm asked me what I thought of her boyfriend.
POLITE COMMAND	Would you please open the window.

24b CONVENTIONAL USES

There are other conventional, or accepted, uses of the period.

1. After abbreviations, initials, and some acronyms (words formed from the initial letters of a name several words long). Check an up-to-date dictionary to see which acronyms omit the period.

ABBREVIATION	Dr. Williams said that John had a torn ligament in his leg.
INITIALS	Have you read any books by C. S. Lewis?
ACRONYM	Charles always buys UNICEF Christmas cards.

2. To divide act, scene, and line in citations from drama (Hamlet, v.ii.10); to divide chapter and verse in Biblical citations (Genesis 2.7); and to divide book and line in citations from long poetic works (*The Prelude*, 5.221). In these instances, however, do not put a space between the numbers and the periods.

TROUBLESHOOTING

Avoid the following common errors with the period.

1. Do not use the period as end punctuation with any other end punctuation, and do not place two periods together at the end of a sentence.

INCORRECT	An outstanding undergraduate student in architecture, Peter decided to work on an M.A..
CORRECT	An outstanding undergraduate student in architecture, Peter decided to work on an M.A.
INCORRECT	Alice, you look as if you've been scalped.!
CORRECT	Alice, you look as if you've been scalped.
CORRECT	Alice, you look as if you've been scalped!

2. When the period follows an abbreviation *within* the sentence, it *is* used with other marks of punctuation.

John grimaced when he saw that his chemistry lab was scheduled at 7:30 a.m.—it was an inhuman hour.

3. When the title of a written composition appears at the top of the page, do not put a period after the title, even if the title is a complete sentence.

4. Do not put a period after nicknames or after other shortened word forms that have become accepted as independent words.

INCORRECT   Al. Smith ran for president in 1928.
CORRECT   Al Smith ran for president in 1928.

INCORRECT   We were working in the lab. until 3 a.m.
CORRECT   We were working in the lab until 3 a.m.

5. Always put the period inside quotation marks.

He sang "Somewhere over the Rainbow."

25/QUESTION MARKS

Like a period, a **question mark** is used as a mark of ending punctuation but only after direct questions.

25a DIRECT QUESTIONS

Use the question mark to follow a sentence that is a direct question, even if the question has the word-order of a statement. (A direct question quotes the speaker exactly.) Question marks go inside quotation marks when the question is part of the quotation.

> Do you really think billboards are more attractive than trees?
> How long will the sale on down jackets last?
> We don't get a reading period before exams begin?
> He asked, "Why are they running?"

When a sentence consists of a series of direct questions, you may either put a single question mark at the end of the entire sentence or put a question mark at the end of each of the questions.

> Did Juan give Inez any explanation for forgetting her birthday, for being half an hour late for their date, for being in a bad mood all evening?
> Did Juan give Inez any explanation for forgetting her birthday? for being half an hour late for their date? for being in a bad mood all evening?

25b CONVENTIONAL USE

Use the question mark with dates or figures that are of doubtful accuracy to authorities. Do not use a question mark with your own haphazard guess at a date or figure when a glance at the dictionary or encyclopedia will furnish exact information.

> Giotto (1266?-1337), one of the great painters of the Italian Renaissance, was famous for his frescoes.

25c SUPERFLUOUS USES

Avoid the following common errors with the question mark.

1. Do not use a question mark to punctuate an indirect question or an exclamation in the form of a question. (An indirect question does not give the speaker's words exactly and usually is a subordinate clause.)

INDIRECT QUESTION	He asked if he could share our cab from the airport to the hotel.
EXCLAMATION	Isn't this a fine predicament!

2. Do not use two questions marks when there is a question within a question. Use only one question mark at the end of the complete interrogative sentence in such a case.

> Who wrote the song, "Where Is Love?"
> Who was it who asked, "When will the meeting begin?"

3. Do not use the question mark in an attempt to be humorous or sarcastic.

INAPPROPRIATE   Our compassionate (?) teacher assigned us homework to be done over the holidays.

REVISED   Our supposedly compassionate teacher assigned us homework to be done over the holidays.

26/EXCLAMATION POINTS

The **exclamation point** is the most dramatic mark of ending punctuation.

26a DRAMATIC OR EMOTIONAL STATEMENTS

Use the exclamation point to end sentences that are exclamatory or that express exceptionally strong commands. Also punctuate interjections and exclamatory words and phrases with the exclamation point. Exclamation points go inside quotation marks only if the exclamation is part of the quotation.

Hurrah!
Out with it!
Jumping Jupiter! Look at him go!
No! I absolutely will not hear another word!
How adroitly he handles his tennis racket!

26b SUPERFLUOUS USES

Avoid the following common pitfalls with the exclamation point.

1. Do not overuse the exclamation point. Doing so makes a passage overblown and weak so that your real exclamations lose their effectiveness.

2. Never use more than one exclamation point after a word, phrase, or sentence. Using two or more in an attempt to add emphasis is a cute feature of junior high school love letters, but it is not acceptable in mature writing.

INCORRECT   Elmer has the sweetest smile in the world!!

CORRECT   Elmer has the sweetest smile in the world!

3. Never use an exclamation point with a period or a question mark at the end of a sentence.

INCORRECT   What do you think you are doing!?

CORRECT   What do you think you are doing!

CORRECT   What do you think you are doing?

4. Do not use an exclamation point to indicate humor or sarcasm.

INAPPROPRIATE   For the party our capable (!!) chef cooked a dinner that gave everyone indigestion.

REVISED   For the party our supposedly capable chef cooked a dinner that gave everyone indigestion.

NAME _____ DATE _____

DIRECTIONS: In the space provided, rewrite the following sentences, correcting errors in the use of periods, question marks, or exclamation points. Write a *C* for correct sentences.

EXAMPLE: Goodness gracious!! Are you really serious about that.

Goodness gracious! Are you really serious about that?

1. When we finally hailed a cab in Times Square, two other couples trying to escape the sudden rain asked if they could share the taxi as far as Park Avenue?

   _____

   _____

2. That gorgeous (?) girl whom Rich. introduced as my blind date turned out to be one of the horrors of the western world!!

   _____

   _____

3. The minister read Ecclesiastes 3, 1-8, and then he asked us if we would read the same passage aloud?

   _____

   _____

4. Just who do you think you are, young man, to say to me, "How's it going, Pops?"?

   _____

5. The concept of the movie theater became a reality in the United States on April 23, 1896 (?) at Korter and Bials' Music Hall in New York City, when Thomas Edison showed several movies to an enthralled audience.

   _____

   _____

6. Maggie—you have met her, haven't you?—is the rudest person on the face of the earth!.

   _____

7. Don't be foolish!; Don't get involved!.

_____

8. New Year's Day is a time when we all should ask ourselves what our goals are? how well we have lived in the past year? and what we should do to improve our lives during the coming twelve months?

_____

_____

_____

9. Though she spent most of her free time playing pop. tunes on the piano, Terri was actually interested enough in the classics to contemplate studying music for her B.A. .

_____

_____

10. Dr. Brown continued, "What will we do about widespread cheating among students? about apathy on the campus? about the ever-increasing inflation of grades?"

_____

_____

11. Although his father was active in the Lions Club, the Shriners, the Rotary Club, and the Chamber of Commerce, Grover considered these service (?) organizations ineffective and vowed never to join any groups like them.

_____

_____

_____

12. Al. Sims, a C.P.A. who worked for years in an office building across from the capitol, quit his job and wrote a best seller called *F.D.R.: Did He Save the U.S. Economy?*.

_____

_____

13. Wow!! You don't even believe that I saw a U.F.O.!

_____

27/COMMAS

The **comma** is a mark of punctuation used within the sentence. As a rule, it functions as a separator; for example, it separates items in a series or phrases and clauses from each other. It also has a number of conventional or accepted uses as a separator.

27a INDEPENDENT CLAUSES

One of the main uses of the comma is to work with the coordinating conjunctions (*and, or, nor*, and *but*) to separate independent clauses, or main clauses, within the sentence. The comma immediately precedes the coordinating conjunction.

> The history exam had six discussion questions, but Jared whizzed through the whole test in 40 minutes.
>
> She is going to medical school now, and then she will specialize in internal medicine.

If both main clauses are short, the comma is often omitted. It is never wrong, however, to put in the comma between main clauses as long as there is a coordinating conjunction between them.

> He ran fast but she was faster.
>
> He ran fast, but she was faster.
>
> She did not like him in the least nor did he like her.
>
> She did not like him in the least, nor did he like her.

When they divide main clauses, the words *so, for*, and *yet* are often regarded as coordinating conjunctions and thus are preceded by a comma.

> Anne was at the doctor's office on time, for she didn't want to miss her appointment.
>
> It was too hot to play tennis, so we went for a swim instead.
>
> Several pieces had fallen out, yet the clock still ran.

TROUBLESHOOTING

Always bear in mind that when you join two independent clauses with a comma, you *must* use a coordinating conjunction with that comma. Otherwise, you will make a serious error called a *comma splice*.

COMMA SPLICE	Traffic is very heavy on that street, the residents are complaining.
CORRECT	Traffic is very heavy on that street, and the residents are complaining.
CORRECT	Traffic is very heavy on that street. The residents are complaining.
CORRECT	Traffic is very heavy on that street; the residents are complaining.
CORRECT	Because traffic is very heavy on that street, the residents are complaining.

Note that the above corrections of the comma splice take four forms. First, a coordinating conjunction is added to follow the comma. Second, two separate sentences are made. Third, a semicolon is used instead of a comma. Finally, one of the two main clauses is revised to make it subordinate to the other.

Such adverbial conjunctions (adverbs serving as conjunctions to relate two main clauses) as *however, nevertheless, thus,* and *therefore* are *not* coordinating conjunctions, and they may trick you into making a comma splice when they occur between main clauses. Remember that when adverbial conjunctions come between independent clauses, they require a semicolon, *not* a comma.

COMMA SPLICE	The downtown area was deserted after dark, thus Allen practically ran the three blocks to the subway.
CORRECT	The downtown area was deserted after dark. Thus Allen practically ran the three blocks to the subway.
CORRECT	The downtown area was deserted after dark; thus Allen practically ran the three blocks to the subway.

If you fail to use either a coordinating conjunction or punctuation between two independent clauses, you will make the serious error called a *fused sentence.* The same methods used to correct comma splices can be used to correct fused sentences: (1) adding a comma and a coordinating conjunction, (2) making two separate sentences, (3) using a semicolon instead of a comma, and (4) making one of the main clauses subordinate to the other.

FUSED SENTENCE	Isabel decided to wash the windows Waldo said he wanted to take a walk.
CORRECT	Isabel decided to wash the windows, but Waldo said he wanted to take a walk.
CORRECT	Isabel decided to wash the windows. Waldo said he wanted to take a walk.
CORRECT	Isabel decided to wash the windows; Waldo said he wanted to take a walk.
CORRECT	When Isabel decided to wash the windows, Waldo said he wanted to take a walk.

27b ITEMS IN A SERIES

Another major function of the comma is to separate three or more items in a series (words of the same class that appear consecutively). These items in a series may take the form of single words, phrases (prepositional, participle, or infinitive, for example), subordinate clauses, or main clauses.

The mod lamp comes in green, orange, or navy. (single words)

Four-year-old Jeff looked for the Easter eggs under the hedge, in the flower bed, and in his sandbox. (prepositional phrases)

The announcer strode briskly onto the stage, picked up the microphone, and greeted the audience with a nervous grin. (verb phrases)

The onlookers saw a student running at full speed down the icy street, enthusiastically waving a letter, and yelling at a girl on the next block. (present participle phrases)

"Mr. Williams," she said coolly, "I have come to examine your classroom, to evaluate your performance as a teacher, and to make a recommendation about renewing your contract for the fall." (infinitive phrases)

The professor announced that the exam would be comprehensive, that it would count for 50 percent of the final grade, and that there would be no exemptions or makeups. (subordinate clauses)

During the hottest part of that sweltering day, the cows lay motionless under the trees, the corn stood parching in the white heat, and the farmer and his son grunted irritably at each other over their fence-mending job. (main clauses)

Although the comma is sometimes omitted before the conjunction and last item in a series, it is always correct to put it in. Moreover, it is often confusing to leave it out.

CORRECT	For lunch we had bread, wine and cheese.
CORRECT	For lunch we had bread, wine, and cheese.
CONFUSING	For lunch we had sandwiches of ham and cheese, salami, bacon and tomato and peanut butter and jelly.
CLEAR	For lunch we had sandwiches of ham and cheese, salami, bacon and tomato, and peanut butter and jelly.

The comma is also used to separate two or more adjectives, provided that the sentence makes sense when read with an *and* between the adjectives or when read with the order of the adjectives reversed.

His persuasive, calm manner impressed his patients.

His persuasive and calm manner impressed his patients.

His calm, persuasive manner impressed his patients.

If the order of the adjectives cannot be reversed, do not separate them by commas.

INCORRECT	His calm, bedside manner impressed his patients.
CORRECT	His calm bedside manner impressed his patients. (Note that you would not say, "His bedside calm manner impressed his patients.")

TROUBLESHOOTING

1. Do not use a comma after the final item in a series.

INCORRECT	Ken, Scott, and Alan, were the only good dancers in the group.
CORRECT	Ken, Scott, and Alan were the only good dancers in the group.

2. Do not use commas if all of the elements in the series are connected with coordinating conjunctions.

INCORRECT	The poorly planned orientation activities were boring, and time-consuming, and uninformative.
CORRECT	The poorly planned orientation activities were boring and time-consuming and uninformative.

3. Do not automatically put in a comma every time you write *and, or, nor,* or *but.* Before inserting a comma, check to be sure that what appears on either side of the conjunction can be read as an independent sentence. Do not use a comma with a coordinating conjunction between compound subjects, verbs, objects, or complements.

INCORRECT	Janice, and her good friend Mindy went to see the late movie. (compound subject)
CORRECT	Janice and her good friend Mindy went to see the late movie.

INCORRECT	The wind howled, and rattled the shutters on the cottage. (compound verb)
CORRECT	The wind howled and rattled the shutters on the cottage.
INCORRECT	Judy did not like Ann's new dress, or her hair style. (compound object)
CORRECT	Judy did not like Ann's new dress or her hair style.
INCORRECT	Richard was the most enthusiastic member of the committee, and the hardest worker. (compound predicate nominative)
CORRECT	Richard was the most enthusiastic member of the committee and the hardest worker.

27c INTRODUCTORY ELEMENTS

One of the main functions of the comma is to divide introductory components from the main clause in the sentence so that the reader's attention is directed without confusion to the main idea. Introductory elements may be single words, phrases of several kinds, and subordinate clauses.

When a sentence begins with an introductory word (adverb, isolate, or conjunction, for example), the writer may choose to emphasize that word by breaking the movement of the sentence with a comma.

Finally Christmas Eve came.
Finally, all of the weary campers were accounted for.

Thus he ended up here at Columbia University.
Thus, he decided to attend Columbia University.

The comma after an introductory phrase is often optional, though there are some guidelines to help the writer. If the phrase is a participle or infinitive phrase, the sentence will usually be clearer if a comma follows the opening phrase. Though it is not wrong to omit the comma after a short introductory verbal phrase, it is never wrong to put it in.

Skipping ahead the child discovered the open manhole. (present participle phrase)
Skipping ahead, the child discovered the open manhole.

Prepared for the worst I opened the letter and began to read. (past participle phrase)
Prepared for the worst, I opened the letter and began to read.

To complain John wrote a bitter note to his boss. (infinitive phrase)
To complain, John wrote a bitter note to his boss.

If two prepositional phrases are one prepositional phrase of more than five words begins a sentence, a comma is usually necessary to insure clarity. It is not necessary, however, to put a comma after one short introductory prepositional phrase (though a comma is not wrong).

In the bottom drawer of the desk in the corner, you will find four ledgers.
By the middle of the game, the Tigers had obviously run away with the championship.

After the game the six couples met at Ken's apartment.
After the game, the six couples met at Ken's apartment.

If an introductory phrase ends with a preposition or a prepositional adverb, a comma must follow it for clarity, regardless of the length of the phrase.

To find out, Kate marched straight into Mr. Martin's office without even knocking.

A subordinate clause beginning a sentence is followed by a comma unless the clause is very short, but it is never wrong to put a comma after even a short introductory clause. When the subordinate clause follows the main clause, no comma is needed, even if the subordinate clause is long.

When the storm began the dog jumped up on his master's bed and tried to hide from the thunder.

When he heard the thunder rumbling in the distance, the farmer began to hope that the parched crops might at last get rain.

The farmer began to hope that the parched crops might at last get rain when he heard thunder rumbling in the distance.

TROUBLESHOOTING

1. Before you automatically put a comma after an introductory verbal phrase, be sure that the phrase is not an infinitive or gerund phrase serving as subject of the sentence. Commas follow modifiers but not subjects.

INCORRECT	Taking a chance, did not frighten Steve nearly as much as it did his companions, who watched from the steps as he cautiously turned the key and pushed the door open.
CORRECT	Taking a chance, Steve cautiously turned the key and pushed the door open while his frightened companions watched from the steps.
INCORRECT	To embarrass her friends, seemed one of Sally's aims, for she constantly pointed out their faults in public.
CORRECT	To embarrass her friends, Sally constantly pointed out their faults in public.

Also remember that a prepositional phrase that serves as the subject must not be followed by a comma.

INCORRECT	In the trunk of the car, was the last place Bill looked for his wallet, but there it was.
CORRECT	In the trunk of the car was the last place Bill looked for his wallet, but there it was.

In short, never mistake the subject of the sentence for an introductory phrase or clause because the subject of the sentence is never separated from the verb by a comma unless the subject is followed by a nonrestrictive modifier, that is, by a modifier that is not essential to the meaning of the sentence.

INCORRECT	Cynthia, was very conceited.
CORRECT	Cynthia was very conceited.
CORRECT	Cynthia, who was very pretty, was also very conceited about her good looks. (Note the nonrestrictive clause *who was very pretty*.)

2. Introductory adverbial modifiers are never followed by commas if they immediately precede an inverted subject and verb.

INCORRECT	Then, came the clincher: the exam would be cumulative.
CORRECT	Then came the clincher: the exam would be cumulative.
INCORRECT	Beyond the distant oasis, plodded the camel caravan.
CORRECT	Beyond the distant oasis plodded the camel caravan.

27d PARENTHETICAL ELEMENTS

Parenthetical or interruptive words, phrases, and clauses are always set off by (enclosed within) commas. Punctuating such elements is easy: a comma (or commas) separates them from the rest of the sentence. To be certain that your punctuation of parenthetical elements is correct, read the sentence aloud, omitting the part you consider parenthetical. If you have correctly punctuated it, the sentence will make sense when read without that element. Parenthetical elements set off by commas include the following:

1. Adverbs and adverbial phrases

This production of *Hamlet*, to be frank, is not to my liking.
I give you permission, moreover, to use my credit card.

2. Contradictory phrases

It is happiness, not wealth alone, that you should strive to attain.

3. Direct address and certain other isolates such as *yes, no*, and *thank you*

Go to school at once, Anton, or you will be sorry. (direct address)
No, I don't want to go to California with you. (isolate)

4. Illustrative words such as *namely, for example*, and *that is*, which introduce examples or illustrations

The ancient Greeks, for example, created many literary forms.

5. Tag questions (which consist of an auxiliary verb and a pronoun)

You will go, won't you?
There is no reason, is there, to suspect foul play?

TROUBLESHOOTING

1. Never use a comma immediately after *such as* or *such . . . as.*

INCORRECT	She likes to travel only to exotic places such as, Easter Island, Timbuktu, and Machu Picchu.
CORRECT	She likes to travel only to exotic places such as Easter Island, Timbuktu, and Machu Picchu.

2. When punctuating parenthetical modifiers, be sure that you put a comma both before and after such modifiers. If you use only one comma, the element is not set off, and the reader will likely be confused.

CONFUSING	He, on the other hand never wears a ring.
IMPROVED	He, on the other hand, never wears a ring.

27e RESTRICTIVE AND NONRESTRICTIVE MODIFIERS

Restrictive modifiers are those words, phrases, or clauses that are necessary to the sense of the sentence because they limit, or restrict, the elements they modify. Nonrestrictive modifiers, or "unnecessary" modifiers, are not necessary only in the sense that what they say about the element they modify does not need to be said in order for that element to be clearly identified. Nonrestrictive modifiers add information to the sentence—they are necessary in that sense—but they modify elements that are already—without the help of the nonrestrictive modifier—clearly identified.

In writing, commas are used to separate nonrestrictive modifiers from the rest of the sentence. Restrictive modifiers are *not* set off from the rest of the sentence by punctuation.

RESTRICTIVE	The boys who were good dancers were invited to the party.
NONRESTRICTIVE	The boys, who were good dancers, were invited to the party.

The first sentence means that *only* those boys who were good dancers were invited. The subordinate clause *who were good dancers* identifies exactly which boys were invited. The modifier is, therefore, restrictive and is not set off by commas. In the second sentence, on the other hand, *all* of the boys were invited. The fact that they are good dancers is "extra," or nonrestrictive, information; the boys are identified without this extra information. That is why, in this case, the *who*-clause is set off by commas.

Compare the differences in meaning in the following sentences:

RESTRICTIVE	NONRESTRICTIVE
Nan tried to explain to the irate professor that all of her note cards which she had left in the coffee house had been stolen or thrown away. (Clause—presumably some cards that she did not take to the coffee house were not lost.)	Nan tried to explain to the irate professor that all of her note cards, which she had left in the coffee house, had been stolen or thrown away. (Clause—here she loses them all!)
The typewriter covered with dust had been in a closet for years. (Phrase—the restrictive phrase identifies which of several possible typewriters had been in the closet.)	The typewriter, covered with dust, had been in a closet for years. (Phrase—only one typewriter is being discussed; the fact that it was covered with dust is simply additional information about it.)
The butterfly Danaus plexippus is usually known as a monarch. (Appositive—there are many butterflies, and the words *Danaus plexippus* distinguishes the one being discussed as the one called a monarch.)	The monarch, a large American butterfly, is also called a milkweed butterfly. (Appositive—the monarch is the only butterfly being discussed and the only one also known as a milkweed butterfly; the appositive *a large American butterfly* simply provides extra information.)

TROUBLESHOOTING

When punctuating nonrestrictive modifiers, be sure that you put a comma both before and after that modifier. If you use only one comma, the element is not properly separated from the rest of the sentence, and your meaning will not be clear.

INCORRECT   Those three soldiers, who were brave in battle all received medals.

CORRECT   Those three soldiers, who were brave in battle, all received medals.

27f CONVENTIONAL USES

Comma usage is sometimes more a matter of accepted practice or conventional use than of grammatical logic. The principal conventional uses of the comma include the following.

1. **Direct Quotations.** A comma separates the phrase identifying the speaker from a direct quotation (a quotation using the speaker's exact words).

The librarian handed me an application form and said, "Please fill this out if you want a card."

2. **Geographic Units.** A comma is used to separate the name of a smaller geographic unit from the name of the larger unit that contains it. It is best also to put a comma after the name of the last geographic unit when this last unit occurs in the middle of a sentence.

She moved from Newark, New Jersey, to Washington, D.C., last month.

3. **Dates.** If the order of the date is month–day–year, separate the day from the year by a comma, and place another comma after the year when the date occurs in the middle of the sentence.

On July 4, 1979, Virginia got married.

If, however, the order is day–month–year, no commas are used.

Virginia got married on 4 July 1979.

When only the month and year are given, the use of the comma is optional.

I was graduated from high school in June 1970.
I was graduated from high school in June, 1970.

4. **Titles and degrees.** Names are separated by commas from titles or degrees that follow them.

Charles I, king of England   Simon Kowalski, M.D.

5. **Numbers.** Use commas to separate digits by thousands when you write numbers over 1,000. Starting from the right, place a comma between every three numerals.

5,322   51,322   1,051,322

6. **Salutations and Complimentary Closings.** In *informal* letters, use a comma after the salutation. (Formal letters often use a colon instead.) Use a comma after the complimentary closing of a letter.

Dear Jennifer,   Very truly yours,
Dear Sir: Affectionately,
Dear Mrs. Olsen,

TROUBLESHOOTING

1. Do *not* use a comma between the name of a state and the ZIP code.

New York, New York 10014

2. If a title precedes a name, do not use a comma. When a Roman numeral or an ordinal numeral is used to differentiate persons or vehicles with the same name, no punctuation is used.

His majesty King James II   *Mariner II*
Pope Pius XII   Louis the Fourteenth

3. Do not use commas to separate numbers in identification numbers, ZIP codes, telephone numbers, street addresses, or years. Do not use commas to separate numerals after a decimal point.

Serial No. 721397   54621 Sunrise Highway
New York, N.Y. 10019   1600 B.C.
Tele. 688-9100   3.66666

4. Always put commas inside quotation marks.

She recited "Birches," and her sister said, "Terrific!"

27g CLARITY

Even when none of the rules already given clearly applies, you can use your common sense to employ commas so as to provide clarity and prevent misreading.

CONFUSING   Out of every forty four were rejected.
CLEAR   Out of every forty, four were rejected.
CONFUSING   With green stamps I got a lamp and my husband got a lawn sprinkler.
CLEAR   With green stamps I got a lamp, and my husband got a lawn sprinkler.

Commas are often used to signal the acceptable omission of repeated words, especially verbs. Here the comma marks the place where the omission is made.

Helga went to Vassar; her brother, to Princeton.

Use commas to separate two or three consecutive occurrences of the same word within a sentence.

Work, work, work—is that all that matters to you?

27h SUPERFLUOUS COMMAS

1. Do not separate an adjective from its noun by a comma.

INCORRECT   Lara felt that going to school was a rewarding, experience.

  CORRECT   Lara felt that going to school was a rewarding experience.

2. Do not use a comma to separate a subject from its verb unless the subject is followed by a nonrestrictive element.

INCORRECT   The baseball fans, began to cheer when their favorite player hit a home run.

  CORRECT   The baseball fans began to cheer when their favorite player hit a home run.

  CORRECT   The baseball fans, who had been sweltering in the sun all afternoon, began to cheer when their favorite player hit a home run.

3. Do not use a comma to separate a verb from its complement or direct object. The direct object may be a word, a phrase, or a subordinate clause.

INCORRECT   Her poem is, a marvel of simplicity.

  CORRECT   Her poem is a marvel of simplicity.

INCORRECT   The customer said, she wanted a pocketbook.

  CORRECT   The customer said she wanted a pocketbook.

INCORRECT   The repairman asked, if the TV set had been working satisfactorily.

  CORRECT   The repairman asked if the TV set had been working satisfactorily.

4. Do not mistakenly identify as a coordinating conjunction one part of a correlative conjunction such as *so . . . that, as . . . as, more . . . than, both . . . and, either . . . or,* and *neither . . . nor.* Sentence elements connected with correlative conjunctions should not be separated by commas.

INCORRECT   Either the raggedly dressed boy with the fishing pole, or the woodsman cutting the tree near the lake must have seen the escapee. (Delete the comma before *or* here to make the sentence correct.)

INCORRECT   Mickey was as delighted with his new tape deck, as Simon was dismayed at its cost. (Delete the comma before *as* to make the sentence correct.)

NAME _____ DATE _____

PART A

DIRECTIONS: Insert commas wherever necessary between independent clauses. Write *C* in the space before correct sentences and *CS* before comma splices.

EXAMPLE: _____ At first she insulted me, later she apologized.

_____ 1. David dreamed that his new car had a mangled left front bumper and, when he awoke, he found that the car did indeed have a big dent on the front.

_____ 2. After the meeting the accountant hurriedly stuffed the papers into his briefcase and scurried out of the mahogany-paneled conference room.

_____ 3. She liked to play the piano, he enjoyed singing.

_____ 4. The cat, however, was terrified of mice and always climbed the curtains to escape the menacing little creatures.

_____ 5. Jane was known for her charm and wit, on the other hand, her brother had all the good looks in the family.

_____ 6. The boy who wore the jeans and sweat shirt and the old man who was walking the poodle exchanged a brief greeting but they were the only ones who spoke.

_____ 7. Before going to bed, Jill watched a terrifying horror movie on TV or she read a good murder mystery.

_____ 8. When Alison finally dragged herself out of bed, she discovered that her car and all the mailboxes along the curb had been buried in a massive snowfall.

_____ 9. The woman who got on the elevator at the fifteenth floor eyed the other passengers for a minute or so and then began to mumble loudly to herself as if she were alone.

_____ 10. "Please help me," she said, smiling, "if you have a few minutes to spare and don't mind getting a little dusty."

_____ 11. The bungling waiter did not light the candle on the table nor did he remove the dinner plates before he served the dessert.

_____ 12. After they had hiked for only a few minutes, the four men found that the winding trail ended abruptly in a gloomy swamp and they looked at each other in silence.

_____ 13. The committee charged the two athletes with cheating, nevertheless they were unable to prove their allegations and the case was dropped.

_____ 14. It was not the expensive candy that pleased Joan but the homemade valentine that Charles had enclosed.

_____ 15. The plane had to circle the airport for more than an hour for the fog hung thick and heavy over the runway.

DIRECTIONS: Practice writing and correctly punctuating sentences that have two main clauses joined either with a semicolon or with a coordinating conjunction plus a comma. In the spaces provided, write good sentences to fit the specifications.

EXAMPLE: (Main clause), and (main clause)

John jogs every morning, and he plays tennis two evenings a week.

1. (Main clause), and (main clause)

_____

_____

2. (Main clause); however, (main clause)

_____

_____

3. (Main clause), but (main clause)

_____

_____

4. (Main clause), yet (main clause)

_____

_____

5. (Main clause), nor (main clause)

_____

_____

6. (Main clause); thus, (main clause)

_____

_____

7. (Main clause), for (main clause)

_____

_____

NAME _____ DATE _____

PART A

DIRECTIONS: Insert commas where necessary between items in a series. Put a *C* before correct sentences.

      EXAMPLE: _____ The short, pudgy man opened the car door, got into the
                          car, and drove off.

_____ 1. In the patch of sunlight, the cat lay on its back, purring loudly washing its face and batting at tall blades of grass blown across its body by the gentle breeze.

_____ 2. Surveying her wardrobe, Judy found, to her dismay, that all her skirts were unfashionably short that two of her heavy wool sweaters had been nibbled at by moths that her most stylish slacks had a broken zipper and that the five-year-old plaid coat no longer matched any of her other clothes.

_____ 3. Curious incomprehensible phrases like "outta sight" "in the bag" "far out" and "out of his tree" echoed in Abdul's mind long after he left the party for new exchange students.

_____ 4. To feel useful to feel needed to feel loved were the hopes of most of those signing up for the counseling.

_____ 5. For breakfast Sam preferred bacon or ham and eggs waffles with butter and syrup melon or juice and scaldingly hot very strong coffee.

_____ 6. "Uncle John and Aunt Louise and Grandfather Todd are all coming to hear your speech," Elsa's mother announced to her.

_____ 7. The sad and bewildered expression on the child's face coaxed the harried irritable nurse into offering a half-smile an almost-cheerful greeting and a lollipop.

_____ 8. A week at Cape Hatteras a four-day hike in the Appalachian Mountains and a three-day trip by raft on the Pee Dee River tanned Matt's skin to a golden brown reduced his weight by ten pounds and soothed away the frustrations of his new responsibilities.

_____ 9. Sarah said that we could pick her up she could pick us up or we could all meet at the theater.

_____ 10. Jake was generous to a fault polite at all times pleasant in trying situations but stubborn to an annoying degree.

_____ 11. He loved the subtle flavor the faint aroma but not the too-smooth almost slimy texture of mushrooms.

_____ 12. Even-tempered analytically minded Joseph could not understand Lori's moods logic or ambitions.

DIRECTIONS: On the lines provided, write sentences according to the specified patterns, and punctuate them correctly with commas. For examples of each of the patterns, see 27b.

1. A sentence with prepositional phrases in a series

_____

_____

2. A sentence with infinitive phrases in a series

_____

_____

3. A sentence with verb phrases in a series

_____

_____

4. A sentence with a series of main clauses

_____

_____

5. A sentence with a series of subordinate clauses

_____

_____

NAME _____ DATE _____

PART A

DIRECTIONS: Insert commas where necessary after introductory elements in the following sentences. Put a *C* before correct sentences.

EXAMPLE: _____ After the long and tedious commencement address, the graduates finally received their diplomas.

_____ 1. Jack and Marty finally having left Anne breathed a deep sigh of relief and hurried back to her other guests.

_____ 2. Running across campus to his waiting students Professor Adams collided with a tree, skinning his nose and dropping his papers and books on the icy ground.

_____ 3. Under a pile of paper clips the thin silver ring lay undiscovered by a frantically searching Susan.

_____ 4. To be among the first commercial passengers to vacation on the moon is Joel's dream.

_____ 5. To tell the truth about here is where I always get lost.

_____ 6. Running across campus to get to class on time is a fine art perfected by the specialists among the late risers.

_____ 7. "Actually I think you have a good case," said the lawyer.

_____ 8. On the way to the airport Allen remembered that his plane ticket was on the dresser back in his room.

_____ 9. Therefore Bob had no choice but to swallow his inhibitions and walk with her to the dance floor.

_____ 10. The movie having already begun they decided not to go in but to go next door for pizza instead.

_____ 11. In the loft Rick liked to snuggle into the hay and listen to the cooing of the pigeons.

_____ 12. Among the first-graders Angela was the only one who had not yet learned to tie her shoes.

_____ 13. Although Mandy had received a sizable raise during her first year on the job she constantly had to supplement her substantial salary by borrowing from her parents.

_____ 14. After losing the heel of her shoe on the way into the restaurant Marilyn calmly smiled at her date and hobbled toward their table.

_____ 15. "Oh it's you," said the irate landlord.

_____ 16. To design a set and get it built for rehearsals within four days was the job confronting the two amateur directors.

_____ 17. While Pat cried John tried to assure her that no one at dinner had noticed her social blunder.

_____ 18. If the street lights had been less bright than they were the astronomy enthusiasts could have seen much more of the meteor shower than they did.

_____ 19. In a minute will be too late.

_____ 20. At the far end of the subway car Jane spied a young woman whom she thought she had known in school.

PART B

DIRECTIONS: On the lines provided, write one sentence to fit each specified pattern. Be sure to punctuate the sentences correctly with commas. For examples of each of the patterns, see 27c.

1. A sentence beginning with two prepositional phrases

_____

_____

2. A sentence beginning with a subordinate clause

_____

_____

3. A sentence beginning with an introductory word (interjection or isolate, adverb, transitional word)

_____

_____

4. A sentence beginning with an introductory infinitive phrase

_____

_____

_____

5. A sentence beginning with a present participle

_____

_____

_____

6. A sentence beginning with a past participle

_____

NAME _____ DATE _____

PART A

DIRECTIONS: Correctly punctuate the following sentences to indicate which words, phrases, and clauses are restrictive and which are nonrestrictive. Cross out commas setting off restrictive modifiers, and add commas, where needed, to set off nonrestrictive modifiers. Write a *C* in the space before correct sentences.

> EXAMPLE: _____ *Pride and Prejudice,* which was Lara's favorite novel, was written by Jane Austen.

_____ 1. The Lone Ranger who was John's favorite hero of the Wild West was always merciful but firm with his captives.

_____ 2. The character that entertained Sandi the most was a bumbling elf who never seemed able to do anything right.

_____ 3. Fedora was a woman, who had risen from a life of poverty to become one of the richest and best educated women in New York City.

_____ 4. Sandwiches, delivered to the dorm, are very expensive.

_____ 5. Brenda, whose boyfriend forgot Valentine's Day, was very depressed.

_____ 6. Sitting in front of a roaring fire in the ski lodge, sipping hot drinks, and taking cat naps are activities, which are enjoyed by nonskiers as well as skiers.

_____ 7. A nude girl who wanted her picture in the paper streaked across the football field just before the players appeared.

_____ 8. Mary Griffith who wanted people to notice her always wore outrageously big, brightly colored hats.

_____ 9. The boys carefully set the traps which they hoped would snare the woodchuck.

_____ 10. Anna who had auburn hair and green eyes was the girl of Ned's dreams.

_____ 11. The girl who had freckles all over her face was the one, Joe asked to dance.

_____ 12. During the spring vacation Lori and Estelle who have roomed together for three years plan a two-week trip during which they will tour cathedrals in Spain and Italy.

PART B

DIRECTIONS: In a sentence or two explain the difference in the meaning of each of the following pairs of sentences.

1. a. The Stop 'N Save store which is open until midnight serves coffee to shoppers.
   b. The Stop 'N Save store, which is open until midnight, serves coffee to shoppers.

_____

_____

_____

2. a. Myra's brother ran away to join the circus which he had seen four times a year for ten years.
   b. Myra's brother ran away to join the circus, which he had seen four times a year for ten years.

_____

_____

_____

3. a. All the spectators, who had cheered for the Tigers, were glum and disappointed when they trickled out of the stadium after the game.
   b. All the spectators who had cheered for the Tigers were glum and disappointed when they trickled out of the stadium after the game.

_____

_____

_____

PART C

DIRECTIONS: Write and correctly punctuate a sentence with the following parenthetical elements. For examples of each of the patterns, see 27e.

1. A restrictive appositive

_____

2. A nonrestrictive appositive

_____

3. A restrictive phrase (participle, infinitive, or prepositional)

_____

4. A nonrestrictive phrase

_____

5. A restrictive clause

_____

6. A nonrestrictive clause

_____

NAME _____ DATE _____

DIRECTIONS: Insert and delete commas as needed in the following sentences. Label correct sentences with a *C.*

> EXAMPLE: _____ She said, "I celebrated my twenty-fifth wedding anniversary on January 20, 1951."

_____ 1. Luci said "Mama doesn't like hard household chores such as mopping the floor, scouring the oven, and washing windows, but she loves to do plumbing, rake leaves, and refinish furniture."

_____ 2. Remember that her office has been moved to 4813 White Oak Circle Richmond Virginia 23201.

_____ 3. Stephen explained, "She bragged for three months about how rich her family is, but that bragging was just a coverup for her feelings of inadequacy."

_____ 4. The woman screamed "Complaints complaints complaints—that's all I hear around here!"

_____ 5. A total of 18431 tickets were sold for the outdoor concert given on May 18 1975.

_____ 6. Abraham Lincoln was born on February 12 1809 near Hodgenville Kentucky, and he died on April 15 1865 in Washington D.C.

_____ 7. We left the woman even more concerned about her son's truancy than before.

_____ 8. On September 3 1977 our company delivered 27100 bricks to your building site at 371 Heywood Road Atlanta Georgia.

_____ 9. She disliked her hometown because it was a dirty, noisy, place.

_____ 10. How great it will be when you at last are John Edwin Trammell Ph.D. on August 21 1982.

_____ 11. Gigi loved, fairy tales more than any other kind of story.

_____ 12. Either Alfredo, or Antonio will do the errand.

DIRECTIONS: Review the chapter on commas and then punctuate the following sentences with commas. Change capitalization as necessary.

> EXAMPLE: Jana lamented, "He is tall, dark, and handsome, but he is also stubborn and unreliable."

1. The old saying claims "Clothes make the man." It is largely true for clothing to a great degree defines and labels a person to his observer.

2. If an observer studies the clothing of passersby on a city street he or she can discover from that array of designer handbags blue jeans food-besmeared uniforms run-down shoes and ill-fitting garments a great deal about the social and psychological conditions of those who wear them.

3. Attracting the attention of all observers a woman for example who is impeccably attired in that kind of high-fashion totally coordinated clothing that in its newness appears slightly strange yet slightly pleasing may be saying with her clothes "Look at me because I am wealthy enough to follow *haute couture.*"

4. Similarly a woman in a gray, conservatively tailored pants suit may be saying with her clothing that she is an ambitious hardworking capable businesswoman who should not be overlooked in the ranks of her corporation.

5. Polished and curled and dressed in expensive clothes two toddlers held in tow by a mother wearing last year's style may wear what their parents probably overly indulgent cannot afford for themselves.

6. Looking at a person's attire may tell us immediately that the person is a postman an airline pilot a rancher a nurse or a waitress.

7. To oppose this idea that clothes are to some extent the man many people particularly the young ignore current clothing trends and wear old inexpensive and often outlandish clothes that do not conform to the society's patterns of dress.

8. Soon however these nonconformist clothes of the early 1970s e.g. blue jeans flannel work shirts and muslin blouses and shirts become themselves the new fashion as more and more people perhaps intrigued with the philosophy behind them or won over by their comfort don the newest nonconformist designs.

9. In addition to the sociological and psychological information they give us about individuals clothes often are also indexes of the prosperity and philosophy of a whole community or nation.

10. For example whole communities of Chinese people living in large American cities such as San Francisco or New York reject American styles and continue to wear traditional Chinese clothing because their native culture is one based strongly upon adherence to tradition.

11. The Chinese who live in the People's Republic of China however have swept away many ancient traditions in an effort to build a Communist society and the revolution of the workers is reflected in the work suits worn by all men and women.

12. Hardships that result from disasters such as war pestilence or earthquakes can drastically affect quality quantity and design of clothing.

13. Working in factories in dresses during World War II for instance was very difficult and impractical for women so they began to work in slacks which were less likely to get caught in machinery and which gave the women freer movement than skirts did.

14. Although the hardships brought about by World War II popularized slacks for women the idea of women's wearing slacks was proposed a whole century earlier by Amelia Bloomer the advocate of temperance and women's rights after whom "bloomers" were named.

15. The history of dress—also the history of people's hardships their luxury their vision of others and their concept of themselves—is strewn with amusing often freakish fads testimonies of people's imagination and their vanity.

16. In the colder climates the first clothes were animal skins crudely fitted on people to protect them from the elements and in the warmer areas early clothes were free-flowing draped garments of loosely woven fibers.

17. The Egyptians knew how to make fabrics from cotton wool and linen but it was the Persians not the Egyptians who replaced draped clothing with fitted garments that had sewn-in sleeves.

18. Whether it has developed to project people's bodies modesty or vanity dress is continuing to change though perhaps nowhere quite as quickly and dramatically as in the United States.

28/ SEMICOLONS

The **semicolon**, made up of a period stacked over a comma (;) has only two basic uses: it divides main clauses from each other, and it separates items in a series when the items already contain commas. Semicolons, however, connect *only* grammatical structures that are of coordinate, or equal, rank. For example, semicolons connect only two main clauses, *not* a main clause and a dependent clause.

> The rising sun shot golden arrows through the low-lying fog; it bathed the surf in an eerie pink light. (connects two main clauses)
>
> Wally said that we would visit Long Creek, where apples are grown and shipped nationwide; the Stump House Mountain Tunnel, which was begun by a railroad company in 1852; and the Walhalla National Fish Hatchery, where trout are bred to stock rivers in the area. (connects a series of direct objects already containing commas)

28a MAIN CLAUSES

Although the semicolon functions in the same way that the combination of a comma and coordinating conjunction does, these two methods of separating independent clauses give the sentence a different tone. Compared to the comma and coordinating conjunction, a semicolon provides a more emphatic pause between the ideas expressed in the two parts of the sentence. A semicolon can also mark a similarity or contrast between ideas more strongly than a comma and coordinating conjunction can.

> Tom, always scowling, had an abrasive personality, and he was so ill-tempered that even his dog developed the same viciousness.
>
> Tom, always scowling, had an abrasive personality; he was so ill-tempered that even his dog developed the same viciousness.

The above examples illustrate correct methods of punctuating two main clauses. The effect the writer wishes to produce is a determining factor in the choice of punctuation.

28b ADVERBIAL CONJUNCTIONS

An adverbial conjunction connects two main clauses and shows the relationship in meaning between the two clauses. Familiar adverbial conjunctions include *however, therefore, moreover, nevertheless*, and *finally*. When an adverbial conjunction comes between two main clauses, a semicolon appears at the end of the first main clause and before the adverbial conjunction. The adverbial conjunction, in turn, is followed by a comma.

> I prefer not go to her party; however, if you think I really should go, I will.

If the conjunctive adverb is located *within* the second clause, it is usually set off by commas.

> I prefer not go to her party; I will go, however, if you really think I should.

28c SEPARATING WORD GROUPS

Keep in mind that a series in which some elements have internal commas is separated by semicolons, not commas.

CONFUSING	The committee consisted of Marge, who suggested the sale, Manuel, who offered the parking lot of his store as the location, and Sven, who has had experience with three other flea markets.
CORRECT	The committee consisted of Marge, who suggested the sale; Manuel, who offered the parking lot of his store as the location; and Sven, who has had experience with three other flea markets.

28d SUPERFLUOUS SEMICOLONS

To avoid misusing the semicolon, keep the following tips in mind.

1. Do not overuse the semicolon. If you use it in every other sentence, it loses its effect and becomes practically meaningless.

2. Do not use the semicolon with a coordinating conjunction except in those rare cases when the first independent clause is complex or long enough to call for both a conjunction and a semicolon. As a rule, the semicolon *replaces* the coordinate conjunction.

INCORRECT	Mary and Tom double-dated with us; but they were boring company.
CORRECT	Mary and Tom double-dated with us, but they were boring company.

3. Do not use the semicolon to connect elements of unequal rank, for example, to connect an independent clause and a dependent clause or phrase. When the semicolon takes the place of the coordinating conjunction, the clauses on either side of it must be grammatically capable of standing alone as independent sentences.

INCORRECT	He was afraid to take the test; especially after he had neglected his studies.
CORRECT	He was afraid to take the test, especially after he had neglected his studies.

4. Do not use a semicolon before a direct quotation.

INCORRECT	He asked; "Are you going to the theater this evening?"
CORRECT	He asked, "Are you going to the theater this evening?"

5. Do not use a semicolon with a listing or summary statement.

INCORRECT	In this store you will find the following items; luggage, handbags, wallets, and umbrellas.
CORRECT	In this store you will find the following items: luggage, handbags, wallets, and umbrellas.
INCORRECT	Determination, motivation, ambition; these are the steps to success.
CORRECT	Determination, motivation, ambition—these are the steps to success.

6. Do not confuse adverbial conjunctions with subordinating conjunctions; the two kinds of conjunctions are punctuated differently. See 9a and 9b for a review of subordinating and adverbial conjunctions.

29/COLONS

The **colon** is made up of two periods stacked one over the other (:). Although it looks like a double period, the colon does not mark the end of a thought the way a period does; instead, it says to the reader, "Keep going. You're about to find the proof for what has just been generalized." In other words, it invites the reader to continue, to find ideas that intensify or expand what has gone before.

Although the colon does not connect independent clauses, it can connect unequal, or noncoordinate, structures such as an independent clause and a phrase, or an independent clause and a list of words or phrases.

29a MAIN CLAUSES

One of the main functions of the colon is to divide two main clauses when the second develops, details, or expands the first. The first word of a complete sentence after a colon may be capitalized or not as the writer chooses.

> The lesson you should learn from this experience is clear: drive more carefully in the future.
>
> He was always a good sport: If he lost a game, he congratulated the winner.

29b LISTINGS AND SERIES

The colon is often used to introduce a list of items, which may be in the form of words, phrases, subordinate clauses, or independent clauses and which may be introduced by the words *the following* or *as follows.*

> There are only three primary colors: red, yellow, and blue.
>
> The defense argued two points: that Williams had a good alibi for the time of the murder and that he had no motive.
>
> Olga's father gave her only two choices: she must continue to go to school, or she must get a job and support herself.
>
> The kinds of drums used in orchestras include the following: snare drums, kettledrums, bass drums, and tenor drums.
>
> Her first sight of the clouds far below the plane was almost bewitching: she felt as if she were sleepwalking in a huge valley of marshmallow mountains.

29c LONG QUOTATIONS

Short quotations and dialogue are usually introduced by commas, but a colon is frequently employed to introduce long quotations.

> Senator Smith, pushing for an antibureaucracy bill, read aloud to his colleagues a relevant passage about George III from the Declaration of Independence: "He has made Judges dependent on his Will alone, for the tenure of their offices, and the amount and payment of their offices, and the amount and payment of their salaries. He has erected a multitude of New Offices, and sent hither swarms of Officers to harass our people, and eat out their substance."

29d CONVENTIONAL USES

In addition to serving as a grammatical signal indicating a close relationship between two elements of a sentence, the colon has a number of conventional uses, that is, uses that come under the category of accepted practice.

1. The colon divides chapter from verse in Biblical citations. (Periods may also be used for this purpose.)

John 3:16 *or* John 3.16

2. The colon divides hours from minutes in expressions of time.

3:48 P.M.

3. The colon is used (instead of a comma) after the salutation in formal letters.

Dear Sir: Dear Professor Wilamowitz:

TROUBLESHOOTING

Do not use the colon to divide a verb from its complement or object *or* to divide a preposition and its object. Use a colon *only* when the first clause is grammatically complete.

INCORRECT	Andy was afraid of: spiders, birds, and frogs.
CORRECT	Andy was afraid of spiders, birds, and frogs.
CORRECT	Andy was afraid of three things: spiders, birds, and frogs.
INCORRECT	Her major goals in life are: getting married, having a successful career, and raising a family.
CORRECT	Her major goals in life are getting married, having a successful career, and raising a family.
CORRECT	Her major goals in life are these: getting married, having a successful career, and raising a family.

NAME _____ DATE _____

PART A

DIRECTIONS: Correctly punctuate the following sentences with the colon and semicolon by inserting semicolons and colons where they are needed or by replacing periods and commas with semicolons and colons. Write a *C* in the margin before any correct sentence.

EXAMPLE: _____ We planned to go abroad this summer; however, we may not go after all for these two reasons; travel is getting too expensive, and my mother is ill.

_____ 1. The modern alphabets that are the building blocks of written global communication were preceded by at least three other kinds of writing systems ideography, writing in which a picture stood for an idea, logography, a method of drawing signs to represent words in an idea, and rebus writing, a syllabic system in which a sign stood for a particular sound.

_____ 2. The Egyptians, the Sumerians, and the Hittites developed writing systems based on picture writing, however, it was the Chinese who built the most complex system of picture writing with some 50,000 characters for words.

_____ 3. The first real alphabetic system of writing was developed by the Greeks around 800 B.C., and early Greek letters evolved into the modern Greek alphabet.

_____ 4. The Etruscans, who had migrated from the eastern Mediterranean to Italy around 1000 B.C., handed down their knowledge of the Greek alphabet to the Romans thus, the Romans were the refiners, not the inventors, of the alphabet that is named for them.

_____ 5. The runic alphabet, an early Germanic writing system, may have evolved in imitation of signs on Greek and Roman coins, or it may have grown out of the Greek and Roman alphabets.

_____ 6. The runes were considered mysterious and magic letters, in fact, the word *rune* means "secret."

_____ 7. Small letters were developed for use with capital letters in the Roman alphabet for two major reasons small, rounded letters were easier to write than capitals, and the smaller letters took less space in books.

_____ 8. Many modern languages, including English, use the Roman alphabet of twenty-six letters, however, modern Chinese, Japanese, Hebrew, Arabic, Greek, and Russian are among the many languages represented by other alphabets and writing systems.

PART B

DIRECTIONS: Practice creating sentences with semicolons and colons.

1. Complete these sentences:

   a. Everything about the girl was extraordinary: _____

   _____

   b. _____; however, _____

   _____.

   c. Bill had three immediate goals: _____

   _____

   d. _____; on the other hand,

   _____.

   e. The view was lovely: _____

   _____

2. Write three original sentences using the colon.

   a. _____

   b. _____

   c. _____

3. Write three original sentences using the semicolon.

   a. _____

   b. _____

   c. _____

30/DASHES

The key to the proper use of the **dash** is the word *informal*, for the dash generally replaces the more formal comma, semicolon, colon, or parentheses. Improperly used, the dash is a poor cover-up for sloppy and undisciplined writing.

The dash may be used alone or in pairs. If the material to be set off by a dash occurs at the beginning or end of a sentence, only one dash is used. If, however, the material occurs within the sentence, a dash is used both before and after the inserted material.

30a PARENTHETICAL STATEMENTS

The dash is used to set off a sharp break in thought or a parenthetical element. Sometimes the material set off by dashes is an appositive.

BREAK IN THOUGHT	Jeremy—he's the high-school teacher who lives next door—has invited me to go camping with him and his family.
BREAK IN THOUGHT	I believe—actually, I'm certain—that you have your shirt on backwards.
APPOSITIVE	The main course—rib roast with Yorkshire pudding, asparagus with hollandaise sauce, and broiled tomatoes—was cooked to perfection.

Notice that these same sentences can be rewritten in a more formal style without dashes.

Jeremy, the high-school teacher who lives next door, has invited me to go camping with him and his family.

I don't just believe that you have your shirt on backwards; I am certain that you do.

The main course, which consisted of rib roast with Yorkshire pudding, asparagus with hollandaise sauce, and broiled tomatoes, was cooked to perfection.

30b SUMMARY STATEMENTS

The dash serves as an informal substitute for a colon before a summary statement or after an introductory list.

Trigonometry, physics, and chemistry—these subjects were the bane of George's existence during his senior high school years.

Health, wealth, and wisdom—all of us value these blessings highly.

30c DIALOGUE

A dash can be used to indicate hesitant speech in dialogue.

"I always thought—he—well—that I was to inherit the bulk of his estate."

"That is—uh—not exactly what I had in mind," Joan told the clerk, eyeing the $85 price tag neatly pinned to the scarf.

TROUBLESHOOTING

1. Be sure that the tone of your composition is suited to the informality of the dash.

2. Do not use the dash, like glue, to patch together parts of wordy, sprawling sentences.

POOR	Amy's Boutique—it's the new shop at the corner of Farris Road and McDaniel Avenue—has had a wonderful sale—a real blockbuster of a sale—on everything in the store—all their slacks, blouses, sweaters, skirts, dresses, and coats.
IMPROVED	Amy's Boutique, the new shop at the corner of Farris Road and McDaniel Avenue, has had a wonderful sale on all their slacks, blouses, sweaters, skirts, dresses, and coats.

3. Do not omit one of a pair of dashes when the dashes are being used to set off parenthetical information within the sentence. Leaving out one of the pair will create a run-together muddle.

INCORRECT	The tour's itinerary—Buckingham Palace, the Tower of London, the Houses of Parliament, Piccadilly Circus, and the British Museum was much too full for the scheduled six hours.
CORRECT	The tour's itinerary—Buckingham Palace, the Tower of London, the Houses of Parliament, Piccadilly Circus, and the British Museum—was much too full for the scheduled six hours.

31/PARENTHESES

Parentheses (singular **parenthesis**) always appear in pairs. They are used in many of the same ways that commas and dashes are, but they play down, or soften, the effect of the enclosed information, whereas the dash, at the other end of the spectrum, points up, or emphasizes, the parenthetical information. The comma, when it encloses parenthetical information, neither softens nor calls attention to it but provides a neutral tone.

> The theft was particularly distressing because the thieves took my four antique silver mugs (they were my great-grandfather's prized possessions) and the Oriental rug my aunt had lent me.

> The theft was particularly distressing because the thieves took my four antique silver mugs—they were my great-grandfather's prized possessions—and the Oriental rug my aunt had lent me.

> The theft was particularly distressing because the thieves took my four antique silver mugs, which were my great-grandfather's prized possessions, and the Oriental rug my aunt had lent me.

31a NONESSENTIAL INFORMATION

Parentheses are used to enclose minor digressions, amplifications, explanations, and other nonessential information.

> Claude Joseph Rouget de Lisle (1760-1836) wrote the French national anthem.

> Peccaries (pig-like animals) are native to both North and South America.

31b NUMERALS AND LETTERS

Parentheses are also used to enclose numbers or letters that number items in a series.

> Among the many kinds of shelters built by American Indians were (1) the *wigwam* of leaves and bark, found in eastern North America; (2) the long, rectangular houses of leaves and bark, also found in the eastern region; (3) huts of brush and matting known as *wickiups*, built in the southwestern United States; (4) the earthen *hogan* of the southwestern region; and (5) the buffalo-skin *tepees* of the plains.

TROUBLESHOOTING

Never use a single parenthesis. Parentheses *must* be used in pairs. If the material enclosed by parentheses forms a complete sentence and is not inserted within another sentence, the first word should be capitalized, and ending punctuation should be placed before the second parenthesis.

> Jorge unexpectedly paid me a visit. (Secretly, I've always admired him.) He didn't stay very long, however.

Otherwise, the first word is not capitalized, and final punctuation, if any, follows the closing parenthesis.

> Heidi (she is an experienced mountain climber) decided to climb the Matterhorn and immediately started to organize a group to go with her.

32/ BRACKETS

The use of **brackets** is limited; they should be used as a supplement to parentheses and not as a substitute for them.

32a EDITORIAL COMMENTS

If you want to insert explanatory material within a direct quotation from another writer, that material *must* be put within square brackets, *never* parentheses. If you want your reader to know that you are aware of an error in the spelling, grammar, or content of the information you are quoting, insert the term *sic*, underlined and enclosed in brackets, into the quotation after the incorrect part.

> "It is clear that they [The Athenians] would lose the battle."

> A recent letter to the editor stated that "unless the United States strengthens it's [sic] military forces, it is doomed to fall early in a confrontation with China or the Soviet Union."

32b PARENTHESES WITHIN PARENTHESES

Use brackets to enclose parenthetical material *within* parentheses.

> *Flaybottomist* is an antique term for a schoolmaster (*1811 Dictionary of the Vulgar Tongue: A Dictionary of Buckish Slang, University Wit, and Pocket Eloquence* [Northfield, Ill.: Digest Books, Inc., 1971]).

The information in parentheses and brackets here could, of course, be put into a footnote, eliminating the need for brackets.

PART A

DIRECTIONS: Punctuate the following sentences with dashes, parentheses, and brackets.

EXAMPLE: The snow was falling⌃it was winter⌃so we decided to stay indoors.

1. Geronimo he's my kid brother's pet toad nearly frightened Mom to death when he leapt out of her lingerie drawer where he had apparently spent the night.
2. Painting, sculpture, architecture, botany, astronomy, geology, and anatomy all these fields were explored with exceptional insight by Leonardo da Vinci 1452-1519.
3. The Vikings also called Northmen, Norsemen, and Danes remembered largely because they terrorized Europe for several centuries from roughly 700 to 1100, were not only excellent at shipbuilding but also at making metal tools and weapons.
4. The hotel room actually, calling it a room requires imagination measured about eight by ten feet and was crammed full of the ugliest, dingiest furnishings imaginable a dirty wicker chair, a creaking bed, a rusted lavatory, and a single naked light bulb.
5. Awakened by sounds of rush-hour traffic, Jill sprang out of bed an hour late at 8:30 a.m. it was the third time she had overslept in a week only to find that the electricity was off in her apartment.
6. My friend John, who has taken his new editorship too seriously, sent my note back to me marked as follows: "The anticipation of your eminent *sic* trip to Boston with my roommates and I *sic* has excited us all—especially me— a lot *sic.* See you Tuesday *sic.* Love, Amy."
7. St. Valentine's Day, celebrated on February 14 the original date was probably February 15 derives from the Roman Feast of Lupercalia honoring the god Lupercus.
8. The class studying the history of the English language was overwhelmed by the amount of work required by Professor Mandel his nickname is Mandel the Mad and the mountain of detailed information in the text Thomas Pyles, *The Origins and Development of the English Language* New York: Harcourt Brace Jovanovich, Inc., 1971.
9. Short-haired breeds of cats include 1 Domestic Shorthair, 2 Siamese, 3 Burmese, 4 Abyssinian, 5 Russian Blue, 6 Manx, and 7 Rex.
10. "Well, I uh really don't want uh can't go with you to the opera Friday," Aaron said to Mindy, blushing at his inability to hide his distaste for classical music.

PART B

DIRECTIONS: Write sentences according to the following specifications.

1. A sentence that uses the dash to set off a list

_____

_____

2. A sentence that uses the dash to set off parenthetical information or a sharp break in thought

_____

_____

3. A sentence that uses the dash to show hesitancy in dialogue

_____

_____

4. A sentence that uses parentheses to set off a digression or other nonessential information.

_____

_____

5. A sentence that uses parentheses to enclose numbers or letters that number a list of items.

_____

_____

PART C

DIRECTIONS: On a separate sheet of paper, rewrite the following sentences using brackets to make the indicated additions and to show the indicated errors in the following quotations.

1. "From 1260 to 1294 he ruled China and Mongolia, making Peking his capitol."
   a. Indicate to your reader that the *he* is Kublai Khan.
   b. Indicate that you recognize that the author has mistakenly used *capitol* for *capital.*
2. "Particularly during his pontificate there was in Rome a great surge of interest in learning and an increased appreciation of the arts."
   a. Indicate to your reader that the *his* refers to Leo X.
   b. Indicate that you recognize the author's subject-verb disagreement.

33/QUOTATION MARKS

Quotation marks have three major uses: to enclose direct quotations from speech or writing, to enclose the titles of shorter or smaller works of art, and to set off words or phrases being used in a special sense.

33a DIRECT QUOTATIONS

1. Put quotation marks around the exact words of a speaker or writer but not around the name of the speaker or writer and the word *said* or its synonym.

"Dixie's constant forgetfulness drives me crazy, but let's invite her anyway," said Don.

2. When the identification of the speaker or writer comes in the middle of the quotation, you must analyze each part of the divided quotation to see what kind of punctuation to use before and after the identification of the speaker. If the elements in quotation marks on both sides of the identification of the speaker are complete sentences, put a period after the identification of the speaker and begin the second part of the quotation with a capital letter as a new sentence. Putting a comma after the identification of the speaker in this instance would make a comma splice (the error of joining two independent clauses with only a comma).

INCORRECT   "Jeff is a great guy," said Julie, "I really love going out with him." (comma splice)

CORRECT   "Jeff is a great guy," said Julie. "I really love going out with him."

3. If the identification of the speaker interrupts a sentence, put a comma both before and after the identification of the speaker and begin the second part of the quotation with a small letter (unless the first word would otherwise be capitalized).

"I've been trying to find a job for the summer," said Jake, "but I haven't had much luck so far."

4. When writing or quoting dialogue, begin a new paragraph with each change of speaker.

"What's your favorite movie of all times?" Thelma asked.
"*Star Wars*," replied Max, "and there isn't even a close second."
"Well, I thought it had its cute moments, but, really, how can you put it in a category with truly great films like *Casablanca, Cabaret,* or *Gone With the Wind*? It's a kiddie show with a few flashy visual effects."
"Thel, your taste is really awful. Maybe you should see *Star Wars* again. It's got about ten levels of sophistication—something for everyone. Why, it's the Lone Ranger and King Arthur all at once."
"See it again? I haven't seen it the first time, and, furthermore, I don't intend to waste three bucks on that drivel."

5. When quoting several paragraphs by the same speaker or writer, put the quotation marks at the beginning of each new paragraph but omit them from the end of each paragraph, except for the final paragraph, where they are used to conclude the entire quotation.

About patriotism, Mark Twain wrote: "Patriotism is merely a religion—love of country, worship of country, devotion to the country's flag and honor and welfare.

"In absolute monarchies it is furnished from the throne, cut and dried, to the subject; in England and America it is furnished, cut and dried, to the citizen by the politicians and the newspaper.

"The newspaper-and-politician-manufactured Patriot often gags in private over his dose; but he takes it, and keeps it on his stomach the best he can. Blessed are the meek."

—"As Regards Patriotism"

6. A quotation of fewer than three lines of poetry or 100 words of prose (some say 60 or 70 words or five or six typewritten lines) is put directly into the text with quotation marks around the quotation and introduced by a comma. Any quotation marks occurring *within* the quotation you are citing become single quotation marks (an apostrophe on the typewriter). (Note: Do not use single quotation marks interchangeably with regular quotation marks. You may, however, often see single quotation marks in books printed abroad, especially those from Great Britain.)

"One of my favorite songs of all times is 'As Time Goes By,' but everyone teases me about being old when I say that," said Ruthie.

7. With direct quotations that are questions or exclamations, use a question mark or exclamation point immediately after the question or exclamation to which it applies, even if the whole sentence has not yet ended. In such cases, do not use a comma.

"Will they ever get here?" Lou asked irritably.

"Don't do that!" Marcy shouted to Carole angrily.

33b LONG QUOTATIONS

A quotation consisting of more than three lines of poetry or 100 words of prose is normally separated from the main body of the text. Such a quotation, called a **block quotation**, is introduced by a colon and begins on a new line. It is indented an extra five spaces on either side and is single-spaced. (Some prefer to double-space block quotations.) The indentation replaces the quotation marks; no quotation marks are necessary with block quotations unless there are quotation marks *within* the quoted material.

That same sensation of loneliness mixed with homesickness is well expressed by Charles Lamb in "Christ's Hospital Five and Thirty Years Ago":

> I was a poor friendless boy. My parents and those who should care for me, were far away. Those few acquaintances of theirs, which they could reckon upon being kind to me in the great city, after a little forced notice, which they had the grace to take of me on my first arrival in town, soon grew tired of my holiday visits. They seemed to them to recur too often, though I thought them few enough; and one after another they all failed me, and I felt myself alone among six hundred playmates.

O the cruelty of separating a poor lad from his early homestead! The yearnings which I used to have towards it in those unfledged years! How, in my dreams, would my native town (far in the west) come back, with its church, and trees, and faces! How I would wake weeping, and in the anguish of my heart exclaim upon sweet Calne in Wiltshire!

33c TITLES

Enclose within quotation marks the titles of shorter works of art and the titles of works that are parts of larger works (for example, titles of articles, essays, short stories, chapters in books, short poems, and short musical works). Some people also prefer to enclose in quotation marks the titles of movies, radio and television programs, paintings, and statues, but these are perhaps more often italicized or underlined.

"UFO's Over Miami: Some New Sightings" (article)

"To Autumn" (short poem)

"Jaws" *or* *Jaws* (film)

"The Thinker" *or* *The Thinker* (statue)

Titles of unpublished works, for example, theses or dissertations, are *always* enclosed in quotation marks. Their length is not a consideration.

33d SPECIAL USES OF WORDS

Put quotation marks around words being used in a special sense, potentially confusing technical words, and coined words. In addition, words being cited as words are often enclosed in quotation marks, although many people prefer to italicize or underline words used as words.

The engravers did not make the "cut" the right size, and it did not fit on the page.
To raise money, the fraternity sponsored a "dog-wash."

The word "unctuous" (or *unctuous*) sounds ugly to my ear.

33e SUPERFLUOUS QUOTATION MARKS

Do *not* employ quotation marks for the following uses:
1. To enclose paraphrases or indirect quotations.

INCORRECT	John said "he hated to wrap packages."
CORRECT	John said he hated to wrap packages.
CORRECT	John said, "I hate to wrap packages."

2. To enclose the title at the top of your paper, though quotation marks should be used around the title if it appears in the text.
3. To enclose the titles of longer works of art, which are italicized (underlined): *Moby Dick* (not "Moby Dick"); *Catch 22* (not "Catch 22").
4. To enclose indented quotations, unless the quotation marks appear in the text being quoted.

5. To enclose certain kinds of titles that are never enclosed in quotation marks or italicized, especially the Bible or its parts or parts or all of other sacred works. Do not put quotation marks around titles of prayers, creeds, signs, mottoes, or names of catalogs, directories, or political documents.

SACRED WORKS	New Testament, Isaiah, The Lord's Prayer, Koran
MOTTOES	All the News That's Fit to Print
SIGNS	No Left Turn
CATALOGS AND DIRECTORIES	Manhattan Telephone Directory
POLITICAL DOCUMENTS	Mayflower Compact

6. To enclose familiar nicknames: William the Conqueror, Honest Abe, my nephew Chip.

TROUBLESHOOTING

1. Remember that quotation marks *always go outside* the period and the comma, whether the entire sentence is the quotation or only a phrase or word at the end of the sentence is the quoted matter.

INCORRECT	Alan said, "But you have to come too".
CORRECT	Alan said, "But you have to come too."
INCORRECT	In the shower Eloise always sang "Tea for Two".
CORRECT	In the shower Eloise always sang "Tea for Two."
INCORRECT	"I've always loved Frost's poem 'Birches'", Helen said.
CORRECT	"I've always loved Frost's poem 'Birches,'" Helen said.

2. Similarly, quotation marks *always* come *before* colons and semicolons. With the question mark and exclamation point, however, the logic of the sentence dictates the placement of the quotation marks.

In the recital Dixie played the lighthearted "Cuckoo Song"; Kirsten, however, chose to perform a funeral march by Chopin.

"Do you know who first recorded 'Dark Moon'?" Larry asked. (Here the entire quotation is the question, so the question mark is included within the quotation marks.)

"Why are you always asking me 'What is Life?'" Harry grumbled. (Here one question mark covers the question within the question and thus comes inside both sets of quotation marks.)

I've never before heard that poem "Who Shot Cock Robin?" (Here only the quoted title is the question.)

What is meant by a "round robin"? (Here the whole sentence is the question, not the quoted phrase.)

"You're insane!" she screamed. (Here only the quoted matter is the exclamation.)

Don't play one more note of "Tiger Rag"! (Here the entire sentence, not the quoted material, is the exclamation; thus, the exclamation point goes outside the quotation marks.)

NAME _____ DATE _____

DIRECTIONS: Punctuate the following sentences with quotation marks, adding periods, commas, question marks, exclamation points, and capital letters where necessary. around the identification of the speaker and at the ends of the sentences.

EXAMPLE: "Don't you think," he asked, "the time is ripe for our enterprise?"

1. All that rude insurance investigator could say to me was Lady, were you driving with your eyes shut Sally said to Beth

2. I know you're down on television Jack replied but don't you find some good qualities in shows like Kojak and All in the Family

3. Josh, who had gone to some top schools, said he had never read the U.S. Constitution or the Declaration of Independence

4. If you will wait here for just one moment, Miss whispered the white-haired teller I shall have someone show you to the vault

5. Balderdash thundered the portly Mr. Cavalier These proposals are just so much balderdash, and I want new ones on my desk by 8 a.m. tomorrow

6. The late President Kennedy once said and if we cannot end our differences, at least we can help make the world safe for diversity

7. It's not an exaggeration said Carol to say that every other phrase Horace says is Give 'em hell

8. If I were you, I'd hold off on buying a car right now David suggested however I'd keep it in the back of my mind in case a really good deal comes along

9. Andi asked Bob if he remembered the song Where Have All The Flowers Gone

10. Stop hitting your sister with your spoon Mark's mother ordered try using it to eat all that cereal that's in your bowl

11. Which Shakespearean character says what's in a name asked Dwight

12. What on earth do you think you're doing, young man shouted Chuck's mother come right into the house this very minute

13. Many people misspell the words penicillin and bouillon

14. I didn't know what to do on my first day at the *News* when the city editor asked me to run down to the morgue and get him last month's *Time*, which had the article South Africa: The Defiant White Tribe

15. These flowers have been here only half a day and they're already wilted Ray said to Katie did you forget to water them after the florist made the delivery

16. I'm sorry to be late Ruth explained to Herman but, to tell the truth, before I came I just had to finish watching Sixty Minutes.

34/APOSTROPHES

The **apostrophe** does several jobs to clarify writing, jobs that cannot be done by any other punctuation mark. Without the apostrophe our plurals and possessives would become muddled, and our contractions would be confusing. Actually, learning how to use the apostrophe is not difficult because its uses—though important—are few.

34a POSSESSIVES

1. Add the apostrophe followed by -s (-'s) to form the possessive of singular nouns and some indefinite pronouns. Although many people prefer to omit the -s and add only the apostrophe when the word ends in an s or z sound, it is not wrong to add -'s (Charles' grin *or* Charles's grin). If the possessive of a word ending in -s or -z is sounded as a separate syllable in speech, the -'s should be added, but if the possessive would not make a separate syllable or if the next word begins with an s sound, you may use just the apostrophe.

the dog's bone (one dog has one bone)	anyone's guess
my boss's temper	everybody's responsibility
Liz' goat	France's history
Morris's paintings	Dickens' *or* Dickens's novels
The hippopotamus's mouth	

2. Add only the apostrophe to form the possessive of *regular* plural nouns.

the dogs' bones (Two or more dogs own these bones.)
the trees' branches   the Smiths' mailbox

3. If the plural is irregular, that is, formed without adding -s or -es, then add -'s to form the possessive.

the children's pony   the mice's cage   the policemen's beats

4. To show joint possession of two nouns, make only the last item possessive, but to show individual possession, make each item possessive.

Gilbert & Sullivan's operettas (They wrote them together.)
Burns and Allen's skits (They performed them together.)
Columbus's and Magellan's voyages (They made the voyages separately, not together.)

To show joint or individual possession when at least one of the words is a pronoun, use a possessive adjective, not a personal possessive pronoun.

INCORRECT	Come see mine and Jim's new house.
CORRECT	Come see my and Jim's new house.
INCORRECT	Let's take both yours and my car.
CORRECT	Let's take both your and my cars.

5. To form the possessive of compound nouns or pronouns, add the possessive to the final item.

the man-of-war's flag   no one else's comments

On the other hand, the possessive of a noun or pronoun *phrase* is often cumbersome if formed with *-'s*; in formal writing, an *of* phrase is preferred.

AWKWARD	*Gone with the Wind's* plot
PREFERABLE	The plot of *Gone with the Wind*
AWKWARD	The intrusion's suddenness
PREFERABLE	The suddenness of the intrusion
AWKWARD	The girl next door's boyfriends
IMPROVED	The boyfriends of the girl next door

6. Gerunds, like other nouns, require the possessive. (A gerund is a noun made from a verb by adding *-ing*.)

INCORRECT	The plane landing so suddenly startled the passengers. (It was the landing, not the plane, that startled the passengers. *Landing* is the subject and *plane* is a modifier of that subject, so *plane* should be in the possessive.)
CORRECT	The plane's landing so suddenly startled the passengers.

The *double possessive*, which employs both the *-'s* and an *of* phrase, occurs when the sentence involves a human possessor of a thing that is among several such possessions. The double possessive is necessary when the phrase could be rewritten using *one of* or *some of*.

For his costume Sam wore some high-heeled shoes of his mother's. (The shoes were among several pairs of his mother's shoes. Note that you could also say "some of his mother's high-heeled shoes.")

Sam also wore a trench coat of his father's. (This double possessive implies that Sam's father has several trench coats for him to choose from.)

Sam also wore his father's trench coat. (Here the single possessive implies that Sam's father has only one trench coat.)

34b CONTRACTIONS

Use the apostrophe to replace missing letters in contractions (words shortened by omitting one or more letters). Be sure to put the apostrophe only at the point where the letter or letters are omitted.

INCORRECT	CORRECT
Im	I'm
does'nt	doesn't
"Peg 'O My Heart"	"Peg O' My Heart"

In informal writing, the apostrophe is also used to indicate the missing century in dates.

INCORRECT	CORRECT
the Great Blizzard of 78	The Great Blizzard of '78
the Spirit of 76	the Spirit of '76

Do not use the apostrophe with the hyphen to express inclusive numbers (dates and pages).

INCORRECT   CORRECT
pp. 125-'32   pp. 125-32
1925-'42   1925-42

Remember, however, that contractions are usually frowned upon in formal writing.

34c SPECIAL GRAMMATICAL ENDINGS

When you use letters or symbols as nouns or verbs, put an apostrophe between the letter or symbol and any grammatical endings (plural, possessive, past tense, participle).

Go through the paper and put the α's and γ's in by hand.

Perry x'ed out the names of members who had not paid their dues.

V's and F's are the most difficult letters for me to type.

CONFUSING Is and Is are often confused.

CLEAR I's and I's are often confused.

TROUBLESHOOTING

1. Do not use the apostrophe to form the possessive of personal or relative pronouns.

INCORRECT   his', her's, your's, yours', our's, ours', theirs' (Note that these forms do not exist at all in correct English.)

CORRECT   his, hers, yours, ours, theirs

2. Do not mistake the possessive pronoun *its* (meaning "belonging to it") for the contraction *it's* (meaning "it is" or "it has") or the relative possessive *whose* (meaning "belonging to whom") for the contraction *who's* (meaning "who is" or "who has").

3. Do not use the apostrophe in forming plurals of nouns or proper names.

INCORRECT PLURALS   the Williams's   the class's
CORRECT PLURALS   the Williamses   the classes

4. Do not use the apostrophe before abbreviated or clipped words listed in the dictionary as words in their own right.

INCORRECT   'fridge   'burger   'coon   'phone
CORRECT   fridge   burger   coon   phone

NAME _____ DATE _____

DIRECTIONS: Rewrite each of the following sentences, replacing the italicized phrase with a possessive noun or pronoun. In addition, add other apostrophes where they are needed.

EXAMPLE: Because two MPs detained her on the way home from the base, Frieda wasnt able to pick up *the suit of Charles* at the cleaners or to get the special cheese at *the shop of Gino* as shed planned.

Because two MP's detained her on the way home from the base, Frieda wasn't able to pick up Charles' suit (or Charles's suit) at the cleaner's or to get the special cheese at Gino's shop as she'd planned.

1. *The Halloween costume of Lewis* was so bawdy that his girlfriends refusing to go with him *to the party of John and Alan* was completely understandable.

_____

_____

2. "The bank cant tell your 5s from your 9s," *the mother of Francis* said, "and its bouncing *checks of yours* because it cant deal with your penmanship."

_____

_____

3. The beauty of the gold cross lay in *the exquisite filigreed border of it*, a tiny lacelike edging that Judson didnt fully appreciate until he held it up to the light.

_____

_____

4. The suddenness of the hiss shot terror into *the soul of Willis* as he turned to face *the foe of him*, a gigantic, writhing snake *the head of whom* was poised to strike.

_____

_____

5. "Ive been *X*d from *the list of the sorority* of people eligible to move into *the house of the chapter*," moaned *the sister of Lois*, "and I dont think anybody elses name was scratched off except mine and *that of Janice*."

_____

_____

6. "You rah-rahd me to death at that miserable football game," Alice snapped at Don, "and now you expect me to go to *the party of Mike and Boris*, where Ill have to hear the official post-mortem on *the defeat of the Rams*."

_____

_____

7. Once theyve learned that the *P*s are really *R*s and the *H*s are really *N*s, beginning students of Russian dont have many difficulties with *the alphabet of it*.

_____

_____

8. After the Catholic Church named November 1 as All Saints Day during the 700s, pagan and religious traditions fused to make October 31 Halloween Day.

_____

_____

9. Although the color of the lenses wasnt that specified in *the order of the optometrist, the satisfaction of his customer* with the substitute hue prevented Dr. Thomas having to exchange them.

_____

_____

10. Among the furnishing in *the first apartment of Cathy and Sean* were *two grotesque mahogany chairs of those of his grandmother* and four bright blue wicker lampshades that his sister hadnt been able to sell *at the rummage sale of her church*.

_____

_____

35/HYPHENS

The **hyphen**'s major uses are to divide words between two lines and to join the elements of various kinds of compounds. Words formerly hyphenated are now often spelled as one word, so check the current usage in an up-to-date dictionary. Because no two dictionaries agree completely on the spelling of all hyphenated words, choose one good dictionary and use it consistently.

Do not confuse the hyphen with the dash. The dash is made by typing two hyphens together, and its functions are not at all the same as those of the hyphen.

35a WORD DIVISION

1. Use a hyphen to divide a word between the end of one line and the beginning of the next. Divide the word only between syllables (check your dictionary for syllabication).

2. Never divide a word of only one syllable, and do not divide a word after a single syllable of one letter.

3. Divide words containing hyphens only at the hyphen.

4. Do not hyphenate personal proper names, numerals, contractions, acronyms, or abbreviations used with numbers.

5. Try to avoid ending more than two lines of type in a row with divided words.

6. Never hyphenate the last word on a page or the last word of a paragraph.

35b PREFIXES AND SUFFIXES

Use a hyphen after the prefixes *ex-*, *self-*, *all-*, *quasi-*, *half-*, and *quarter-* and also between any prefix and a proper name. Use a hyphen before the suffixes *-elect* and *-odd*.

All-powerful	un-American	president-elect
ex-husband	trans-Pacific	thirty-odd
self-interest		

35c CLARITY

Use a hyphen within a word to prevent ambiguity or misreading and to avoid a double *i* or the same consonant three times in a row.

tall-tale teller (one who tells tall tales)

tall tale-teller (a tall person who tells tales)

semi-illiterate (not semiilliterate)

fall-like weather (not falllike)

35d COMPOUNDS

1. A hyphen is usually employed between the elements of compounds in which one element is a letter or a numeral. However, practice varies, and it is best to check your dictionary when you are uncertain.

A-frame   PT-109   C sharp (but C-sharp major)

2. Use a hyphen to connect compounds in which both or all of the elements are of equal grammatical weight.

poet-philosopher   Tiger-Gamecock game

3. Use a hyphen to connect compound modifiers when they come *before* the noun they modify, but do not hyphenate them when they follow the noun or when they are used adverbially.

run-of-the-mill applicant   a fly-by-night business
a six-ounce container *but* The container held six ounces.
a first-rate hotel *but* The hotel was first rate.

Do not hyphenate the compound modifier, however, if the first word is an adverb ending in *-ly*, even if the modifier precedes the noun.

a fully grown tree   the quickly developed formula

4. In extremely long compound adjectives, you may substitute quotation marks for hyphens.

an I-don't-know-where-to-begin cough *or* an "I don't know where to begin" cough

5. Compound words that are correctly written as single words or as two separate words should not be hyphenated. Here again, a dictionary is your best guide.

INCORRECT	CORRECT
pre-test	pretest
to-morrow	tomorrow
over-whelm	overwhelm

6. Hyphenate the parts of written-out compound numbers up to ninety-nine and the parts of written-out fractions (unless either the numerator or the denominator is already a hyphenated compound).

thirty-nine *but* one hundred ninety-five   seventy-four
two-thirds *but* a third   five twenty-thirds

7. The so-called suspended hyphen is used when a series of compounds all have the same second element. Space between the first hyphen and the following word.

third- and fourth-semester courses   two- or four-year college

35e INCLUSIVE DATES AND PAGES

A hyphen is used to express inclusive dates or pages.

pages 315-22   1941-45

35f SPELLED-OUT WORDS

Use a hyphen to indicate the spelling-out of a word and to indicate stuttering.

His name is spelled G-e-n-e, not J-e-a-n.   "B-b-but you p-p-promised!"

NAME _____ DATE _____

DIRECTIONS: Insert hyphens in the following sentences as necessary for correct spelling and clarity. Consult your dictionary if you need to. Label correct sentences with a *C*.

EXAMPLE: _____ That is not an easy–to–believe story.

_____ 1. Janice thought that the trip would be a once in a lifetime opportunity.

_____ 2. The bank is cutting back on both its long and short term loans.

_____ 3. The historical society plans a complete recreation of the eighteenth-century village.

_____ 4. Will you please relay the message that the store cannot relay the carpet until Tuesday?

_____ 5. On her thirty first birthday, Cindy woke up with a depressed, over the hill feeling.

_____ 6. One hundred and seventy odd people showed up for the dance and reveled in the fairy tale setting until the wee hours.

_____ 7. *The Cockroach That Ate New York* was a B grade film admired by only hard core fans of monster movies.

_____ 8. The cold hearted interviewer bluntly told Sue: "Don't call us; we'll call you."

_____ 9. On Monday night the local anticrime committee voted to demand that the new sheriff be released from his four year contract.

_____ 10. Mandy is a very good natured, even tempered, self sufficient young woman.

_____ 11. The Griffins are building an A frame house on a forty acre tract only three and two thirds miles from John's job.

_____ 12. "Joe, you are bright enough to be an A plus student," the obviously concerned counselor said, "but you seem to have a very poor self image that keeps you from doing the high caliber work that you are capable of producing."

_____ 13. "I don't give a rip about your pie in the sky ideals!" shouted Jennifer. "I just want my hard earned share of reality."

_____ 14. "Either a three or a four bedroom house will do," Mark said to the realtor, "but my two dog, three person menagerie absolutely will not fit into anything smaller."

_____ 15. The newly married couple thought they could afford a house with three or four bedrooms, but the sky-high prices for homes drove them to a dingy, too-small apartment in a crime-ridden neighborhood.

_____ 16. Anna's thirteen year old brother won a four year scholarship to study painting with the world famous David Eakins.

_____ 17. Mark's sister, who is thirteen years old, has a real devil may care attitude about everything except horses.

_____ 18. The German U boat stalked the English freighter through the storm tossed seas off the Algerian coast.

_____ 19. He is not only anti Democrat and anti Republican but also anti feminist.

_____ 20. The sky was cloudless, and the blue green sea was swellless.

_____ 21. He composed a sonata in B flat major, but his wife objected to the key of B flat, preferring A flat.

_____ 22. Samuel Taylor Coleridge (1772 1834), an English poet philosopher of the Romantic period, wrote the long poem *The Rime of the Ancient Mariner.*

36/ ITALICS

In printing, **italic** letters slant toward the right, as opposed to the regular, nonslanting letters called roman letters. In handwriting or typing, italic type is indicated by underlining.

36a TITLES

Italicize (that is, underline) the titles of books, magazines, periodicals, plays, long poems, long musical compositions, and the names of individual ships, airplanes, and spacecraft. (Do not italicize the word *the* when it appears as the first word in the title of a newspaper or periodical unless it is actually a part of the official title.) Many people also prefer to italicize (rather than enclose in quotation marks) the names of statues, paintings, motion pictures, and radio and television programs.

BOOKS	*Gone with the Wind, Middlemarch*
NEWSPAPERS	*The New York Times,* the *Daily News*
PERIODICALS	*Newsweek, The New Yorker*
LONG MUSICAL COMPOSITIONS	*The Nutcracker, La Bohème*
PAINTINGS	*Sunflowers, The Bellelli Family*
STATUES	*David, The Thinker*
RADIO OR TV PROGRAMS	*Sixty Minutes, Saturday at the Opera*
MOVIES	*Close Encounters of the Third Kind*

Note that the names of types or makes of ships and aircraft and the abbreviations S.S., U.S.S., and H.M.S.S. are capitalized but not italicized, even when they are used with the name of an individual ship:

H.M.S. *Guerrière*   S.S. *United States*

36b EMPHASIS

Italics serve to emphasize a word or phrase, especially in dialogue. Use italicization for emphasis sparingly in expository writing because its overuse destroys the desired effect and gives an impression of immaturity.

"It's not *what* he says that irritates me so much," Alice snarled. "It's *how* he says it."

36c WORDS AS WORDS

Italics may be used with words, letters, or numbers that refer to the words, letters, or numbers themselves.

The modifier *only* is often misplaced.
The number *three* has had mystical qualities in many cultures.

Words used as words may also be enclosed in quotation marks. Whether you use italics or quotation marks, be consistent.

36d FOREIGN WORDS

Italicize foreign words or phrases (but not an entire sentence) that are not completely accepted as English words. Your dictionary will indicate whether the word should be italicized. If you translate the word or phrase, put the translation in quotation marks after the italicized foreign word or phrase.

> *Le bon mot,* literally, the "good word," generally means "witticism" and was the trademark of Oscar Wilde.
>
> We learned to our sorrow that *sosta vietata* means "no parking."

36e SUPERFLUOUS ITALICS

Do not italicize the following:

1. The names of sacred books or political documents

The Koran   The Bill of Rights

2. Foreign proper names of persons or places

Copenhagen, Denmark   Pablo Picasso

3. Your own title when it appears at the top of the first page of your paper

TROUBLESHOOTING

Words or phrases already enclosed in quotation marks should not be italicized.

INCORRECT	Tom loves to watch the *"The Days of Our Lives."*
CORRECT	Tom loves to watch "The Days of Our Lives."
CORRECT	Tom loves to watch *The Days of Our Lives.*

DIRECTIONS: Underline words that should be italicized in the following sentences.

EXAMPLE: She loved the film <u>Gone</u> <u>With</u> <u>The</u> <u>Wind</u>.

1. The court appointed Eric Baldwin to serve in loco parentis for the child.

2. Some people pronounce each of the words pear, pare, and pair differently.

3. Anna's favorite piece of sculpture in the Chicago museum is Adam, done in bronze by Auguste Rodin, but Joe, objecting to its intense realism, prefers the early Gothic works, especially The Visitation of the Virgin Mary.

4. It must have been thrilling to sail on one of the great American clipper ships like the Flying Cloud or the Andrew Jackson.

5. Although Laszlo had always kidded Helga about watching soap operas, he got hooked on one in the student lounge one afternoon, and now nothing—not even Helga's almost unbearable taunts—stands between him and Search for Tomorrow.

6. The Denver Post was the first to break the story, but the Phoenix Sun and the Arizona Republic gave the scandal more intensive coverage.

7. "Chris, did you see that cooking feature in the February edition of McCall's?" Gloria asked. "It almost convinced me that I can make petit fours that I won't be ashamed to serve."

8. The word carpenter came into English through the Norman French, but it originated in the Latin word carpentarius, or "carriage-maker."

9. "Old films like On the Waterfront, All the King's Men, and It Happened One Night are superior to modern movies," Eric argued, "because, unlike the best old films, the ultrarealistic modern movies seldom leave anything to the imagination."

10. To say "the fat is in the fire" meant, in early use, that a plan had failed (e.g., Heywood's Proverbs and Epigrams, 1562), but by the mid-nineteenth century it had come to be used to describe a situation in which one person's thoughtless act was certain to enrage another.

11. Beethoven's opera Leonore was later renamed Fidelio.

12. Schopenhauer, a nineteenth-century German philosopher, had an extremely pessimistic Weltanschauung, or "world view."

13. It took Wiley Post one week in 1933 to pilot his Lockheed, the Winnie Mae, on the first solo round-the-world flight.

37 / SLASHES

The **slash** (also called *slant, diagonal, virgule, solidus*, or *oblique*) is a highly specialized mark of separation.

37a ALTERNATIVES

The slash is one way to indicate alternatives. The expression *and/or* is the most frequently used term of this type, but in formal writing the slash should be avoided by rewriting the sentence. Usually either *and* or *or* is sufficient.

QUESTIONABLE   For dessert you can have cake and/or ice cream.
PREFERABLE   For dessert you can have cake, ice cream, or both.

37b QUOTING POETRY

The slash serves to separate lines of poetry quoted in running text.

"And then my heart with pleasure fills, / And dances with the daffodils."

37c FRACTIONS

Use a slash to separate the numerator from the denominator in fractions included in running text.

A scruple is a unit of weight equivalent to 20 grains or 1 37/125 grams.

38 / ELLIPSES

Ellipses are a series of three spaced dots used to indicate that a word or words have been omitted from a direct quotation. It is not necessary to use ellipses at the beginning or end of a quotation to indicate that you are quoting only part of a paragraph or line of poetry, but any omissions *within* the quotation itself must be marked with ellipses. When using ellipses, however, be sure not to distort the meaning of your source by your omissions.

Consider the following passage from Margaret Mead's *Blackberry Winter* and the following illustrations of the use of ellipses in quoting the passage.

I had decided to keep my own name. This made a flutter in the press, partly because I had stated my decision as a matter of preference rather than principle. I had got the idea from an angry cousin of my mother's; in describing what an impractically idealistic young woman Mother had been, she had said, "If your mother were getting married today, she'd even keep her own name!" I resented the tone in which she was putting my mother down, and I said to myself, "Why not?" Keeping my own name, in which Luther concurred, led to endless explanations, on and on through life. But I was merely acting on my mother's belief that women should keep their own identity and not be submerged, a belief that had made her give her daughters only one given name, so that they would keep their surnames after marriage.

If ellipses are made *within* one sentence, use only three spaced dots (periods on the typewriter) no matter how brief or long the omission. To make an omission in the fifth sentence in the passage above, punctuate like this:

Keeping my own name . . . led to endless explanations, on and on through life.

To use just the first sentence in the passage and then to skip to the third sentence, you must put a period after the first sentence and then write ellipses —four periods altogether—though you do not space before the period at the end of the sentence.

I had decided to keep my own name. . . . I had got the idea from an angry cousin of my mother's; in describing what an impractically idealistic young woman Mother had been, she had said, "If your mother were getting married today, she'd even keep her own name!"

To indicate that one or more lines of poetry have been omitted, use an entire row of spaced dots.

Little Miss Muffet
Sat on a tuffet,
. . . .
Along came a spider
. . . .
And frightened Miss Muffet away.
                    —Nursey rhyme

Never use ellipses as a substitute for a dash or any other mark of punctuation.

39/DIACRITICS

Although English uses no diacritical marks—special symbols used with letters to indicate pronunciation—many foreign languages do require them. They must be accurately transcribed when one uses foreign words and phrases. The most common diacritical marks are shown here with examples.

ACUTE ACENT	été, étoile, café
GRAVE ACENT	voilà, père, kilomètre
CEDILLA	français, garçon
CIRCUMFLEX	côte, gâteau, fenêtre
TILDE	mañana, español
UMLAUT	Küssen, für, Hängen
HAČEK	Dvořak, Stredočesky

40/COMBINING MARKS OF PUNCTUATION

The marks of punctuation used to separate phrases, clauses, and sentences are commas, semicolons, colons, dashes, periods, question marks, and exclamation points. Some of them can be used together, and then accepted practice regulates the order in which they appear. Other punctuation marks, however, must not occur together. The rules that follow should provide helpful guidelines regarding when and how to combine marks of punctuation or to use them alone.

1. When they are needed, a question mark and exclamation point are always used in preference to other marks and replace these other marks.

"Is it really that important to you?" I asked. (Question mark replaces comma before identification of the speaker.)

I won't listen to another word on the subject! (Exclamation point replaces period.)

2. Within a sentence, the period as a mark of abbreviation can be used with other marks of punctuation.

I hear she finally got her Ph.D.—what a surprise after all those years!

Her many problems, e.g., poor health, old age, and lack of money, were too much for her in the end.

When, however, the last word in a declarative sentence is an abbreviation, only one period is used at the end of the sentence.

I asked her to forward my mail to me in Boston, Mass.

3. Dashes should not be used with commas, semicolons, or parentheses.

INCORRECT   You must go immediately,—not next week—, to Chicago.
CORRECT   You must go immediately, not next week, to Chicago.
CORRECT   You must go immediately—not next week—to Chicago.

4. Never put commas, semicolons, or colons before parentheses within a sentence. These marks of punctuation, however, may *follow* parentheses within a sentence if the sense requires them to do so.

INCORRECT   Because she was afraid she had contracted German measles, (rubella) she voluntarily isolated herself to avoid spreading the disease.
CORRECT   Because she was afraid she had contracted German measles (rubella), she voluntarily isolated herself to avoid spreading the disease.

There is one exception to the preceding rule. When parentheses are used to separate letters or numbers introducing items in a series, commas may precede the parentheses.

He sponsored legislation that he thought would (1) reduce unemployment, (2) reduce crime by increasing the number of jobs, and (3) reduce welfare payments because of a higher rate of employment.

5. *Always* place commas and periods *before* closing quotation marks, no matter what the logic of the sentence is.

Inga wrote a short story entitled "It's Later Than You Think," but she was unable to get it published. (The comma precedes the quotation marks even though it applies to the entire clause and not just the quoted material.)

6. Always place semicolons or colons *after* closing quotation marks.

Inga wrote a short story entitled "It's Later Than You Think"; however, she was unable to get it published.

7. Question marks and exclamation points are placed before or after quotation marks in accordance with the logic of the sentence.

Have you read Keats' "Ode to a Nightingale"? (The question mark follows the title because it refers to the entire sentence, not just to the title.)

She quoted the famous line "What's in a name?" (The question mark is part of the quotation and thus comes within the quotation marks. Note that no period is used at the end of the sentence.)

41/TYPING PUNCTUATION

Well-typed papers that follow the accepted practices for typewritten material make a favorable impression on the reader (including the instructor). There are specific rules for the correct spacing of marks of punctuation in typed copy. Consult section 41 of Millward's *Handbook for Writers* or any other reference source for the rules for typing punctuation.

NAME _____ DATE _____

DIRECTIONS: Punctuate the following sentences correctly.

EXAMPLE: While he was sleeping, he cried out, "Help me! I'm drowning."

1. After he had given the furnace a thorough going over the repairman told Mrs Townes that he would have to order a new humidifier for it

2. Chuck knew he had three choices to demand a raise and a promotion to continue to knuckle under to simpering Mrs. Smiths ridiculous orders or to quit and begin job hunting all over again

3. Cora thought that the concert was the best shed ever heard John on the other hand maintained that it was a disgracefully poor performance

4. After alls been said and done Al said Ill bet Im going to be sorry that I ever said Id be the publicity chairman for this years Firemens Ball

5. Planning her meals for the coming week was Dabneys most time consuming weekend chore

6. Peter said What makes me nervous about being around Bob is that every other comment he makes is either Im cool or How does that grab ya

7. The Turning Point a well made film that is set in the world of ballet is an excellent statement about the choices women and by extension all people have to make with their lives

8. Casting long shadows over the inklike stagnant water the cypress trees draped with Spanish moss looked like aged sentries guarding the swamp

9. After what seemed like a never ending production of Mozarts The Marriage of Figaro George and Sybil hungry and tired had a quick supper at Perrones Deli and hurried home

10. I never want to see you again Sally yelled hurling the heart shaped box of chocolates at Paul who stared at her in disbelief

11. At the corner of the house in the tall grass is where the cat seems to hide all the treasures that she pilfers from the house

12. At the corner of the house in the tall grass the cat hid her latest treasure pilfered from the house a box of dental floss

13. The old house which had been lashed by the storm winds and sea spray for more than a century had become to local residents a symbol of mans ability to endure adversity

14. She asked me if I wanted to go to see her uncles new horses Hester said grimacing at the very thought of an afternoon spent trudging around the stables

15. Wow Ive been waiting for two years for that course to be offered at the YWCA said Vickie I cant believe Im finally going to get to take it

16. Eric asked Joan to mail his books and papers to him at 1423 McDaniel Ave Clemson S C 29631

17. Looking up from his homework' Charlie asked Mom what does the word picaresque mean

18. William Hogarth 1697 1764 was a British painter and engraver whose most famous works are the series of pictures The Rakes Progress and Marriage a la Mode

19. The Belle of Amherst a play about Emily Dickinsons life is a one character play that quotes extensively from the poet's letters and well known poems such as The Soul Selects Her Own Society I Like to See It Lap the Miles and Because I Could Not Stop for Death

20. The January wind howled and rattled at the windowpanes but around the fire an aura of safety and snugness soothed everyones fears

21. Every night John went to bed punctually at 11 p m however he often lay in bed for more than an hour before he was able to fall asleep

22. Every night John went to bed punctually at 11 p m however active or tired he felt

23. Every night John went to bed punctually at 11 p m however because he was a fanatic about getting enough sleep

24. To tell the truth was to be in a lot of trouble with others to lie on the other hand was to be in trouble with himself

25. To tell the truth Don Anna said I believe you enjoy deceiving people

26. Which play is it in which Shakespeare wrote Frailty thy name is woman Laura asked her roommate

27. Sixteen year old Harry cranked up his grandfathers old car and rattled into town to try to find his mother

42/CAPITALIZATION

Although the trend over the last two centuries has been toward less and less **capitalization** in English, it is still necessary to capitalize the first words of sentences and of most lines of poetry. Further, nearly all proper names should be capitalized.

42a FIRST WORDS

Capitalize the first word of every sentence or deliberate sentence fragment, although capitalization of the first word of a complete sentence following a colon is optional.

> Don't forget to write your mother, your brother, and your aunt.
>
> You were told to do that at once. In other words, immediately.
>
> His landlord was not bluffing: He just got an eviction notice.
>
> His landlord was not bluffing: he just got an eviction notice.

Capitalize the first line of every line of poetry if it was capitalized in the original.

> I wandered lonely as a cloud
> That floats on high o'er vales and hills,
> When all at once I saw a crowd,
> A host, of golden daffodils;
> —William Wordsworth, *"I Wandered Lonely as a Cloud"*

42b PERSONAL NAMES AND TITLES

1. Capitalize the names, nicknames, and epithets of persons. Capitalize a person's name after a prefix *unless* the compound is listed in your dictionary without a hyphen.

> William Wordsworth   anti-Stalin
> Frederick the Great   antichrist
> Stan the Man

2. Capitalize words derived from proper names unless the word is spelled in your dictionary without a capital letter.

> Jeffersonian democracy   Marxism
> diesel engine   jeremiad

3. Capitalize the titles of officials, nobility, and relatives when they *precede* the person's name or substitute for the name of a specific individual. (If the office is a very high one, the title is sometimes capitalized even when used without the following name, though as a rule a title used alone is a statement of the office or relationship and is not capitalized.)

> General Grant *but* the general   Daddy *but* his father
> Uncle Toby *but* my uncle   King Charles *but* the king
> the President of the United States *but* the bank's president

4. Capitalize academic degrees or titles that appear after a person's name.

Andrew Martin, M.D.   John Mills, Doctor of Laws

42c NAMES OF GROUPS

1. Capitalize the names of national, linguistic, and racial groups and of adjectives formed from these names.

American	Eskimo	Polynesian
Mongol	Semite	German
Indian	Indo-European	Austrian

2. Capitalize the names of officially organized groups of any kind but not of unofficial or loosely organized collections of people.

Columbia University	a college
United States Army	the army
Young Women's Christian Association	my swimming club
United Nations	our country

42d RELIGIOUS TERMS

Capitalize names or epithets of deities, organized religious groups, sacred texts and ceremonies, and adjectives derived from these nouns. (It is not necessary to capitalize pronouns referring to deities unless confusion would otherwise result.)

God, Christ, Jehovah, Allah, the Apostle John
Judaism, Roman Catholicism, Protestant, Islam, Buddhism
the Bible, Koran, Exodus, Upanishads
the Lord's Prayer, the Ten Commandments
Moslem, Jewish, Christian, Buddhist, Biblical

42e NAMES OF PLACES

Capitalize the names of nations, states, provinces, counties, cities, towns, streets, highways, parks, mountains, rivers, lakes, and other recognized political and geographical divisions.

Brazil	Yellowstone National Park
Arizona	Mount Everest
the Province of Ontario	the Mississippi River
Cook County	Lake Michigan
New York City	the Far East
Fifth Avenue	Cape Hatteras
the New Jersey Turnpike	the Malay Peninsula

Capitalize the names of individual buildings, monuments, ships, and aircraft.

the Eiffel Tower	Lincoln Memorial
the Empire State Building	*Mariner III*

42f TITLES OF WORKS

Capitalize all the words—except articles, conjunctions, and short prepositions—in the titles of essays, articles, chapters, books, periodicals, newspapers, films, television programs, plays, musical compositions, and works of art. When, however, an article, conjunction, or preposition is the first word of the title, it is capitalized.

"Archaic Art in Ancient Greece"	*Death on the Nile*
Gone With the Wind	"Masterpiece Theatre"
The Talisman	*As You Like It*
Time	"My Old Kentucky Home"
Daily News	*The Prodigal Son*

If a work is divided into parts, the parts are also capitalized.

Introduction	Chapter 2	Volume IV
Part II	Act III	Index

42g OTHER NAMES

1. Capitalize the names of days of the week, months of the year, official holidays, and geological time divisions (but not the words *era, period, epoch,* and so on).

Sunday	March
Columbus Day	the Fourth of July
Mesozoic era	Cretaceous period
Pliocene epoch	

2. Capitalize the names of treaties, laws, historical documents, historical epochs or events, and legal cases.

the Treaty of Paris	the Reign of Terror
the Social Security Act	the Seven Years' War
the Monroe Doctrine	*Miranda v. Arizona*
the Middle Ages	

3. Capitalize the names of flags, awards, and official brand names (but not general names) of products.

Old Glory	Kleenex	a federal grant
Pulitzer Prize	the flag	tissue

4. Capitalize the official name of an academic course but not the general subject matter unless that subject is itself a proper noun, as in the case of languages.

Chemistry 301 *but* He is studying chemistry.
French 211 *and* I enjoy my French class.

42h SINGLE LETTERS

Capitalize the pronoun *I*, the interjection *O*, letters used to designate grades in a course, letters used to define a following noun, letters used to designate musical notes, and letters used to designate major keys in music (letters indicating minor keys are not capitalized).

A-line skirt	Vitamin A	C major
V-neck	T square	c minor

Capitalize letters of abbreviations if the words for which they stand would be capitalized when spelled out. (Some abbreviations, however, are always capitalized even though the full words for which they stand are not capitalized.) Always capitalize *A.D., B.C., R.S.V.P.,* and the abbreviations for time zones. Capitalize, too, the first letter of abbreviations for chemical elements. The abbreviations for academic degrees are capitalized even if they do not follow names. Finally, capitalization of the abbreviation for the word *number* is optional.

A.D. 14 (anno Domini 14)
R.S.V.P. (Répondez s'il vous plaît)
EST (Eastern standard time)
NaCl (sodium chloride)
B.A. in Fine Arts (a bachelor's degree in fine arts)
No. 20 *or* no. 20

TROUBLESHOOTING

1. Do not capitalize the first word of a sentence inserted *within* another sentence by means of dashes or parentheses.

We got the old heap loaded with our worldly goods—it squeaked and groaned with every added box—and struck out to find fame and fortune in the wilds of Kentucky.

2. Do not capitalize the first word of the second part of a direct quotation divided by the words *he said* (or their equivalent) unless the second part begins a new sentence.

"Spencer managed to trip over the cuff of his jeans," Lorraine giggled, "and he fell into that vat of blue dye."
"Spencer managed to trip over the cuff of his jeans," Lorraine giggled. "His falling into that vat of blue dye was one of the funniest accidents I've ever seen."

3. Do not capitalize occupational titles that appear *after* a person's name.

Edward Kennedy, senator from Massachusetts
Elena Sanchez, our new club president

4. Do not capitalize the general names of occupations or of social and academic classes.

She is studying to be a doctor.
He will have to decide upon his major by the end of his sophomore year.
He is a member of the British upper class.

5. Do not capitalize the names of the points of the compass unless these names refer to specific geographic regions.

We drove south for the first 250-mile leg of our trip to the West.

6. Do not capitalize the names of the seasons of the year; the words *world, sun, moon, universe,* or *star*; or the word *earth* unless it is being used as the name of a planet in contrast with other planets.

The sun rose at 5:15 a.m. yesterday.
She claims to be able to read the stars.
How much of the earth's surface is covered with water?
What is the distance between Mars and Earth?

7. Do not capitalize the names of centuries or the names of most general historical periods. Check your dictionary for the capitalization of historical periods. Tradition rather than logic determines the capitalization rules for historical periods.

the twentieth century   the nuclear age
the Dark Ages   the Restoration
the Romantic Movement

8. Do not capitalize the terms for diseases, conditions, medical tests, and so on, unless the term contains a proper name.

smallpox   Schick test
rabies   Parkinson's disease

NAME _____ DATE _____

DIRECTIONS: In the following sentences, rewrite the words which need capitalization above the incorrect words.

EXAMPLE: ~~during~~ my trip to ~~new york~~, I visited the ~~museum~~ of ~~modern~~
During   *New York*   *Museum Modern*

~~art~~, the ~~statue~~ of ~~liberty~~, and the ~~bronx botanical gardens~~.
Art   Statue   Liberty   Bronx Botanical Gardens

1. "don't forget what alexander pope wrote in his poem *an essay on criticism*,"

   warned elsa. "he's the one who said, 'good-nature and good-sense must ever

   join; / to err is human, to forgive divine.'"

2. islam, also called mohammedanism, is a monotheistic religion whose one god

   is allah and whose central beliefs are set forth in the koran, the divine truth

   revealed to mohammed (570?-632).

3. igor stravinsky, the famous russian composer, greatly influenced the trends of

   modern symphonic music by employing complex, often dissonant tones and

   rhythms in such works as *the firebird* (1910) and *rites of spring* (1913).

4. plant-eating dinosaurs were often attacked by flesh-eating ones like the tyran-

   nosaurus, a beast that lived during the cretaceous period of the mesozoic era.

5. the flight of *apollo IV* had been scheduled for 6:36 a.m. (est), but blast-off

   was delayed after about 1,000 protesters, mostly cubans who lived near the

   space center, had a confrontation with guards from the nearby army base.

6. "i was really scared that i had diabetes or something," sally confessed, "when

   dr. bertland asked me to have a glucose-tolerance test."

7. as the strains of "amazing grace" poured forth from the rural baptist church, fran reflected on her protestant upbringing in the south and wondered how she would like living in the north and working at her new job in buffalo.

8. after the assassination of julius caesar on the ides of march in 44 b.c., marc antony and octavian, caesar's eighteen-year-old heir, controlled the roman army and, thus, the roman empire for more than ten years.

9. the ptolemaic philosophy of the universe—it taught that earth was a stationary mass at the center of crystalline spheres within which the sun and the planets moved—was being seriously questioned by the end of the middle ages.

10. dixie had never worked until she was a junior at the university, and then the only job she could find was a part-time position in the chemistry laboratory.

11. in the sixteenth century a young scientist named andreas vesalius, a native of brussels, became the father of modern anatomy, dissecting human cadavers before his students' eyes and publishing his findings in *the fabric of the human body*.

12. arthur baker, chairman of the local theater's board of directors, hosted a dinner for the cast of *equus* on the last saturday of the play's run.

13. the front-runner for the office of adjutant general in the state was eston marchbanks, a general in the army reserves.

14. the golden arches of mcdonald's were visible from i-26, evoking a chorus of howls for hamburgers and milkshakes from four small, squirming backseat travelers.

43/ABBREVIATIONS

Although many abbreviations are not acceptable in formal writing, they are useful in informal writing. Periods follow most abbreviations, but acronyms (abbreviations made up of the first letter or letters of each word of a series of words) are often spelled without them. The dictionary indicates whether or not an abbreviation or acronym is spelled with periods.

43a ABBREVIATIONS TO USE

1. Always abbreviate the following titles before personal names: *Mr., Mrs., Ms., Dr.,* and *St.* and *Ste.* (for Saint and Sainte). Always abbreviate *Junior* and *Senior* and titles of degrees when they immediately follow full personal names. Separate the name from the abbreviation with a comma.

William E. Cely, Sr.   William E. Cely, Ph.D.

2. Always abbreviate the following expressions of time and temperature when they are accompanied by a numeral.

p.m.	11:46 p.m. *or* 11:46 P.M.
a.m.	9:10 a.m. *or* 9:16 A.M.
EST (Eastern standard time)	CST (Central standard time)
MST (Mountain standard time)	PST (Pacific standard time)
A.D. (anno Domini)	A.D. 435 (A.D. precedes the year.) in the sixth century A.D.
B.C. (before Christ)	435 B.C.
35°C. (centigrade or Celsius)	35°F. (Fahrenheit)

However, do not use these abbreviations unless they are accompanied by a number.

INCORRECT	They are leaving for Florida tomorrow a.m.
CORRECT	They are leaving for Florida tomorrow morning.
CORRECT	They are leaving for Florida at 9:30 a.m. tomorrow.

43b ABBREVIATIONS TO AVOID

1. Do not abbreviate the first or last names of persons unless these persons are best known by their initials.

O. Henry   *but*   William Sydney Porter

2. Do not abbreviate the names of countries, states, cities, towns, or streets in general writing.

INCORRECT	She hopes to vacation in Fla. this winter.
CORRECT	She hopes to vacation in Florida this winter.

3. Do not abbreviate the names of months, days, or holidays.

INCORRECT	Are you visiting me on Mon. or Tues.?
CORRECT	Are you visiting me on Monday or Tuesday?

4. Do not abbreviate the names of parts of a written work. Use *volume*, not *vol.*; *chapter*, not *ch.* or *chap.*; and so on.

| INCORRECT | Turn to Chap. 5. |
| CORRECT | Turn to Chapter 5. |

5. In nontechnical writing, terms for measurement should not be abbreviated. Use *foot*, not *ft.*; *ounce*, not *oz.*; *teaspoon*, not *tsp.*; and so on. In technical writing, however, such abbreviations are often acceptable.

| INCORRECT | She lost fourteen lbs. in a month. |
| CORRECT | She lost fourteen pounds in a month. |

6. Symbols such as &, ¢, %, =, +, @, or # should not be used in general writing although they are acceptable in business writing, in technical writing, and in tables that are used in nontechnical writing.

| INCORRECT | I hear that the soap now costs 50¢ a bar. |
| CORRECT | I hear that the soap now costs 50 cents a bar. |

7. Do not use such abbreviations as *gov't, con't, co.,* or *inc.*

| INCORRECT | He was named president of the co. |
| CORRECT | He was named president of the company. |

43c SPECIAL PROBLEMS

1. Write the name of a company just as the company writes it, including abbreviations like *&, Inc.*, and *Corp.* if they are part of the official company name.

2. Do not place a period after nicknames or abbreviations that have become accepted words in their own right. Your dictionary can guide you when you are in doubt.

Rob, Ed, Rich, Pam, exam, lab, taxi

43d ACRONYMS

Very common **acronyms**—abbreviations made up of the first letter or letters of each word of a series of words—are abbreviated, even in formal writing: NATO, NFL, TVA. If the acronym or abbreviation is not well known but is used several times within a paper, spell it out when it first occurs, placing the abbreviation or acronym in parentheses just after the full name. Afterwards use the acronym or abbreviation alone.

He was active in the work of the National Association for the Advancement of Colored People (NAACP). In fact, he worked for the NAACP for many years before he died.

44/CONTRACTIONS

Contractions are a kind of abbreviation that represent the loss of a sound or syllable in speech. They are usually avoided in formal writing, except for expressing dialogue, but are often used in informal writing. When you do use contractions, be sure to place the apostrophe at the exact point where the letter or letters have been omitted.

1. Among the most frequently used contractions are those consisting of a verb and a following *not*. The word *not* is abbreviated, but the verb is *never* abbreviated.

aren't	wasn't	hasn't	mustn't
isn't	didn't	hadn't	needn't
weren't	don't	can't	oughtn't
won't	doesn't	couldn't	shouldn't
wouldn't	haven't	mightn't	

2. Another common type of contraction is composed of a pronoun and an auxiliary verb (such as *be, have, will*). The verb is abbreviated, but the pronoun is *never* abbreviated.

I'd	you'd	he'd	who'd
I'm	you're	he's	who's
I've	you've	she'd	who've

3. Other pronouns and noun subjects also form contractions with *is* and *has*. Here, too, the full form of the subject is followed by *-'s*.

Everyone's gone home. = Everyone has gone home.
Marjorie's a good sport. = Marjorie is a good sport.

In spelling out contractions in formal papers, be sure to use the correct full form. Some contractions stand for different full forms: Both *is* and *has* are contracted as *-'s,* and both *had* and *would* are contracted as *-'d.*

He's late again. = He is late again.
He's done it again. = He has done it again.
I'd rather not go. = I would rather not go.
I'd better not go. = I had better not go.

NAME _____ DATE _____

DIRECTIONS: Rewrite the following sentences, abbreviating words incorrectly spelled out and spelling out abbreviations and contractions incorrectly used in formal essay writing.

EXAMPLE: Mister Roberts is going to Ariz. for the gov't. seminar.

Mr. Roberts is going to Arizona for the government seminar.

1. When Randolph E. Jones, Senior, arrived at the L.A. airport, he hailed a taxi to rush him to the corp. headqtrs. on Perriman Blvd., where he was to confront the major stockholders of Avakian Media, Inc.

   _____

   _____

2. Although the thermometer registered only 78°F., the tourists swarming around the Smithsonian Inst. and other popular attractions in Wash. were fanning themselves and flocking to every available patch of shade and air-condition'd lobby.

   _____

   _____

3. Sen. Brown, concerned about the economic power of the OPEC cartel, proposed that the gov't hire several top scientists to study the potential of solar & nuclear energy.

   _____

   _____

4. Doctor Samuel N. Bernstein, one of the leading pediatricians in the U.S., was asked to head a UNICEF team being sent to the disaster areas in S. America.

   _____

   _____

5. By Nov. 3 both the FBI and IRS were sure that Dr. Bowen hadn't been able to leave N.Y. and that they'd be able to locate him within a few days.

   _____

   _____

6. In preparation for her Xmas baking, Mrs. Wilson had bought fifteen lbs. of white and brown sugar, 200 ft. of foil wrap, and two gals. each of sherry and brandy.

_____

_____

7. Sgt. Simmons, declared A.W.O.L. by Col. Peters when he didn't appear for either Mon. drill or Tues. duty, was cleared of the charge after he was found trapped in a storage closet with 100 gals. of green paint.

_____

_____

8. Walt couldn't believe his eyes: paycheck #1246836, bearing his name, totaled 67¢, though the computer had paid $268 to the IRS and FICA.

_____

_____

9. *A History of Amor* by Edwin Appleton et al. is extremely entertaining though the authors should've directed more of their energy toward the accuracy of their information, especially in Chaps. 1, 4, & 6.

_____

_____

10. He'd been gone about two hrs. when Doctor Mason got a call from the S. Dak. highway patrol asking for information about his whereabouts.

_____

_____

11. In over 50% of the interviews, inmates of the Southgate Correctional Inst. said that they'd been abused or neglected as children.

_____

_____

12. The people who've moved into the old Smith house don't seem to care that their grass is two ft. high or that they're the only ones on Dellwood Ave. who have a yard full of trash.

_____

_____

45/NUMBERS

Deciding whether to spell out numbers or to write them as figures poses problems because different kinds of writing have different conventions about the form numbers should take. Figures predominate in more technical kinds of writing such as papers on scientific experiments or mathematics. In very formal writing like wedding invitations, certificates, or highly formal essays, all numbers are usually spelled out.

The rules for usage of numbers vary so much that the best rule is consistency throughout a given paper. There are, however, some conventions that serve as guides in the use of numbers.

45a WHEN TO SPELL OUT NUMBERS

Spell out numbers that can be expressed in one or two words. (Many people prefer to write out numbers through ten and use figures for numbers over ten.)

Numbers that begin sentences, regardless of the length of the number or its relationship to other numbers in the sentence, should be spelled out. (Often rephrasing the sentence so that it does not begin with a number makes it less awkward.)

INCORRECT	25 years ago I came to live in New York City.
CORRECT	Twenty-five years ago I came to live in New York City.
CORRECT	I came to live in New York City 25 years ago.

Approximate or indefinite expressions of number should always be spelled out.

The Vaughans had owned that store for over a hundred years.

45b WHEN TO USE FIGURES

1. Use figures to express streeet numbers, room or apartment numbers, telephone numbers, amounts of money, the temperature, percentages, sports scores, Social Security or other identification numbers, air flight or train numbers, ZIP codes, television channel numbers, page numbers, chapter numbers, and volume numbers.

He lives at 780 Riverside Drive, New York, New York 10032.
She owes me $250.
Channel 13 is my favorite television channel.
Turn to page 211 in Chapter 7.

2. Use figures to express numbers before an abbreviation of any kind.

48°7'W   3 kg
8 mm film   60 mph

3. Use figures to express mixed whole numbers and fractions or numbers with a decimal point.

She is 3½ hours late.
I'm getting 7.5 percent interest on my time deposit at the bank.

4. Use figures in tabular material and in numbering lists or series.

5. Use figures to show a distinction between one set of numbers and another set within the same context.

Buy three 4-ply sheets and six 2-ply sheets.

6. Use figures before *a.m.* and *p.m.* in expressions of time. When, however, the number comes before *o'clock* or is used with phrases like *half past, a quarter after, twenty of,* and *in the morning,* which do not employ decimals, spell out the number.

3:00 p.m.   three o'clock
4:15 a.m.   a quarter after four

7. There are several conventional ways to express dates.

January 20, 1921
20 January 1921 (No comma if the day precedes the month)

When, however, the day precedes the month and no year is given, spell out the number.

January 20th *but* the twentieth of January

Avoid, however, *January 20th, 1921* or *January twentieth, 1921.*

45c INCLUSIVE NUMBERS

Inclusive numbers indicate a series of continuing dates or pages. With inclusive numbers, it is always correct to write the full figure for both the beginning and ending number of a series. However, if the number is over 110, those digits of the ending number that are identical to digits of the beginning number can be omitted when the inclusive numbers are connected by a hyphen. Numbers in the units and tens positions must always be repeated.

194–1968 *or* 1964–68   pages 331–339 *or* 331–39

Full figures should be written if the words *from* and *to* are used. Do not combine *from* with a hyphen.

INCORRECT   from 1964–68
INCORRECT   from 1964-1968
CORRECT   from 1964 to 1968

45d ORDINAL NUMBERS

Ordinal numbers are those that indicate the order of the numbers rather than amounts: *first, second, third,* and so on. **Cardinal numbers** indicate amounts: *one, two three,* and so on. Most ordinals are formed by adding *-th* to the number: *seventh, tenth, hundredth,* though some have irregular spellings (*first, second, third*). When a cardinal number ends in *-y,* change the *-y* to *-i* and add *-eth* (*twentieth, thirtieth*).

Most ordinals are abbreviated by adding *-th* to the figures (*5th, 20th, 100th*), but the abbreviated forms of the ordinals for *one, two,* and *three* are irregular (*1st, 2nd, 3rd*). No periods are used after the abbreviations for ordinals.

Ordinals may be used as nouns, adjectives, or adverbs without any change in form. Adding an *-ly* when using them as adverbs is unnecessary.

Sheila got the scholarship because, first (not *firstly*), her grade point ratio was the highest and, second (not *secondly*), because she worked constantly and effectively in ten different organizations on campus.

Although the rules for spelling out ordinals are generally the same as those for cardinals, spell out ordinals, even large ones, when indicating governmental units, military groups, and religious organizations (*the First Baptist Church, the Thirty-ninth Congress*).

45e ROMAN NUMERALS

The figures we usually employ to express numbers (1, 2, 58, 411) are called **Arabic numerals**. **Roman numerals** are letters used as numbers. Only seven letters, either capital or small, are used in writing Roman numerals:

I (i) = 1	C (c) = 100
V (v) = 5	D (d) = 500
X (x) = 10	M (m) = 1,000
L (l) = 50	

A line over any Roman numeral indicates that its value should be multiplied by 1,000.

$$C = 100 \qquad \overline{C} = 100,000$$

There are several basic rules for reading Roman numerals.
1. Add repeated numerals together (II = 2; XXX = 30)
2. Add numerals when a smaller number follows a larger one (VIII = 8; DLX = 560)
3. Subtract a smaller number from a larger number that follows it (IX = 9; CXL = 140)

Capital Roman numerals are used in numbering volumes, parts, and sometimes chapters of books, acts of plays, and main headings in outlines. The date of construction of a building is often indicated in Roman numerals, and publication dates in older books are often written in capital Roman numerals. Small Roman numerals are used for preliminary pages in books (for example, introductions, tables of contents), scenes in plays, and fifth-level headings in outlines.

Volume IV of the *Cambridge Ancient History*   on p. iv of the Preface

Part XI, Chapter I   *As You Like It*, III:i

NAME _____ DATE _____

PART A

DIRECTIONS: Rewrite the following sentences and correct numbers incorrectly expressed. Put a *C* before correct sentences.

EXAMPLE: _____The lawyer met 2 of the defendants in the case at ten a.m. on Friday.

The lawyer met two of the defendants in the case

at 10 a.m. on Friday.

_____ 1. According to the police, the letter, postmarked twenty-three March 1978, had been typed using 4 different typewriters.

_____

_____

_____ 2. Although John had assured Kate that he would pick her up promptly at five p.m., at seven o'clock he had still not arrived.

_____

_____

_____ 3. Although the 3 top players were out with injuries, the Red Raiders kicked a field goal in the final two seconds to win the soccer match three to two.

_____

_____

_____ 4. Live performances of the ten major ballet companies in the country are televised each Wednesday at 9 o'clock on channel seven.

_____

_____

_____ 5. Although they had planned to build a twelve-room ranch-style home, Patti and Michael bought a sixty-one-thousand-dollar house that was over 100 years old.

_____

_____

_____ 6. Anna figured that since her 2 roommates had moved into the apartment the water bill had risen forty percent and the electricity bill twenty percent.

_____

_____

_____ 7. 32 parks in northern Florida and southern Georgia were closed to the public for about 6 months while zoologists searched for representatives of 7 species of birds feared near extinction.

_____

_____

_____ 8. In this small western town, booming with the construction of 3 nearby power plants, a newcomer would have to pay one hundred and ten thousand dollars for a 2,200-square-foot house if the cost was fifty dollars a square foot.

_____

_____

PART B

DIRECTIONS: Translate the following Roman numerals into figures.

1. CDIX   _____

2. CCLXIV   _____

3. MCDXIV   _____

4. DCDXLIX   _____

5. MMCMXLI   _____

258

46/SPELLING

Most people have some words that they can never spell correctly, but careful writers keep a dictionary close by and use it often. Poor spellers always ask, "How should I know to look up a word if I don't know that it's misspelled?" Such a question usually exaggerates the writer's inability to spell, however, for people who really want to improve their spelling usually can find a pattern to the kinds of words they misspell, words they learn to check in the dictionary until they are finally sure of the correct spelling.

One good way to help overcome spelling problems is to keep a small notebook handy to use in listing words you have misspelled in your writing. Write the correct spelling in your notebook for future reference, and you will soon have a list of your own most frequently misspelled words to review in your spare time. You can also develop your own devices, or "crutches," to help with troublesome words. For example, the crutch "*a rat* lives in the middle of *separate*" will help you remember how to spell *separate*, often misspelled as *seperate*. A third way to improve your spelling is to study carefully a few rules that can help with words that are a particular problem for you.

46a SPELLING AND PRONUNCIATION

Many spelling errors result from the fact that there is a poor correspondence in English between spelling and pronunciation. Particularly troublesome words are those that have certain letters or combinations of letters.

1. Silent letters (knee, psychiatrist, island, filet, bomb)

2. Letters omitted through incorrect pronunciation (quantity, government, surprise, mathematics)

3. Letters added through incorrect pronunciation by analogy with other words.

INCORRECT	CORRECT
atheletic	athletic
forrest	forest
priviledge	privilege
similiar	similar

4. Letters, both vowels and consonants, that are pronounced the same but spelled differently in different words

cheese/breeze	agony/lavatory
promotion/admission	desperate/admirable

5. Letters that are transposed, or reversed, in slurred pronunciation or letters that are silent and are transposed because the writer cannot remember where the silent letter goes

INCORRECT	INCORRECT
perrogative	prerogative
revelant	relevant
sutble	subtle

46b FOUR STANDARD SPELLING RULES

Although each of the four following rules has exceptions, all are helpful.

1. **-ie- and -ei-.** If the sound is long *e*, as in *bee*, then *i* precedes *e*, except after *c*. After *c*, the spelling is *ei* (*priest, thief, conceive*).

Exceptions include *seize, weird, caffeine, protein, codeine, financier*, and (if long *e* is used in the pronunciation) *either, neither, leisure.*

If the sound is not long *e* but is another sound, especially long *a*, as in *day*, then *e* precedes *i* (*eight, rein, neighbor*). Exceptions are *friend, sieve, mischief.*

If the *i* and the *e* are pronounced as two separate vowels, the rule does not apply (*fiery, science*). If *c* is pronounced like *sh* in *she*, then *i* precedes *e* (*ancient, sufficient*).

2. **Changing final -y to -i.** When a word ends in -*y* preceded by a consonant, change the *y* to *i* before adding a suffix. If the suffix begins with *i*, however, keep the *y*, except before the suffix -*ize* (crafty/craftiness; vary/varying; agony/agonize).

If the *y* is preceded by a vowel, *y* does not change to *i* (annoy/annoyance; gray/grayish).

Exceptions to the rule include (a) the plural forms of proper names ending in -*y* do *not* change -*y* to -*i*- (*Larrys, Henlys*), (b) a few short words in which -*y* is preceded by a vowel *do* change -*y* to -*i*- before some endings (*pay/paid; day/daily*), and (c) a few short words ending in -*y* vary in their spelling with suffixes.

    dry/dryness *but* dryer *or* drier
    sly/slyness *but* slyest *or* sliest

3. **Dropping final -e.** If a word ends in a consonant followed by a silent -*e*, drop the -*e* before endings beginning with a vowel but keep -*e* before endings beginning with a consonant (*fate: fatal, fateful*).

Exceptions include (a) the words *acreage, awesome, mileage, ninth, wholly, dyeing* (from *dye*), and *singeing* (from *singe*); (b) words in which *c* and *g* have a "soft" pronunciation: *noticeable, courageous*; (c) words ending in -*dge* before the suffix -*ment: acknowledgment, judgment*; (d) words ending in -*ue: argue/argument, true/truly*; (e) words ending in -*oe* before the suffix -*ing: shoe/shoeing, canoe/ canoeing.*

4. **Doubling consonants.** If, after the suffix has been added, the stress is on the last syllable before the suffix *and* if the last consonant is preceded by a single vowel, double the consonant before adding a suffix that begins with a vowel (*occur: occurred, occurring, occurrence*).

Do not double the consonant before a suffix beginning with a consonant (*man/manhood*). Do not double the consonant if it is preceded by another consonant (*harm/harmless*). Never double the letter *x* (*mix/mixing*).

Do not double the consonant if it is preceded by two vowels (*roar/roaring*).

Exceptions to these rules include (a) regardless of where the stress is, many words ending in -*l* vary in their treatment: the final -*l* may be unpredictably doubled (*excel/excellence*) or the word may be correctly spelled either with or without doubling the -*l* (*revel/reveled* or *revelled*); (b) except for -*ing* and -*ish*, suffixes beginning with -*i*- usually do not double the preceding consonant.

    hop/hopping   moral/morality
    snob/snobbish   addict/addictive

1. Most nouns form their plurals and most verbs their third-person singular present tense by adding *-s* to the stem, even if the word ends in *-a*, *-i*, and *-u* (*skis*, *cabanas*, *jumps*).

2. Words ending in *-ch*, *-s*, *-sh*, or *-x* add *-es* to form the plural or third-person singular if, in speech, the ending makes an extra syllable (*catches*, *flashes*, *taxes*, *kisses*). One-syllable words ending in a single *-s* or a single *-z* preceded by a vowel may double the final consonant before adding *-es*, but you should check your dictionary because practice varies (*quizzes*, *gases* or *gasses*).

3. Verbs ending in *-f* or *-fe* add *-s*, but some nouns add *-s*, other nouns drop the *-f* or *-fe* and add *-ves* (*beliefs*, *knives*, *chiefs*), and some nouns form plurals either way (*scarfs* or *scarves*). Check your dictionary to be sure.

4. Follow your dictionary on words ending in *-o*. Some nouns and verbs ending in *-o* preceded by a consonant add *-es*, some add *-s*, and some take either (*potatoes*, *memos*, *volcanos* or *volcanoes*).

5. Most compound words form their endings according to the rules for the last element of the compound (*outdoes*, *sit-ins*), but a few compounds in which a noun is the first and most important element add a plural to the first element instead of the second (*brothers-in-law*, *ladies-in-waiting*, *passersby*).

6. A few words have irregular plurals (*mouse/mice*, *tooth/teeth*, *child/children*, *man/men*).

7. Words borrowed from other languages often retain their plurals or have an alternative English plural (*cactus/cacti*, *crisis/crises*, *datum/data*, *phenomenon/phenomena*, *plateau/plateaux* or *plateaus*, *larva/larvae*, *appendix/appendices* or *appendixes*, *stigma/stigmata* or *stigmas*). Some borrowed words have the same form in the singular and plural (*corps*, *series*, *status*).

8. A few nouns have the same form in the singular and plural (*barracks*, *means*), particularly the names of kinds of wildlife (*salmon*, *fish*, *deer*). Tribal or national names from foreign countries often have the same form in the singular and plural (*Swahili*). If the word ends in *-ese*, no plural ending is added (*Japanese*).

46d PREFIXES AND SUFFIXES

Many of the most commonly misspelled words are those that consist of a prefix, a stem, and a suffix.

Prefixes. The spelling of the root word or stem is *never* changed by the addition of a prefix (<u>mis</u>interpret, <u>trans</u>act, <u>inter</u>national). Many prefixes keep their form regardless of the stem to which they are attached (*be-*, *counter-*, *dis-*, *for-*, *fore-*, *hyper-*, *inter-*, *mis-*, *out-*, *over-*, *poly-*, *post-*, *pre-*, *semi-*, *trans-*, *tri-*, *ultra-*, *un-*, *under-*, and *uni-*, for example). Other prefixes become like the first letter of the stem to which they are attached (*ad-*: <u>ad</u>mit, <u>ac</u>cept, <u>an</u>nounce, <u>ap</u>ply; *com-*: <u>com</u>pare, <u>co</u>operate, <u>con</u>tain, <u>cor</u>rect; *en-*: <u>en</u>grave, <u>em</u>brace; *in-*: <u>in</u>organic, <u>im</u>possible, <u>ir</u>regular; *ob-*: <u>ob</u>tain, <u>oc</u>cur, <u>op</u>pose; *sub-*: <u>sub</u>marine, <u>sus</u>pect, <u>sug</u>gest, <u>sup</u>port; *syn-*: <u>syn</u>thesis, <u>sym</u>metry, <u>syl</u>lable).

The most troublesome prefixes are those that are pronounced alike or nearly alike but are spelled differently.

ante-/anti-	hyper-/hypo-
en-/in-/un-	for-/force-
enter-/inter-/intra-/intro-	per-/pre-/pro-/pur-

De- and *di-* present special problems because the pronunciation is often of no assistance and because the prefixes have so many different meanings. You must learn the correct spelling for each word or check your dictionary for words beginning with these prefixes.

Suffixes. Many suffixes are troublesome because they are difficult to recognize and may even be spelled differently in different words. There are, however, a few helpful rules for spelling suffixes.

1. The suffix *-ly* (never *-ley*) is usually simply added to the word (*poor/poorly, fortunate/fortunately*). If the word ends in *-ll*, add only *-y* (*shrill/shrilly*). If the word ends in *-le* preceded by a consonant drop the *-e* and add *-y* (*humble/humbly*). An exception is *whole/wholly*.

If the word ends in *-y*, the regular rule for changing *y* to *i* applies. Exceptions are *sly/slyly, wry/wryly, day/daily*. Adjectives ending in *-ic* always take the suffix *-ally* (*basic/basically*). The one exception is *public/publicly*.

2. The suffix *-able* is used after common nouns and verbs and also for newly coined adjectives (*comfortable, patchable*). The suffix *-ible* is most often used with stems that do not occur as independent words (*compatible, legible*) and with stems that have a corresponding noun ending in *-ion* (*corruption/corruptible*).

If the stem ends in "hard" *c* or *g*, the suffix is always *-able* (*despicable, navigable*).

If the stem ends in "soft" *-ce* or *-ge*, *e* is retained before *-able*, but dropped before *-ible* (*noticeable, forcible*).

3. Many verbs and all newly formed verbs end in *-ize* (*characterize, modernize*), but if the word is a noun or can be used as a noun, it usually ends in *-ise* (*paradise, exercise*). Exceptions include the two verbs *analyze* and *paralyze* and a few verbs that end in *-ise* (*advise, rise, despise*, for example). The *z* in the endings *-ize* and *yze* is replaced by *s* when a word ending in *-ist, -istic, -ism*, or *-is* is made from the original word (*characterize/characteristic*).

4. Most adjectives end in *-al* (*final, tidal*), and nouns made from verbs usually end in *-al* (*refusal, denial*). Verbs with the meaning of repeated action end in *-le* (*sniffle, babble*).

5. The suffix *-ous* is the suffix for many words (*anonymous*). If the ending is spelled *-uous*, the *u* can be clearly heard in pronunciation (*ambiguous*). In words ending in *-ious*, either an *e* sound can be heard or a preceding *c, t*, or *x* is pronounced as *sh* or there is a preceding "soft" *g* (*copious, conscious, religious*). When *-ous* is added to words ending in *-er*, the *e* is sometimes lost, though some words may be spelled either with or without it (*wonder/wondrous, thundrous* or *thunderous*). Some adjectives are spelled with *-eous*, rather than *-ious* (*advantageous, outrageous*).

6. Before a suffix beginning with *-i, -e,* or *-y*, add *k* to words ending in *-ic* or *-ac* (*panic/panicking, frolic/frolicking*).

46e VARIANT SPELLINGS

Many words have two or even more acceptable spellings. The first spelling listed in your dictionary is always acceptable. Unless your instructor advises otherwise, use the first spelling.

NAME _____ DATE _____

DIRECTIONS: The following passage contains twenty-two spelling errors caused by the mismatch between spelling and pronunciation. Circle the misspelled words, and then spell them correctly on the lines below the passage.

I am not exagerating when I say that I can turn a simple excursion into a disasterous occasion. Two weekends ago I organized a trip to the country for five of my friends and myself. We planned to eat a picnic lunch and then explore the countryside. Lunch proseeded without acident; we spread our blanket under a hansome maple tree, ate our sandwiches, and enjoyed the rural scenery. After eating, Ellie and Joe said they perfferred to take a quiet nap, but the rest of us persuaded them to walk to a nearby hill. Although we were all prespiring by the time we reached the top, we now felt adventurous and wanted to continue down the other side and into the woods beyond. We were suprised to discover that descending the hill was even more tiring then ascending it. Marty skinned his nuckles climbing over a barbed-wire fence and began muttering about the penalties of trespassing and the dangers of lockjaw. But we trudged on toward the woods. As we scrambled over some rocks near the enterance to the woods, Francine asked how many of us would reconize a raddlesnake if we should see one. There was a long silence, but finally we voted to continue our expedition. As we entered the woods, we found that the underbrush was very dense and damp. Because we were all wearing either sneakers or mocassins, we decided to return to more open country.

By this time, the sky had clouded over and we could hear the rumble of thunder. We had no raingear or umberellas with us, so we all started to run back toward the car. As we panted up the hill, we realized that the lightening was very close and we were in an exposed area. Then the storm broke. Drenched by the rain and num with cold, we stumbled back over the hill and down the other side. When we reached the car, we discovered that Bobbie had somehow gotten seperated from the rest of us. Ellie had aquired a nasty-looking cut on her left arm and I had lost my perscription sunglasses. After an anxious half hour during which we imagined all kinds of facsinating tradegies, Bobbie at last appeared, limping and in a very bad mood. The next weekend we all went to Marty's house and watched television.

1. _____   9. _____
2. _____   10. _____
3. _____   11. _____
4. _____   12. _____
5. _____   13. _____
6. _____   14. _____
7. _____   15. _____
8. _____   16. _____

17. _____

18. _____

19. _____

20. _____

21. _____

22. _____

NAME _____ DATE _____

DIRECTIONS: Some of the words in the following list are misspelled, and some are spelled correctly. Every misspelled word violates one of the four standard spelling rules. If the word is misspelled, write the number of the rule that applies in the space to the left of the word and write the correct spelling in the space to the right of the word. If the word is spelled correctly, write *C* in the space to the left.

1. Rule for -*ie*- and -*ei*-
2. Rule for changing final -*y* to -*i*-
3. Rule for dropping final -*e*
4. Rule for doubling consonants

EXAMPLE: ___*1*___ decieve *deceive*

_____	1. conceited _____		_____	16. monkies _____
_____	2. chimnies _____		_____	17. changable _____
_____	3. wordyness _____		_____	18. lovly _____
_____	4. occurrence _____		_____	19. forgoten _____
_____	5. safty _____		_____	20. gleamming _____
_____	6. jinxxed _____		_____	21. fiercness _____
_____	7. peircing _____		_____	22. ninteen _____
_____	8. applyed _____		_____	23. freight _____
_____	9. duties _____		_____	24. shiping _____
_____	10. admiration _____		_____	25. believable _____
_____	11. foreignner _____		_____	26. retrieval _____
_____	12. efficeint _____		_____	27. foollish _____
_____	13. fanciful _____		_____	28. exciteable _____
_____	14. greivous _____		_____	29. truely _____
_____	15. writting _____		_____	30. puting _____

_____ 31. curlling _____   _____ 36. brieffer _____

_____ 32. fameous _____   _____ 37. beginer _____

_____ 33. nieces _____   _____ 38. emptyness_____

_____ 34. displays _____   _____ 39. lonelyer _____

_____ 35. carryed _____   _____ 40. valuable _____

NAME _____ DATE _____

PART A

DIRECTIONS: Write the correct plural form of the following singular nouns. Use a dictionary if necessary.

Example: cry _*cries*_____

1. barracks _____
2. batch _____
3. blue jay _____
4. campus _____
5. car pool _____
6. catalogue _____
7. charwoman _____
8. class _____
9. echo_____
10. father-in-law _____
11. fox _____
12. fudge _____
13. gnu _____
14. goose_____
15. gorge _____
16. fez_____
17. journey _____
18. khaki _____

19. kitchenette _____
20. knife _____
21. loaf _____
22. moustache _____
23. mouthful _____
24. parka _____
25. party _____
26. passerby _____
27. phase _____
28. proof _____
29. reef_____
30. salmon_____
31. sheriff _____
32. solo_____
33. stomach _____
34. Sunday _____
35. technique _____
36. wrench _____

PART B

DIRECTIONS: Write the correct singular form for the following plural nouns. Use a dictionary if necessary.

EXAMPLE: indices ___*index*___

1. alumnae _____

2. criteria _____

3. curricula _____

4. genera _____

5. insignia _____

6. media _____

7. memoranda _____

8. parentheses _____

9. stimuli _____

10. stomata _____

PART C

DIRECTIONS: Write the correct third-person singular present indicative form for each of the following verbs.

EXAMPLE: take ___*takes*___

1. believe _____

2. compel _____

3. defy _____

4. exercise _____

5. fix _____

6. grasp _____

7. knife _____

8. mumble _____

9. occur _____

10. overdo _____

11. realize _____

12. repay _____

13. short-circuit _____

14. stand by _____

15. unlatch _____

16. veto _____

NAME _____ DATE _____

PART A

DIRECTIONS: Underline the prefix in each of the following words. Write two words with the same prefix and another word with the same stem but a different prefix.

EXAMPLE: <u>pre</u>pare _*prefix, present*_ _*compare*_

1. admit _____

2. contain _____

3. countersign _____

4. deceive _____

5. discord _____

6. expel _____

7. foresight _____

8. inspire _____

9. interview _____

10. mistake _____

11. outsleep _____

12. overeat _____

13. perfect _____

14. postscript _____

15. proclaim _____

16. reply _____

17. subject _____

18. supervise _____

19. transfer _____

20. unnatural _____

PART B

DIRECTIONS: Combine the following words with the suffixes indicated to create new words. Make all necessary spelling adjustments.

      EXAMPLE: cool + -ly   *coolly*

1. advertise + -ment _____

2. analyze + -is _____

3. astonish + -ment _____

4. bet + -or _____

5. bid + -er _____

6. brute + -al _____

7. change + -able _____

8. commune + -ism _____

9. coy + -ness _____

10. create + -tion _____

11. defy + -ance _____

12. ethic + -ly _____

13. happy + -ly _____

14. hope + -ful _____

15. imagine + -ary _____

16. man + -ish _____

17. mercy + -less _____

18. monster + -ous _____

19. ninety + -eth _____

20. pit + -ed _____

21. plenty + -ful _____

22. prestige + -ous _____

NAME _____ DATE _____

DIRECTIONS: Use your dictionary to help you decide which of the words in parentheses, often confused with each other, is the correct choice for the blank.

EXAMPLE: The ___*effect*___ (affect, effect) of the accident was completely unexpected.

1. Although the _____ (to, too, two) sisters were _____ (to, too, two) angry _____ (to, too, two) speak to each other, they drove together for fifty miles _____ (to, too, two) the Christmas festivities at _____ (their, there, they're) parents' home.

2. _____ (Threw, Through) no fault of the rider's, Limrick _____ (threw, through) a shoe just as the members of the saddle club started _____ (their, there, they're) ride _____ (threw, through) a narrow and treacherous gorge.

3. Kent does not know _____ (weather, whether) or not he will be able to come with us to _____ (your, you're) beach house, especially if the hazardous _____ (weather, whether) continues.

4. _____ (Who's, Whose) going to sit still for three hours to _____ (hear, here) a monotonous speaker like Sam Kaufman _____ (cite, sight, site) all his opinions about ethics in industry—particularly when we have _____ (all ready, already) _____ (heard, herd) them a million times!

5. After Cleve and Sandi had hiked along the _____ (road, rode) _____ (awhile, a while), Cleve realized that _____ (anyway, any way) they proceeded when they reached the junction would lead _____ (buy, by, bye) the old rock quarry.

6. _____ (Buy, By, Bye) 2 a.m. when the _____ (affects, effects) of the drug had worn off, Giorgio was beginning to taste the sweet _____ (avenge, revenge, vengeance) he would have in confronting the enemy agents with the evidence he had managed to hide from _____ (their, there, they're) scrutiny.

7. In _____ (fiscal, physical) 1979 the company paid a _____ (capital, capitol) gains tax of $25,000.

8. "_____ (Its, It's) the _____ (principal, principle) of the thing!" shouted Todd's father. "Don't you have _____ (cents, sense, since) enough to see that everyone _____ (accept, except) you has a job—even Rob, who is still taking at least one _____ (coarse, course) each term at TEC!"

9. "Standing _____ (*their, there, they're*), only _____ (*to, too, two*) _____ (*conscience, conscious, conscientious*) of the slowly growing _____ (*hole, whole*) in the seat of my pants, I knew that disaster was _____ (*eminent, imminent, immanent*)," recited Alex, who liked nothing better _____ (*than, then*) to _____ (*poor, pore, pour*) _____ (*forth, fourth*) the details of his experiences.

10. The legislative committee _____ (*censored, censured*) Senator Mc-Fadden for his _____ (*amoral, immoral*) conduct in the Hunt case, but he maintained that he was _____ (*holey, holy, wholly*) innocent.

11. "I wish we could settle our differences with a _____ (*dual, duel*)," snarled Van, his _____ (*notable, noted, notorious*) temper raging. "Though _____ (*your, you're*) remark didn't _____ (*faze, phase*) my sister, I thought it a _____ (*flagrant, fragrant*) insult!"

12. Although Dr. Willis had _____ (*formally, formerly*) _____ (*assured, insured*) his collection of art for a large sum, he now tried to _____ (*assure, insure*) his insurance agent that his latest acquisition, a _____ (*statue, stature, statute*) of Venus, required a new policy.

13. "_____ (*Maybe, May be*) _____ (*your, you're*) _____ (*right, rite, wright, write*)," Ben said, "but I still think the _____ (*hole, whole*) _____ (*incidence, incident, instance*) _____ (*regretful, regrettable*), and I don't want to discuss it _____ (*farther, further*)."

14. Breaking into _____ (*tears, tiers*), the widow confessed to her lawyer that she was being _____ (*persecuted, prosecuted*) beyond endurance by a _____ (*troop, troupe*) of fraudulent investors, gold-digging relatives, and three unbearably _____ (*official, officious*) tax agents.

15. Following the _____ (*tortuous, tortured*) _____ (*trail, trial*), the _____ (*loan, lone*) horseman decided to _____ (*quiet, quit, quite*) his search until daybreak, so he bedded down in a _____ (*quiet, quit, quite*) secluded clearing.

16. After looking over the _____ (*cite, sight, site*), the _____ (*corps, corpse, corpus*) of dam engineers agreed that the surrounding _____ (*desert, dessert*) would _____ (*fair, fare*) better as a result of irrigation.

17. The commander's _____ (*temerity, timorousness, timidity*) in storming the village was in _____ (*vain, vane, vein*); enemy troops had already _____ (*raised, razed*) it and taken _____ (*its, it's*) inhabitants along on their _____ (*decent, descent*) from the mountain.

18. The _____ (*fatal, fateful*) accident in which Joseph Kearns died occurred when the three boys, out of _____ (*patience, patients*) with their teacher's stodginess, plotted to _____ (*perpetrate, perpetuate*) the joke of the century on him.

47/CHOOSING THE RIGHT WORDS

Diction is the choice and use of words in speaking or writing. The words we choose tell our audience a great deal about us—whether we are careful or sloppy, rude or gracious, thoughtful or silly. Good diction gives our audience the message we ourselves want to convey; it makes our words work for us. Good diction is not, however, something we learn once and for all. Even professional writers spend their entire lives experimenting with words and refining their diction. The beginning or inexperienced writer must also pay careful attention to the use of words. Most problems with diction involve appropriateness, exactness, economy, or freshness.

47a USING APPROPRIATE WORDS

What is appropriate in speech is not always appropriate in writing. For example, in speech we often say "It's him," but the appropriate form in writting is "It's he." Or we might tell a friend "Those guys really know their stuff," but in writing we would convey this message by "Those people are certainly experts."

In both speech and writing, what is appropriate diction in one situation is not necessarily appropriate in another situation. There are levels of diction, each level being appropriate for particular occasions, audiences, and topics.

Formal English is the language of most serious scholarly and technical writing. It is dignified and precise, and attempts to be as objective as possible.

> FORMAL ENGLISH
>
> It is hardly surprising, then, that dance is the oldest of the arts, the one which binds us most closely to the rest of nature. The stars were wheeling in the sky, birds were dipping and gliding and the vine describing its delicate spiral when man was still an incoherent brute. It is in our blood to move and to be moved by movement. Through participation we enter into the energy-field of life itself, and through empathy we can share its mysteries. Galileo's cry "It moves!" could be echoed by the response "It dances!" For dance is structured movement, and structured movement is the basis of all existence.
> —Alexander Bland, *A HISTORY OF BALLET AND DANCE IN THE WESTERN WORLD*

This passage illustrates many of the features characteristic of much formal English: (1) precise and conservative use of words, (2) fairly long and carefully constructed sentences, (3) avoidance of colloquialisms and slang, and (4) avoidance of contractions like *it's* and *don't*. In general, formal English favors the first-person plural (*we*) or the third person (*one, he she, it, they*) over the first-person singular (*I*) or the second person (*you*). Although writers of good formal English often use "big" words, they do so only for the sake of precision, not simply to impress the reader.

Informal English is the language of most magazine articles, newspaper editorials, and many essays. It is more casual and subjective than formal English.

> INFORMAL ENGLISH
>
> On the beach you can see that we are all pretty much the same when it comes to beauty, and that the scrumptious Southern California boys and girls who pass for Americans on television are a gang of frauds.
>
> It's worth being cooked and eaten occasionally to have this truth verified. I hope any 97-pound weaklings in the audience will put down their barbells, go out to the beach and look for themselves, instead of at themselves for a change, and then wink at that voluptuous dish before it's too late. If after winking, they look, they will probably see she's not exactly voluptuous so much as a little overweight front and aft, but humanly amenable to a little companionship.   —Russell Baker, *"On the Beach," The New York Times*

This passage illustrates several features characteristic of informal English: (1) less precise use of words than formal English (for example, people are not literally *cooked and eaten* at the beach), (2) more loosely constructed sentences, (3) occasional use of colloquialisms or even slang (for example, *scrumptious* and *dish*), and (4) use of contractions (*it's* and *she's*). The use of the first-person (*I*) and the generally humorous tone here are also more characteristic of informal than of formal English.

Colloquial English is natural, conversational English. However, it is the language of speech, not of writing, and though it is not disreputable or substandard as speech, you should avoid colloquialisms in writing. Colloquial English includes fillers like "you know" and "I mean," and words are often used inexactly.

These three levels of English—formal, informal, and colloquial—overlap a great deal. Both informal and colloquial English often include **slang**, the most casual type of vocabulary, and all three levels of English may make use of **idiomatic expressions** (expressions peculiar to a language). Slang should generally be avoided in writing because most slang expressions are vague and give the impression that the writer is too lazy or unimaginative to think up something better. Examples of slang in the late 1970s are the following: "It's the pits" (a description of the worst possible situation); "I'm really frosted" (meaning "I'm angry"); "Those are bad" (*bad* meaning "good" or "stylish"). Slang is short-lived; for example, "I'm frosted" supplants earlier slang expressions like "I'm ticked off" or "I'm teed off."

The term **idiom** usually refers to accepted phrases that do not follow the regular patterns of the language or whose meanings cannot be predicted from the meanings of the separate words of which they are composed. Examples of idiomatic expressions are "I'll pick you up at eight" (this certainly doesn't imply that one person will physically move another); "pass the buck" (blame, not a deer, is at issue here); and "lose your head" (fortunately, this means only to get very excited). These examples are informal or colloquial because of the nature of the expressions, but idioms also occur in formal writing.

College writing is expected to range between high-informal and low-formal English. Avoid slang, use few colloquialisms, and avoid inconsistencies in diction, or mixing words that clearly belong at different levels of language or style.

47b USING EXACT WORDS

In any kind of writing, it is important to use *exact* words to express your meaning, not words that only approximate the meaning you intend. Synonyms often have roughly the same **denotations** (direct, literal meanings) but very different **connotations** (emotional associations that we make with the words). For example, *walk* is a word with fairly neutral connotations, but *waddle* makes us think of a fat person moving, and *amble* makes us think of a leisurely stroll. Similarly, *sauntered, strolled, shuffled,* and *hoofed it* all have different connotations, though they have similar denotations.

Do not use a thesaurus or dictionary simply to find a bigger or more impressive-looking word than the one you might ordinarily use. Thesauruses in particular give little information about connotations and, if you are not already familiar with a word that you find, you are likely to select an inexact word with the wrong connotations. For example, suppose you were writing about your annoyance at having to walk two blocks to get your mail but wanted a fancier word than *annoyance*. You might find the word *disapprobation* listed as a synonym in a thesaurus, but it would not be an exact word to express your feelings because it has connotations of censure, condemnation, blame. In general, a thesaurus should be used only to help you find words you already know but cannot remember at the moment. Unfamiliar words are best learned by reading, where the context provides information about the connotations.

Euphemisms are words or phrases with pleasant or neutral connotations that we use to avoid words that are distasteful. Most euphemisms in America have to do with death, bodily functions, and social problems. Some examples are *pass away* or *pass on* for *die, irregularity* for *constipation,* and *inner city* for *slum.* Generally, you should avoid euphemisms in college writing.

Doublespeak is a kind of euphemism used to hide one's own faults and deceive others. For example, when the CIA refers to assassination as "termination with extreme prejudice," it is doublespeaking. When an advertisement claims that "first quality garments are one-third off their price if perfect," the ad is using doublespeak to avoid calling the merchandise irregular or flawed.

Much poor writing is caused by the overuse of abstract and general terms. **Abstract words** refer to qualities or conditions, and **general words** refer to entire groups or classes. Such writing can be greatly improved by substituting **concrete words** (words that refer to tangible, material things) and **specific words** (words that refer to particular, limited examples of a group or class).

ABSTRACT	GENERAL	CONCRETE	SPECIFIC
physical fitness	exercise	tennis	my daily singles game
youth	young people	preteens	Gilda, an eleven-year-old

Although abstract and general words are necessary for introducing and summarizing a topic and in classification and definitions, you should be as specific and concrete as possible when writing the body of your essays. Overly general writing is dull and unimaginative, and overly abstract writing is so vague that the reader often wonders what the point of it is.

OVERLY ABSTRACT	Joshua often rebels against authority.
IMPROVED	Joshua often bites his teacher.
OVERLY GENERAL	The woman behaved very strangely.
IMPROVED	The tiny brunette put on two pairs of glasses and then began to tear pages out of her *TV Guide* and chew them slowly and methodically.

47c USING WORDS ECONOMICALLY

To keep your writing economical, or concise, do not use more words or bigger words than you need to say what you want to say. The simplest and plainest words are usually best.

Avoid **deadwood,** or unnecessary words, by going through your first drafts and eliminating everything that is not essential to meaning and tone. Phrases like "I think," "in my opinion," and "it seems to me" are redundant because if you are the author, whatever you are writing is obviously your opinion and need not be pointed out as such. Overuse of the expletives *it* and *there* and the use of omnibus words bring about wordy prose. **Omnibus words,** words that are general and abstract and rarely add any information, include *aspect, case, fact, factor, thing, type, quality, sort, manner, kind, crucial, fine, nice, great, important, significant, basically,* *definitely, rather, somewhat,* and *very.* Get into the habit of replacing these words with specific, concrete words.

DEADWOOD   The fact is that there was a sort of nice quality about the neighborhood and this was basically the most important factor in our decision to move there.

IMPROVED   We decided to move into the neighborhood because it seemed so friendly and easy-going.

Circumlocution is the type of deadwood that results from using big words or long phrases instead of simple words.

CIRCUMLOCUTION   I have not yet been informed whether my request for an extension of the deadline for the paper has been reviewed favorably by my instructor or not.

IMPROVED   I still do not know whether I can turn my paper in late.

Also avoid **tautology**, or the unnecessary repetition of a concept. Tautology results, for example, when a noun is modified by an adjective that means the same thing as the noun does (*cold ice, necessary essentials*). But tautology is not limited to nouns and adjectives.

TAUTOLOGY   In his personal opinion, 8:00 p.m. at night is too late an hour for supper.

IMPROVED   In his opinion, 8:00 p.m. is too late for supper.

47d USING FRESH WORDS

Like vegetables, words are always more appealing when they are fresh. Writers achieve fresh diction not by inventing new words but by avoiding clichés, vogue words, nonce words, and "fine" writing.

Clichés are overused, ready-made expressions that both speakers and writers use without thinking much about them. Most clichés were imaginative expressions when they were first invented, but by being used over and over again, they have become tired and worn out. Chances are that if one word that pops into your mind suggests an entire phrase, you have a cliché; instead of using it, try to think of another expression or phrase. There are a number of clichés that we use on almost a daily basis.

work like a dog	hustle and bustle
last but not least	wear and tear
all work and no play	facts of life
pride and joy	sigh of relief
short and sweet	crack of dawn
quick as a wink	white as snow
black as the ace of spades	easier said than done
better late than never	like a bull in a china shop
green with envy	sweet sorrow
vicious circle	happy medium
sneaking suspicion	face the music
crying shame	soft place in my heart

it goes without saying	burn the midnight oil
as a matter of fact	believe it or not
needless to say	first and foremost

Of course, there are dozens more than the ones listed. Many come from the Bible or are quotations from famous authors; others are proverbs.

Vogue words are words or expressions that suddenly become popular but that after being used and overused for a brief period of time fall out of favor again. Current vogue words and phrases are *clout, ego trip, input*, and *to orchestrate*. Avoid vogue words because they are unoriginal and are the mark of a lazy writer.

Nonce words are words made up on the spur of the moment. Most are formed when one part of speech is made into another by the addition of suffixes such as *-ize, -ish, -ment, -tion, -y*.

NONCE WORD We wanted to <u>perpetualize</u> the tradition of a yearly reunion.

CORRECT We wanted to <u>perpetuate</u> the tradition of a yearly reunion.

Rather than making up a nonce word, find a word in the dictionary that has the precise meaning you wish to express.

Fine writing, sometimes called **flowery writing**, should be avoided. Big words and long, rambling, overly "poetic" sentences do not impress intelligent readers.

FINE WRITING Like a wondrous pink machine, the muscles pulled back, the pink skin lifted high over John's cheekbones, and the pearly white of his teeth became visible.

MEANING John smiled.

47e FIGURES OF SPEECH

Figures of speech are expressions in which words are used not in their literal sense but to add freshness and vividness to writing.

Metaphors and **similes**, the most familiar figures of speech, are alike in that both compare dissimilar things. However, while a metaphor states that *X* is *Y* ("the sky is a blue umbrella"), a simile says that *X* is like *Y* or *X* appears to be *Y* ("the sky is like a blue umbrella").

Dead metaphors are proverbial expressions and clichés that have been so overused that we often do not even think of them as metaphors. For example, the sentence "You are a jewel to carry the ball for me like this" contains two dead metaphors, *jewel* and *carry the ball*. A **mixed metaphor** is the use of several different and incompatible comparisons in one construction.

MIXED METAPHOR Just like <u>a bolt of lightning</u>, <u>the handwriting on the wall</u> was suddenly <u>as clear as a bell</u> to Eugene.

Strained metaphors and similes are the result of comparing two things that do not share enough common characteristics or of making comparisons that give the wrong connotations.

STRAINED METAPHOR Frank's stomach is <u>a vacuum cleaner that sucks up all the food in sight</u>.

STRAINED SIMILE Lori's eyes looked <u>like two big brown bowling balls</u>.

47f TONE AND POINT OF VIEW

Tone is the attitude that we, as writers, express toward our subject, our reader, and even ourselves. **Point of view** is the position from which we see our subject. Both tone and point of view are reflected in our choice of words as well as in the information we include—or fail to include. Tone and point of view should be established at the beginning of the paper and should remain consistent throughout it. The proper tone and point of view for any piece of writing depends on the topic, the purpose of the writing, and the audience. Whatever the topic and audience, however, avoid excesses of tone. That is, do not be overly sarcastic, overly sentimental, or overly personal.

Compare the difference in tone and point of view in the following two passages discussing the effects of the Black Death in the fourteenth century.

> The effect on both urban and peasant life was great, but by no means cataclysmic—it increased existing tendencies under new strains, and not least in Germany, where in the frantic panic there swept across most of the land the atrocious outburst of massacres of the hated Jews, accused of causing the plague. The major part of their settlements were exterminated, while the remnant fled eastward. Throughout Europe there was the debasement which follows great disasters: for a while men were more reckless, less dutiful, more callous.
> —C. W. Previté-Orton, *THE SHORTER CAMBRIDGE MEDIEVAL HISTORY*

> The hostility of man proved itself against the Jews. On charges that they were poisoning the wells, with intent "to kill and destroy the whole of Christendom and have lordship over all the world," the lynchings began in the spring of 1348 on the heels of the first plague deaths. The first attacks occurred in Narbonne and Carcassonne, where Jews were dragged from their houses and thrown into bonfires. While Divine punishment was accepted as the plague's source, people in their misery still looked for a human agent upon whom to vent the hostility that could not be vented on God. The Jew, as the eternal stranger, was the most obvious target. He was the outsider who had separated himself by choice from the Christian world, whom Christians for centuries had been taught to hate, who was regarded as imbued with unsleeping malevolence against all Christians. Living in a distinct group of his own kind in a particular street or quarter, he was also the most feasible target, with property to loot as a further inducement.
> —Barbara W. Tuchman, *A DISTANT MIRROR: THE CALAMITOUS 14TH CENTURY*

The tone of the first passage is more distant and less personal than that of the second. The author briefly states the fact of the persecution of the Jews and its result (extermination or flight eastward). The point of view is in general highly objective, although the author does reveal his opinions about the behavior of people during this period through such words as *atrocious, debasement*, and *callous*. The tone of the second passage is much more personal. The author rouses the reader's sympathy and indignation by providing specific details of the persecution and through the use of such phrases as *dragged from their houses, vent the hostility*, and *unsleeping malevolence*. The point of view is much more subjective; the author implies that she understands the motives behind people's behavior during the period.

NAME _____ DATE _____

PART A

DIRECTIONS: The following paragraph is written in formal English. Underline the words and phrases that characterize it as formal English. Then, on a separate sheet of paper, write one version of this paragraph in informal English and one version in colloquial English.

Walking along the beach, one sees as many kinds of activities as there are people frequenting the shore. Sand castles emerge from the creative fingers and plastic shovels of toddlers and their slightly older siblings. Flapping in the sea breeze, colorful umbrellas shelter pale-complexioned people of all ages who read, sleep, or watch the pedestrians, joggers, and swimmers. A young couple or two lie in the sun listening to rock music blaring from a transistor radio and, oblivious to the presence of other people, surreptitiously steal kisses from one another. Frisbees fly in the breeze, caught by suntanned girls with windblown hair or by Irish setters eager to perform for their masters. In addition, and perhaps the most fascinating characters in the tableau, there are the immaculately coiffured and fashionably attired young women. Not a hair is out of place, not a red fingernail is chipped, and not a bathing suit is damp as these models lie rigidly in the sun. The beach is indeed a parade of humanity.

PART B

DIRECTIONS: Choose one of the following topics and, on a separate sheet of paper, write three separate paragraphs of six to eight sentences each—the first in formal English, the second in informal English, and the third in colloquial English—about the topic using the same information in each paragraph.

1. Vending machines

2. Space debris

3. Company baseball teams

4. A first-grade schoolroom

PART C

DIRECTIONS: List six idioms and six examples of current slang.

      EXAMPLE: Idiom _Give him a hand._

                Slang _It's the pits._

Idioms   Slang

1. _____   1. _____

2. _____   2. _____

3. _____   3. _____

4. _____   4. _____

5. _____   5. _____

6. _____   6. _____

NAME _____ DATE _____

PART A

DIRECTIONS: On a separate piece of paper, rewrite each of the following sentences twice. Make the first revision have favorable connotations and make the second revision have unfavorable connotations. Try to avoid slang terms.

EXAMPLE: She has many pieces of old furniture.

Favorable: *She has many antiques.*

Unfavorable: *She has a lot of secondhand furniture.*

1. Miranda is an attractive girl even though she is overweight and wears unsuitable clothes.
2. An interesting-looking man walked into the shop and began looking carefully at the crystal wine glasses.
3. The professor's careful attention to grading her students' papers was widely known.
4. Leo's room was not especially tidy or clean.
5. Phillippe was a quiet person who was rarely aggressive.

PART B

DIRECTIONS: Underline euphemisms and doublespeak in the following sentences. On the line after each sentence, explain what the underlined terms really mean.

EXAMPLE: Harry's Auto Sales has a large selection of pre-owned cars.

_____

1. The Obloys have three children, but the youngest child, a girl, has a severe emotional handicap.

_____

2. Still wet with perspiration from the rigors of the game, Leroy said that he would not accept any contract that would mean a downward financial adjustment.

_____

_____

3. "That policy is no longer operative," the police chief told the mayor.

_____

_____

4. The game warden was responsible for the direct reduction of deer in the county.

_____

5. Bert, who was habitually intoxicated, always offended everyone with his halitosis and nicotine-stained dentures.

_____

_____

PART C

DIRECTIONS: Each of the following paragraphs is too general and abstract. On a separate sheet of paper, rewrite each, keeping the same overall tone but adding specific, concrete words and details. Your paragraphs should be a little longer than the originals.

> EXAMPLE: Else and Mike always have great parties. They invite a wide assortment of people and always have the most interesting food and entertainment. Going to a party at their house is loads of fun.

A party at Else and Mike's place is often like a visit to the United Nations. One is likely to meet a guru, a German scientist, and a Spanish dancer at almost any party. And the hors d'oeuvre table looks like a cover for a gourmet magazine: trays of rumaki, crêpes, and chutney are interspersed with bottles of wine. A pool tournament rages in one room, while dancers cavort on the patio. Their parties usually last until the sun comes up because no one wants to leave.

1. Mr. Ellison is a very unusual person. A bachelor, he has been known as the neighborhood eccentric for at least twenty years because of his strange habits. He even looks odd. In spite of his many peculiarities and unusual features, however, people like him.

2. The farm was exactly what we wanted. It was large enough for us to have animals, and the several barns and outbuildings were ready for use. The house was pleasant, and we loved the woods and pastures that surrounded it.

3. The Wilkins Corporation was not at all the place I had thought it would be when I accepted my job as a computer operator. People in the firm are too ambitious, and it is hard to find people who really enjoy their jobs. I can hardly keep up with all of the office politics. Lately I dread getting up and going to my job there because it is a very unpleasant situation.

NAME _____ DATE _____

DIRECTIONS: Rewrite the following sentences, eliminating deadwood, omnibus words, circumlocution, and tautology.

> EXAMPLE: There were already in existence at the time of Bob's invention three machines that basically could do the same functions that Bob's invention performed, but one feature of his invention made his invention a much more desirable machine than any of the others.
>
> *One feature made Bob's invention more de-*
> *sirable than any of the three similar machines.*

1. There is perhaps no one single natural object in nature that terrifies people yet entices them to sightsee, study, and even worship it more than that erupting mountain of fire, the volcano.

   _____

   _____

2. Because of the fact that volcanoes are basically unpredictable, neither volcanologists who study volcanoes nor the inhabitants who live in the areas around the volcanoes know how a volcano will act over a period of several years' time.

   _____

   _____

3. It is a true fact, however, that no volcanic eruption begins with a massive explosion: there are warning signals that forewarn scientists that an eruption may occur—local seismic shocks in the area around the volcano, the formation of cracks in the earth's surface, and the expulsion of gas, steam, and fragments from within the volcano to the area outside it.

   _____

   _____

   _____

4. Twenty to forty miles beneath a volcano there are reservoirs of hot magma, or melted rock, that heat and release gases that cause everything around them underneath the earth's crust to be pressurized to the point of finally exploding.

   _____

   _____

5. When the gases explode, they create a passageway, called a conduit, through the earth's crust to the surface, forcing the magma up through the newly made passage to the surface, where it becomes lava.

_____

_____

6. The situation at the time of an eruption is that when the lava reaches the surface, it cools and hardens as it covers the surrounding area around the opening.

_____

_____

7. Fine dust, which is forced into the air by the explosion, makes the air black, and gases such as carbon dioxide, hydrochloric acid, hydrofluoric acid, and hydrogen also fill the air.

_____

_____

8. Those volcanoes that have eruptions on a regular basis are called *active* volcanoes, those that erupt fairly regularly from time to time are known as *intermittent* volcanoes, those that may or may not erupt again at a future time are called *dormant*, and those volcanoes that likely will not ever erupt again are called *extinct*.

_____

_____

_____

9. Most volcanoes are found in parts of the world around great chains of mountains, and the largest chains of mountains are usually located near the seacoast.

_____

_____

10. It is true that there are many volcanoes in such places as the South Pacific islands, Japan, and the Philippines, but volcanoes also exist in the western United States, Mexico, South America, and Alaska, and they are even in the Antarctic.

_____

_____

NAME _____ DATE _____

DIRECTIONS: The following descriptions are inadequate because they are too general and abstract. Rewrite each using similes and metaphors to make the descriptions more vivid. Try not to write strained or mixed metaphors and similes.

> EXAMPLE: The trees looked beautiful swaying in the breeze, and they smelled fresh and clean.
>
> *The cherry trees swayed in the breeze like graceful dancers, and their blossoms filled the air with a scent unmatched by any expensive perfume.*

1. Ruthie and Patti were very proud and excited when they unlocked the front door of their house for the first time.

   _____

   _____

   _____

2. When they first saw their new grandson, Jim and Maria were very happy and joyful.

   _____

   _____

   _____

3. Because she does not like her teaching job and cannot get into the art schools she wants to attend, Alison is extremely frustrated.

   _____

   _____

   _____

4. When Barbara rose from her chair, the first student to give a speech in her new public speaking class, she was very nervous. Her hands were clammy and her knees felt weak.

   _____

   _____

   _____

5. Jeffrey likes all animals, for to him the company of animals is superior to that of many human beings.

_____

_____

_____

6. As she walked along the shore in the rain, Linda felt lonely and depressed.

_____

_____

_____

7. As he waited for his interview for the position of financial administrator, David was frightened and dreaded facing the panel of interviewers.

_____

_____

_____

8. Because they had never been to Europe before, Jessica and Jerome were very excited about their forthcoming four-week tour.

_____

_____

_____

9. Kate's boss was always so fussy about every little detail in her department that she had begun to dread discussing administrative problems with him.

_____

_____

_____

10. The crowd at the football game was really excited by the action on the field, and they cheered a lot.

_____

_____

48/ THE DICTIONARY

Your dictionary that you cart around only at the request of teachers and reluctant-ly consult for spelling problems is truly one of the miracles of modern civilization. It is a treasure-house of information about the history of language, shades of meaning, usage problems, grammar, pronunciation, capitalization, spelling, abbreviations, geography, biography, weights and measures, chemical elements, signs and symbols, and various alphabets.

48a COLLEGE DICTIONARIES

Although a paperback dictionary is handy to carry to class and to the library, it is still important to have a standard hard-cover college dictionary. Your family's old dictionary won't do because it will be out of date. Take the plunge. Buy your own. Browse through the standard college dictionaries to see which one is best suited to your needs. Standard college dictionaries differ in format and specialties, so choose the one most pleasing to your eye, the one easiest for you to use, the one best suited to your field of study. There are five excellent college dictionaries that you should consider.

> *The American Heritage Dictionary of the English Language*
> *Funk & Wagnalls Standard College Dictionary*
> *The Random House College Dictionary*
> *Webster's New Collegiate Dictionary*
> *Webster's New World Dictionary of the American Language*

All of these are frequently updated, so be sure to buy the latest printing. After buying your dictionary, don't just put it on your bookshelf. Read the introductory material so that you will understand how to get the most from each entry.

48b UNABRIDGED DICTIONARIES

Although your college dictionary should be sufficient for most of your needs, occasionally you may want to consult a larger, more extensive dictionary. The current unabridged dictionaries are usually located in the reference section of the library.

> *Funk & Wagnalls New Standard Dictionary of the English Language*
> *The Random House Dictionary of the English Language*
> *Webster's Third New International Dictionary*
> *The Oxford English Dictionary*

The last dictionary on the list, commonly abbreviated as *OED*, is an amazing tool that every college student should know something about. Its twelve volumes and several supplements record in detail the history of the English language. For each word, the dictionary names the source and the year in which the word first appeared in written English. New meanings and variations gradually added to the word are also documented by the titles and dates of works in which the particular use is to be found. Such a tool is invaluable in reading anything written before our own century. If you were to read an eighteenth-century history or philosophy text, for example, the word *nature* might be confusing unless you had consulted the *OED* to see what meaning that word had at the time when the work was written and how that definition differs from the twentieth-century definition.

49/WORDS INTO SENTENCES

Learning to write grammatically correct sentences is important, but good writing goes much further than good grammar. Learning grammar is like learning the rules to a game like backgammon or chess: once you have learned how to move the pieces, you can play the game. However, simply knowing how to move the pieces is not enough to enable you to win. You must learn the strategy of the game. The strategy of writing is called **rhetoric**. Rhetoric is the tools we employ to make our writing forceful and effective. If we ignore the importance of rhetoric, our writing will be monotonous and ineffective.

Good rhetoric, the art of using language effectively, is putting the best possible words into the kinds of sentences that are most suitable for the subject matter and for the reader. The chief components of good rhetoric are clarity, emphasis, and variety.

49a CLARITY

Clarity is the single most important quality of good rhetoric, for if your readers do not understand what they read, emphasis and variety will not help.

Sentences are made unclear by several kinds of errors.

1. Grammatical errors detract from clarity. These include incorrect pronoun reference, improper agreement, misplaced modifiers, and the like.

2. Improper punctuation (omitting punctuation where it is needed or putting it where it does not belong) confuses the reader.

3. Improper use of transitional words and careless use of coordinating conjunctions confuse readers by giving them false signals. For example, the following sentence is confusing because the word *so* makes the sentence imply that the Grand Canyon is popular today only because Major Powell explored it.

> The Grand Canyon was first explored by Major J. W. Powell in 1868, and so it is a big tourist attraction today.

4. The overuse of nouns as modifiers of nouns can be confusing, especially when several nouns in succession are used as modifiers. For example, the phrase *the bureau's winter weather prediction* is unclear because it could mean either "the bureau's weather prediction during the winter" or "the bureau's prediction of what the winter weather will be."

5. Awkwardly placed modifiers are also confusing, particularly if they are long and split up a verb phrase or separate a verb from its object or complement.

CONFUSING   The tax collector may, if taxes go unpaid for more than a year, impound personal property for sale at public auction.

REVISED   If taxes go unpaid for more than a year, the tax collector may impound personal property for sale at public auction.

6. Irrelevant details distract the reader from the main idea. Only modifiers and details that have some relationship to the main idea should be included.

> Paula, who is an excellent French student, has won national acclaim as a ballerina. (Her excellence in French is irrelevant to her success as a dancer.)

7. The overuse of long sentences, especially those with a great deal of subordination, confuses the reader. Sentences over thirty or forty words long should be broken up into shorter sentences.

8. Overreliance on speech patterns in writing may confuse the reader because what is perfectly intelligible in speech may be confusing when written.

> Despite the increase in drug traffic, the police force and treatment facilities for drug addicts have been reduced. (Although this sentence would be clear in speech, when it is first read, it seems to say that there has been an increase in drug traffic, the police force, and treatment facilities.)

49b EMPHASIS

When we speak, we emphasize certain words by our intonation and gestures, but when we write, we do not have these tools at our disposal. To achieve **emphasis** (stress on certain ideas) in writing, the writer must use such rhetorical tools as the arrangement of words in the sentence, the choice of words, and, less often, punctuation and other graphic devices.

Use the following methods to gain emphasis.

1. Graphic devices such as underlining, capital letters, and exclamation points. These add to emphasis but should be used very sparingly.

2. Careful placement of elements in the sentence. The end of a clause or sentence is usually the most emphatic position. The beginning is the next strongest position because that is where the topic is normally introduced. The middle of the sentence is the least emphatic position. Place elements you wish to emphasize either at the end or beginning of the sentence, and avoid putting less important elements in these positions.

LESS EMPHATIC	President Kennedy was killed in 1963, after he had been in office for less than three years.
MORE EMPHATIC	In 1963, after he had been in office for less than three years, President Kennedy was killed.

Placing subordinate clauses and modifying phrases before main clauses usually makes sentences more emphatic.

LESS EMPHATIC	Elmer broke four ribs when he fell off the trampoline.
MORE EMPHATIC	When he fell off the trampoline, Elmer broke four ribs.

Transitional words like *nevertheless, however, therefore*, and *furthermore* should appear at or near the beginning of a clause to ensure clarity and to avoid having them in the emphatic end position.

LESS EMPHATIC	The checks clearly were for the wrong amounts. The woman cashed all of them, nevertheless.
MORE EMPHATIC	The checks clearly were for the wrong amounts. Nevertheless, the woman cashed all of them.
MORE EMPHATIC	The checks clearly were for the wrong amounts. The woman, nevertheless, cashed all of them.

An occasional inverted sentence (a sentence in which the normal word order is changed) can add to emphasis, though you should be certain that it is grammatical and that it fits into the context. Use such inversion cautiously.

LESS EMPHATIC	Though Leslie is capable, she is lazy.
MORE EMPHATIC	Capable though Leslie is, she is lazy.

3. Use of climactic order. Put words, phrases, and clauses in an ascending order of importance with the most important points last.

UNEMPHATIC	Most of all, Evelyn wanted a college diploma, a stimulating career, and a week's vacation in a tropical resort.
EMPHATIC	Most of all, Evelyn wanted a week's vacation in a tropical resort, a college diploma, and a stimulating career.

4. Proper use of coordination and subordination. Put important ideas in main clauses and less important ideas in subordinate clauses and phrases. Avoid coordination unless ideas are really equal and you want to emphasize both ideas to the same degree.

UNEMPHATIC	Harry has grown a beard, and he looks dreadful.
EMPHATIC	Because Harry has grown a beard, he looks dreadful.

5. Avoidance of the passive voice. Unless the focus of attention is on the receiver of the action, unless the doer of the action is unknown, or unless a lengthy phrase or clause would otherwise be the subject, the active voice should be used. In some kinds of technical writing, however, it is conventional to avoid the first person (*I*), and the passive may be the only alternative.

ATTENTION ON RECEIVER	Although he disliked biology, Harvey was fascinated by physics.
DOER UNKNOWN	The notice was posted early this morning.
LENGTHY CLAUSE AS REAL SUBJECT	Norma was amazed to learn that the value of her old silver mirror was so high.
AVOIDANCE OF FIRST PERSON	After 24 hours, the contents of the beaker were again weighed.

In general, overuse of the passive creates dull, wordy writing that lacks proper emphasis.

UNEMPHATIC PASSIVE	It was stated by the chairperson that profits had been reduced by the recession.
IMPROVED	The chairperson stated that the recession had reduced profits.

6. The use of balanced sentences and parallelism. In balanced sentences, the main ideas are given equal importance. One of the chief ways of achieving balance is by parallelism, or using the same grammatical structure for all elements that have the same function.

Children begin by loving their parents; after a time they judge them; rarely, if ever, do they forgive them.

—Oscar Wilde, *A Woman of No Importance*

Poetry should surprise by a fine excess, and not by singularity; it should strike the reader as a wording of his own highest thoughts, and appear almost a remembrance.

—John Keats, *Letter to John Taylor*

7. Use of a short sentence before or after a series of longer sentences. This device adds emphasis by providing a change in pace.

> One day, late in 1904, Michael Stein announced to Gertrude and Leo that there was an unexpected balance of eight thousand francs in their account. <u>They were overjoyed.</u> It was an unexpected windfall, proving the wisdom of their having set up housekeeping together.
> —James R. Mellow, *CHARMED CIRCLE: GERTRUDE STEIN AND COMPANY*

49c VARIETY

Variety in sentence length and structure helps keep writing from becoming monotonous. No matter what the content, if all of the sentences in an essay are the same length or if they are all simple sentences or all compound sentences, the reader will lose interest. The biggest problem with variety for beginning writers is the use of too many short, choppy sentences. Such sentences make the writer seem unsophisticated.

Variety in sentence length may be achieved by **sentence combining**, or putting short sentences together in various ways.

1. Use a coordinating conjunction to make a compound sentence out of two or more simple sentences.

2. Use a subordinating conjunction to make a complex sentence out of two simple sentences.

3. Use the technique of embedding, by which a simple sentence is made into a modifier, an appositive, an absolute construction, an adjectival phrase, or an adverbial phrase within another simple sentence.

Usually a group of simple sentences can be combined in several ways. The kind of emphasis you wish to create should determine which method of combination you use.

SIMPLE SENTENCES	Niobe was proud of her many sons and daughters. She boasted about them to Leto.
COORDINATION	Niobe was proud of her many sons and daughters, and she boasted about them to Leto.
SUBORDINATION	Because she was proud of her many sons and daughters, Niobe boasted about them to Leto.
EMBEDDING	Niobe, proud of her many sons and daughters, boasted about them to Leto.

Although sentence combination is the most important method for achieving variety in sentence structure, there are several other devices that are useful in creating variety. Each of these devices is rather dramatic, however, and should be used sparingly.

1. **Rhetorical questions** are questions used for emphasis. No answer is expected.

SIMPLE SENTENCES	Everyone has heard of Leonardo da Vinci. Most people do not know that he pioneered studies of flying machines.
RHETORICAL QUESTION	Who has not heard of Leonardo da Vinci? But few people know that he pioneered studies in flying machines.

2. **Inversion** occurs when you put a complement or direct object before the subject and verb, changing the normal word order of the sentence.

SIMPLE SENTENCES
Herb gave Anne a vacuum cleaner for her birthday. She did not want a vacuum cleaner.

INVERSION
Herb gave Anne a vacuum cleaner for her birthday. A vacuum cleaner Anne did not want.

3. **Sentence fragments**, although usually unacceptable, can sometimes be used to achieve emphasis, humorous anticlimax, or transition. If you use fragments, however, it is a good idea to make a footnote identifying fragments as such so that your professor will know that you can tell complete sentences from fragments.

EMPHASIS
Ralph asked me to iron his jeans. Iron jeans!

ANTICLIMAX
Susan had learned how to change an automobile tire. Well, nearly.

TRANSITION
We have listed the charms of skunks as pets. Now for their bad habits.

DIRECTIONS: Lack of clarity in the following two paragraphs, which were written by students, detracts greatly from the ideas and feelings that the authors are attempting to express. On the lines provided, rewrite the two paragraphs to make them clear. Decide what the main point of the paragraph is and state it clearly in the first sentence. Correct errors in grammar, punctuation, and spelling. Use proper transitions, avoid using too many long sentences, and avoid overreliance on speech patterns. Use specific, concrete diction, not abstract terms or clichés; get rid of wordiness; and maintain *one* level of English throughout each paragraph.

1. Four o'clock in the morning sleeps blanketed by darkness, cushioned with emptiness, a usually peaceful part of the day, I find that it almost escapes the sense of time alltogether. Whole conceptions of night time or sleep time making so many of early morning hours block into one long hour generally slept through. Even when one is awake for these hours, distinguishing a relevence becomes unnecessary. This time is free time. All of the moments happen with gentleness, tumble about, and join together, rising and unfurling like baby ferns, opening into daylight.

_____

_____

_____

_____

_____

_____

_____

_____

_____

_____

2. Since a person is making the choice of life or death for another individual, abortion has cause alot of turmoil. Some people feel that the fetus is not an individual or really even a life, therefore abortion is alright. Others say that the fetus is indeed a life and an individual and it should not be denied the right to life. Abortion is an important issue which should not be ignored. It is just as important as the question of dying with dignity. The Edelin trials brought everyones attention to abortion and finally decided it was time to make a decision on weather or not to legalize it.

_____

_____

_____

_____

_____

_____

_____

_____

_____

_____

NAME _____ DATE _____

PART A

DIRECTIONS: Decide which sentence in each of the following pairs is the most important. Then on a separate sheet of paper rewrite the two sentences twice, making the less important sentence into a subordinate element—a clause in the first sentence and a phrase in the second.

EXAMPLE: Herman really liked being fat. Herman was terribly overweight.

subordinate clause

Although he was terribly overweight, Herman really liked being fat.

phrase

Terribly overweight, Herman really liked being fat.

1. Mr. Gilliam was fastidious about his clothing. He did not care how worn and ill-kept his shoes were.
2. Nora was always irritable. Nora never got enough sleep.
3. The newspaper carrier always seems to throw the paper into the neighbor's yard or into a puddle. Mr. Tweedel has made numerous complaints to the circulation office.
4. The woman's remarks to the clerk grew louder and uglier. The clerk sent for the manager.
5. The fire fighters finally arrived on the scene. They were confronted with one of the worst fires in the city's history.

PART B

DIRECTIONS: On a separate sheet of paper, rewrite the following sentences, replacing the unemphatic passive voice with the active voice.

EXAMPLE: Ted was given a going-away party by his friends.

Ted's friends gave him a going-away party.

1. The arrests were made by police as the result of an intensive undercover investigation.

2. Miriam was warned by her supervisor that her tardiness in reporting to work had been noticed by several staff members.

3. Because of the painstaking work that had been applied to the sculpture by the artist, he was awarded a special grant by the local artists' guild.

4. After the bird had been fed by Dora, she read for a while before the marketing was done and dinner was prepared by her.

5. After the top of the mountain had been reached by Patti and Michael, canned pudding and animal crackers were wolfed down and a long rest was enjoyed as the view was leisurely studied.

PART C

DIRECTIONS: Practice methods for achieving emphasis by writing sentences, on a separate sheet of paper, according to the specifications given for each.

> EXAMPLE: Use climactic order to achieve emphasis in a sentence explaining why a certain place appeals to you.

Table Rock State Park is among my favorite recreational places because it is close to my home, it has great nature trails, and it is incredibly beautiful.

1. Use a graphic device (underlining, capitalization, or exclamation points) to achieve emphasis effectively in a sentence that discusses the disadvantages of owning a particular kind of pet.

2. Use inversion to achieve emphasis in a sentence about dealing with a sales clerk.

3. Use climactic order to achieve emphasis in a sentence about observing or playing sports.

4. Use the passive voice effectively to focus emphasis on the subject of a sentence about the presentation of an award or scholarship to you or to someone you know.

5. Use balance and parallelism to achieve emphasis in a sentence about the difference between duty and obligation or between pride and vanity.

NAME _____ DATE _____

PART A

DIRECTIONS: Read each of the following groups of simple sentences. On a separate sheet of paper, rewrite them, using subordination, coordination, and embedding.

> EXAMPLE: My friend Joe is a most interesting person. He was in the marines for eight years. Everyone thinks that he is very tough and insensitive. Joe is actually a very tenderhearted person. He is particularly alarmed at the thought of animals being mistreated by their owners.

My friend Joe, who was in the marines for eight years, is a very interesting person. Although everyone thinks that he is very tough and insensitive, Joe is actually a very tenderhearted person who is particularly alarmed at the thought of animals being mistreated by their owners.

1. The new industry will be a tremendous asset to the Knoxville area. It will employ about 8,000 people at two sites. The employees will manufacture and market radial tires for cars. Production is expected to begin by the spring of 1983.
2. The first recorded Olympic Games were in 776 B.C. Historians believe they may have begun much earlier. The first games were 200-yard foot races. The Greeks held the games every four years. The games were held on the plains of Olympia in Elis. Within about 70 years of the first recorded games, competition was expanded to include jumping, discus throwing, javelin throwing, and wrestling. Boxing and chariot racing were added later.
3. The Olympic Games became corrupt by the fourth century A.D. The Emperor Theodosius abolished them in A.D. 394. They were not held again until 1896. Eight countries sent athletes to participate in the revived games in Athens. The revival of the games was largely the result of efforts by Baron Pierre de Coubertin of France.
4. The Olympic Games today maintain many of the Greek traditions. A runner enters the stadium to light the Olympic flame. He lights it with a torch brought from Elis, Greece, the home of the games. Many of the original games still challenge the competitors. Of course, today many new games have been added. Women have participated since 1900. The games are now divided into summer and winter competitions. The Greek spirit, however, still dominates the Olympics.

PART B

DIRECTIONS: Demonstrate variety by means other than sentence length. On a separate sheet of paper, write three paragraphs as specified.

1. Write a paragraph of from six to eight sentences in which you discuss either (1) people who are intolerably cheerful at 7 a.m. or (2) why rainy days are fun. In your paragraph use the device of inversion to create variety.
2. Write a paragraph of from six to eight sentences in which you discuss either (1) memories of your first-grade classroom or (2) yourself as a ten-year-old. In your paragraph use a rhetorical question to create variety.
3. Write a paragraph of from six to eight sentences on either (1) the appeal of science fiction or (2) the upsurge of interest in houseplants. Use a deliberate fragment as a device to create variety in your paragraph.

PART C

DIRECTIONS: Choose one of the following topics and on a separate sheet of paper write one or two paragraphs (each should be from six to eight sentences long), incorporating the following: one rhetorical question, at least three compound sentences, at least three sentences that contain subordinate clauses, one inverted sentence, at least two participial phrases, one absolute construction, and one deliberate fragment (put an asterisk after the fragment so that your instructor will know that you know you have written a fragment).

1. Space debris

2. The joys of playing Frisbee

3. The problems of the apartment dweller

4. My favorite hero

50/PARAGRAPHS

Paragraphs are conventional and essential in writing. They are both a physical and mental convenience for readers, physically providing a break that allows readers to keep their places on the page more easily and mentally signaling that one unit of thought has been completed and another is about to begin. Paragraphs also help writers to arrange their material in a logical manner.

Despite great differences among paragraphs in content, organization, and length, every good paragraph is unified, coherent, and complete.

50a UNITY

Unity in a paragraph means that all elements in the paragraph contribute to the central idea and that the paragraph is internally consistent. You should test the unity of your paragraphs by asking yourself what the idea is that your paragraph is attempting to communicate and by checking sentence by sentence to see that every one is related to the development of that idea.

POORLY UNIFIED PARAGRAPH

My father tried several vocations before he finally settled on farming as the most fully guaranteed disaster of a job anyone could ever try. When he was younger, he had worked in a textile mill. My brother works in textiles now, perhaps because he was influenced by my father. My dad tried cotton farming and dairy farming. Many Southern farmers grew cotton at the time, and Dad was one of many who nearly went broke several times. Cotton farming requires good soil, good weather, and a calm temperament. But at least it need not involve working with animals, as dairy farming does.
—Student paper

The opening sentence of the paragraph above leads the reader to expect that the entire paragraph will be about farming. But the second and third sentences introduce a new topic (textile work). Following sentences then go back to the original topic.

The following paragraph is well unified because the topic is introduced in the first sentence, and every sentence thereafter relates directly to that topic.

UNIFIED PARAGRAPH

People who wait on tables at summer resorts have a vocabulary that is completely strange to the outsider. The beginning waiter or waitress soon learns that the *zoo* is the place where the help are fed instead of where animals are fed. A *service plate* is a large plate put under a regular dinner plate or other dish. *Monkey-dishes*, which sound like something that belongs in the *zoo*, are simply small round bowls in which vegetables are served. Diners might think that they are getting something really special if they heard that it was to be served *supreme*, but it may be only a glass of tomato juice because *supreme* means only that the item is placed in a large goblet of cracked ice.
—Student paper

A **topic sentence** is the sentence in a paragraph that introduces or summarizes the idea that the rest of the paragraph develops. Generally, the topic sentence is the first sentence in the paragraph, as in the paragraph above. Topic sentences may, however, also appear in the middle or at the end of the paragraph. Occasionally, especially in descriptive writing, the topic sentence will not be stated but will only be implied.

Notice how the topic sentence in each of the following three paragraphs serves to tie the entire paragraph together. The final paragraph has no explicit topic sentence; if there were a topic sentence, it could only be something like "This is what the room looked like."

TOPIC SENTENCE AT BEGINNING OF PARAGRAPH

Physical dependence on drugs may develop relatively quickly, although not necessarily as quickly as most uninformed adults assume. It is not uncommon to encounter people who have been taking opiates every few days for eighteen months or more without having become physically addicted. Physical dependence on barbituates develops only if the individual has been taking excessively large doses. Physical addiction to alcohol is usually a late occurrence, seen in people who have been consuming progressively larger quantities for many years. —Student paper

TOPIC SENTENCE IN MIDDLE OF PARAGRAPH

Two years ago, if you wanted to play tennis in New York City, you did not have to wait in line. Today you must sign a roster by midday in order to be guaranteed a court at 5:00 p.m. The only alternative is to pay $1 for each hour that you reserve a court. Clearly, tennis has become one of the most popular sports played in New York City. Last summer I had to drive out of Manhattan on Sundays to play tennis because of the long lines at the public courts. Private indoor tennis courts have been doing so well financially that more of them are scheduled for construction every year. —Student paper

TOPIC SENTENCE AT END OF PARAGRAPH

In soap operas, the men all seem to be doctors or lawyers and, for some reason, they all resemble Gore Vidal. (On the other hand, the main business of hospitals and courtrooms is marital, rather than medical or judicial.) You will never see an unemployed man wandering around the streets of soap-land selling homemade granola cookies. Plumbers and other skilled workers are hard to come by. All in all, the soap operas present a very distorted image of the American work force. —Student paper

NO TOPIC SENTENCE

Wing chairs were scattered casually throughout the room, and an old walnut china cabinet lovingly crafted by a long-gone ancestor stood proudly in one corner. An immense hand-braided rug covered the floor, revealing only in the corners the wide floorboards that creaked whenever they were stepped on. The fireplace was made of fieldstones of uneven size and varying colors. White lace curtains were tied back on the windows; the panes themselves were hand-rolled glass, and many an antique dealer had stopped by the house to offer a good price for them.

—Student paper

50b COMPLETENESS

Completeness in a paragraph means that it is adequately developed by details, explanations, definitions, and evidence, and that it does not leave the reader wondering what the writer means. The amount of development needed to make a paragraph complete varies from paragraph to paragraph and subject to subject. Completeness does not mean *long* paragraphs; it means *whole* paragraphs. The reader should not have the feeling that there is more that should be said.

Compare the following two paragraphs, the first of which is inadequately developed, and the second of which is complete.

Dolphins are among the most fascinating of creatures that exist on our planet. They seem to have their own language. They will attack sharks. And, most of all, they seem to have a special fondness for human beings.

Dolphins, with their sleek, graceful splashes and maneuvers, are among the most fascinating creatures that exist on our planet. Human beings are attracted to the dolphin for several reasons. For one thing, dolphins seem to have their own language, a system of whistles and grunts with which they apparently communicate with each other. People have tried for years to interpret this language. Another characteristic of dolphins that makes us respect them is that they will, if necessary, attack sharks, creatures from whom most other sea dwellers will flee. Most appealing of all is the dolphin's evident fondness for human beings, a fondness that has frequently led to a swimmer's thrill at finding himself or herself involved in playful aquatics with one or more of these intelligent creatures.

50c PARAGRAPH DEVELOPMENT

Most writers know enough about their subject to develop interesting, complete paragraphs, but many just put down the information in the order in which ideas occur to them. This kind of writing by free association defeats the purpose of paragraphs—to present material in a logical, orderly manner so that the reader can easily grasp and appreciate what is being said and how it is being said.

There are eight **types of paragraph development** and five **sequences of development** that enable writers to create logical, easy-to-follow, complete paragraphs.

1. In **development by detail**, one of the most common methods of paragraph development, the topic sentence, which is usually at the beginning, is expanded by specific illustrations or examples. For example, in the following paragraph, the author summarizes the paragraph in his first sentence (the view was very appealing), and then lists the details that made it appealing (patio, grass, trees, garden, roses, lake).

The view from his kitchen window was, to be sure, suburban domestic, yet to him it was lovely, serene, and safe. The patio below the window sported a small table and two chairs, inviting to a pair of friends who wanted to sit gazing out over the cropped grass that flowed down a gentle slope to the small lake. Tall trees cast mottled shadows on the lawn. A small vegetable garden would, in the summer, be visible in one of the wider sunny spots. Roses bloomed in beds and sweetened the summer air with their scent. And there, beyond it all, the lake lapped gently at the edge of the grassy bank.

2. **Development by comparison and contrast** is used to discuss subjects that share some features in common and belong to a common and easily identifiable class. If the similarities between the things being compared are so obvious that they need not be mentioned, the discussion may focus on the differences alone. Many paragraphs discuss both similarities and differences. Two ways of handling information in the comparison-and-contrast paragraph when both similarities and differences are discussed are to (1) discuss differences and similarities point by point (X is green and Y is yellow; X is tall and Y is short) and (2) discuss the features of one subject first and then the features of the second subject (X is green and tall; Y is yellow and short). In the second method, a new paragraph often begins with the introduction of the second subject. In the paragraph below, the similarities of the sonnet and the limerick are first stated, and then their differences are listed.

Like the sonnet, the limerick is a very rigid, inflexible verse form: A six-line limerick is as unthinkable as a fifteen-line sonnet. Both are relatively old verse forms in English—the unmistakable rhythms and meter of the limerick appear as early as the seventeenth century. However, while the sonnet is normally a serious, almost academic product transmitted solely through writing, the limerick is funny (if not downright bawdy), irreverent, and is most often transmitted orally. Finally, the sonnet was borrowed into English from other European languages, whereas the limerick is a truly native English verse form.

3. **Development by analogy** is similar to development by comparison and contrast in that a comparison of two different things is made in both. However, analogy attempts to explain the unfamiliar in terms of the familiar, and the comparison is usually between two things that do not belong to the same class.

The small ships that set sail from London that year on their perilous way to the New World were like butterflies involved in a migration to unknown but sensed destinations. They fluttered their sails across a vast unfriendly ocean, driven by what must have been almost an instinct, a will to survive and beget new generations. Like the great-grandchildren of the butterflies, the generations to come would in their turn set sail across a vast space, so immense that their wings would seem pitifully frail within it, to light at last on a new, yet very old world.

4. **Development by process** is a step-by-step description of how something is done, usually in a chronological sequence. In the paragraph below, von Frisch describes the process by which he and his coworkers determined that bees distinguish colors. Note that von Frisch also uses details and explanations in his development by process.

On our table we place a blue card and around it we arrange gray cards of all shades from white to black. On each card we set a little watch glass, but only the glass dish on the blue card contains food (sugar-water). In this way we train the bees to come to the color blue. Since bees have a very good memory for places we frequently change the relative positions of the cards. But the sugar is always placed on the blue card so that in every case the color indicates where food is to be found. After some hours we perform the decisive experiment. The cards and the glass dishes soiled by the bees are taken away. We place on the table a new series of clean cards of different shades of gray, each with an empty glass dish, and somewhere among them we place a clean, blue card provided, like all the others, with an empty glass dish. The bees remember the blue color and alight only on the blue card, distinguishing it from all shades of gray. This means that they have a true color sense.
—Karl von Frisch, *BEES: THEIR VISION, CHEMICAL SENSES, AND LANGUAGE*

5. **Development by classification and partition** occurs when individual items are grouped on the basis of their similarities and differences (classification) or when larger groups are divided into smaller components (partition). Both are similar to comparison and contrast, and both can be forms of definition. As the paragraph below illustrates, the way in which any particular subject matter is classified depends on the purpose of the paragraph: a biologist would certainly classify insects differently than the author does here.

For me, all insects can be divided into two groups—those that are objects of terror and those that can at least be tolerated, even if they are not necessarily regarded with affection. The distinction has nothing to do with whether the insect is poisonous or otherwise dangerous. Nor does it have anything to do with size; mayflies and ticks are equally horrifying, while moths and midges are equally acceptable. Nor does the distinction depend on any biological classification: crickets and cockroaches both belong to the order Orthoptera, but crickets are at worst a minor annoyance, yet cockroaches send me into hysterics. No, the distinction is one of early familiarity: spiders, mosquitoes, black flies, bumblebees, moths, ants, and crickets were all my childhood companions, and I have a live-and-let-live attitude toward them all. I encountered cockroaches, mayflies, ticks, carpenter bees, katydids, and earwigs after my attitudes toward my fellow creatures had hardened, and I am terrified of them all.

6. **Development by cause and effect** usually begins with the statement of an effect, followed by information about its cause. Often there are multiple causes or effects in the same paragraph. In the paragraph below, for example, a number of different causes are listed for a single effect (anxiety in college).

Graduating high-school seniors may have considerable anxiety about their future, anxieties which, after they have entered college, may become full-blown fears of failure and inadequacy. There are several causes for freshmen's fears. They may be living away from home for the first time in their lives, away from the comfort and support of their families, yet they may still be burdened by their expectations. They may be faced with academic requirements stiffer than any they have known; sometimes they are faced with a new vocabulary for their subjects so that their very language seems inadequate. And they may be faced with personal decisions as important as they are new. The vague fears they had while still in high school may take shape and threaten to overwhelm them once they are in college.

7. In **development by definition**, examples or negative examples (what the term does *not* mean), analogies, and comparisons and contrasts are used to explain the meaning of a term. Extended definitions often include classification, partition, and statements of cause and effect. The following paragraph defines the word *pun* by explanations using different words, by examples, and by classification and partition (distinguishing puns from literary devices like paronomasia).

A *pun* is the humorous use of a word or group of words in such a way as to suggest two or more different meanings simultaneously. For example, in the statement *His driving test was a real hit—he hit a tree, a mailbox, and two pedestrians, hit* means both "success" and "strike." Another variety of pun uses entirely different words that sound alike or nearly alike; in the sentence *Her father was a rich perfume manufacturer, but he didn't leave her a cent*, the pun arises from the fact that *scent* and *cent*, although completely different words, are pronounced the same. All puns are humorous; when plays on words are to be taken seriously, they are no longer called puns but go by such fancy names as *antanaclasis, paronomasia*, and *syllepsis*.

8. In **development by a mixture of types**, two or more kinds of development are combined within a single paragraph. If you develop your paragraph with a mixture of types, however, be careful that you do not make too abrupt a switch from one kind of development to another in the middle of a paragraph. The following paragraph is developed primarily by detail, but the author also uses comparison and contrast to describe the unfamiliar object.

His eye was caught by an object suspended by a metal chain from the ceiling. It was elliptical in shape, smaller than a football but larger than a grapefruit—about eight inches from one long end to the other. The surface was as hard and shiny as glazed pottery but pitted like the surface of an orange.

It was very pale brown in color, almost the color of an egg. His curiosity getting the upper hand, he walked over, reached up, and held it. It was surprisingly heavy. As he looked more closely, he saw that the chain had been inserted through a small hole in the upper end and that the object was hollow with walls perhaps one-eighth inch thick.

In addition to the seven types of paragraph development, there are five principal kinds of sequences of paragraph development.

1. **General-to-particular sequence**, the most common type of sequencing in nonfiction writing, begins with a general statement, which is supported by details and illustrations in the rest of the paragraph.

> Of all the places liberated during the reconquest of the Philippines, probably none held more poignant memories for MacArthur than Corregidor. Here he had directed the long defense of Bataan in those early difficult days of 1941. It was from its South Dock that he had boarded the PT boat that took him to his new assignment in Australia. In a hard-fought engagement, the 503d Airborne Regimental Combat Team, assisted by elements of the 34th Regimental Combat Team, retook the island by parachute and amphibious assault. MacArthur's promise to the Philippine Garrison to return with help had now been accomplished.
> —Major Vorin E. Whan, Jr., Editor, *A SOLDIER SPEAKS: PUBLIC PAPERS AND SPEECHES OF GENERAL OF THE ARMY DOUGLAS MACARTHUR*

2. **Particular-to-general sequence** begins with a series of particular details and ends with a general statement (usually the topic sentence).

> One garment form, the tunic, was common to all early cultures regardless of the contact between them. Each kingdom, tribe, or country adapted and refined this early garment to meet the needs of the established social order. The loincloth was also a basic form devised by early man as a simple body covering. Both of these simple garments and the square or rectangular cape were logical forms. The tunic, made of a length of woven material or animal skin, folded in half, sewn up the sides, with a slit for a neck opening, was a direct design. The cape, which was the obvious refinement of the rhino or animal skin, was also an evolutionary apparel item. It is not surprising that these types of clothing appeared in many different geographical locations as the earliest means of covering, protecting, and decorating the person. As each culture developed weaving techniques and refined them, the decorative aspects of clothing received greater attention. As the trade between areas expanded, one culture adopted and improved the refinements of another. Improvisation of garment forms to meet the needs of the people were made in direct proportion to the level of cultural sophistication.
> —Marybelle S. Bigelow, *FASHION IN HISTORY: APPAREL IN THE WESTERN WORLD*

3. **Climactic sequence** builds up to a climax. The most intense or highest point of interest is saved for the final sentence, which is often the topic sentence of the entire paragraph.

> The soldiers had no time for gaping. Round about them lay the enormous relics of a dead past, but Cairo, sybol of an enchanting future, beckoned. Between them and their glittering goal stood the army of the Mameluke sultans. This colorful force was made up of ten thousand horsemen, brilliantly drilled, armed with glittering yataghans, mounted on prancing steeds of noble stock. The commander was the ruler of Egypt himself, Murad. Accompanied by twenty-three of his beys, he rode at the head of his swarm on a swan-white horse, his green turban glistening with precious stones. Napoleon pointed to the pyramids. He exhorted his men, as a general, a master of mass psychology, and as a European face to face with world history. "Soldiers," he said, "forty centuries are looking down upon you!"
> —C. W. Ceram, *GODS, GRAVES, AND SCHOLARS*